OUTWARD ANXIETY

INNER CALM

A Practical Guide to a Happier Life

By Steve Crociata

To Nikki
my big sister and
designated worrier

OUTWARD ANXIETY
INNER CALM
A Practical Guide to a Happier Life

Author - Steve Crociata
Publisher - McCleery & Sons Publishing

International Standard Book Number: 0-9712027-6-1
Printed in the United States of America

When I first met Steve Crociata, I had read his careful rendering of one man's practical guide to happiness, but I confess wondering whether the time was right for another book about survival and recovery. After all, whole sections of the popular bookstores are devoted to such work, much of it excellent. The World Trade Center was struck just days before I flew to Santa Monica to meet with Steve. Looking over the manuscript on the flight, I hoped for someone, or something to erase a part of the gloom that had begun to possess my spirit.

Then I met this fine and illustrious man, and his genuine goodness did its magic. Steve Crociata has endured troubling, long waits in doctors offices; he has fought his way through a myriad of see-sawing diagnostics. And he emerges as a man of calm and fortitude, a man who speaks simply about plain truths and light years of hope. Knowing Steve now is one of my joys. I can pick up the phone and draw from his humor and camaraderie, knowing that I will feel better after every talk we have.

Reading Steve's hilarious descriptions of inflated Hollywood vanity is the paradoxical appeal of Outward Anxiety, Inner Calm. Here, Steve will make you laugh aloud. He knows the secrets and foibles of the "beautiful people". So, be prepared to enjoy some mischievous humor. Steve's lessons on "conscious" living aren't dull or dry, because he has discovered contagious merriment. This book is balanced with seriousness and fun.

It's my sincere hope that many readers, particularly those who either face illness or love the afflicted, will find solace and joy in "Outward Anxiety, Inner Calm." During the present times of challenge for America, there are better tonics than reaching for the medicine bottle, or losing one's self in pleasure-seeking. These are the healing remedies of heart-felt words, delivered, as they only can be, by men and women who walk in good -- and who speak from their honest inner core. Read this book and take it's lessons -- large and small -- to the aching regions of your soul. You will be better for the experience.

Steve Tweed
Editor
McCleery and Sons

TABLE OF CONTENTS:

INTRODUCTION

I really love scrambled egg sandwiches. I can easily eat them four days a week and be perfectly satisfied. I've found that if I take a little care and follow a simple recipe, the result is more satisfying than if I just scrambled some eggs and cooked them up. To get fluffier, smoother eggs, I let the eggs get to room temperature, add a little half & half, a little seasoning, a little flour, and cook the eggs on high heat in a hot pan. In doing these simple things I find I enjoy the taste and texture so much more. A few minutes of preparation makes the experience much more satisfying. That also means I care enough to take the time to try to make the best eggs I could and don't just settle for what most of us think of as scrambled eggs. Anyone can make scrambled eggs and most of us do, anyone can follow a simple recipe to improve them, but most of us don't. There is a reason for that. The majority of people don't even realize there is a better way to prepare that basic dish we've all grown up with.

Once a person experiences the differences, then that will likely become their preferred method of preparation and they will incorporate that recipe from now on. What does that have to do with happiness? You'll see.

Just as there are simple ways of improving the eggs we've always prepared in the traditional way, there are simple ways for improving our lives that we've always led in the traditional way. There are methods we can incorporate to make our lives more satisfying and the experience more enjoyable. Most don't do that for the same reason as most don't make better scrambled eggs. They don't know how. But, with some instruction and a little care our lives can improve immeasurably. There's no trick to it, but there is a method. You only have to know the recipe. If you care enough about yourself and your loved ones to improve the experience of your life and are willing to incorporate the little things that will increase your enjoyment of it, you'll be much more satisfied with the end product. And, as you'll discover, it's not a subtle change, it's a profound change.

If you care enough about your happiness to try to ensure the enjoyment of it on an ongoing basis, you'll find you never again have to settle for less than the best. The recipe for living a happy and tranquil life couldn't be easier and more straightforward. A little care and preparation can ensure that when you sit down to the banquet that life can be if it is lived correctly, it has so much more richness and texture, you'll find that that's the way you'd prefer it to be from now on.

You'll develop a renewed taste for life and will never want to go back to the former coping mechanisms that you've always relied on. If you find the methods you've been employing to be less and less satisfying in coping with the everyday problems we all encounter, you'll find that with a few simple changes, the experience that is your life will go down much smoother, and the taste will be much more to your liking.

If you can think of happiness as the Final Jeopardy question (last analogy for a while), once you've learned how to live in a way that allows you to extract the maximum enjoyment from it, you'll feel confident enough to bet everything. You'll know the category like the back of your hand, and discover for yourself the correct answer to the puzzle of finding happiness.

I'm a history buff and my main area of interest is the American Revolution. If that subject ever comes up on the Jeopardy show, I have total confidence in my ability to answer even the most obscure question. Knowledge translates to confidence and confidence with knowledge translates to success.

We all have the capacity to live happy lives. It's not just for other people. You have just as much chance as the next person to reach that elusive goal. Other people are no better than you, even if some seem to be better at most things. Competence in life does not necessarily translate to happiness. As a matter of fact, once you read and understand the concepts detailed in this book, your chance of success in maintaining happiness is far greater than the average person's. If you've gotten to a point where the stresses of everyday life have taken almost all the enjoyment out of it, and feel ongoing happiness is no longer even a option, you'll be very happy to find that with some work on your part, that is not the case at all. And, the best part is that when you understand and employ the concepts you will read here, happiness will no longer be transitory and unsustainable, but will follow along with you wherever you go.

The problem with the vast majority of us is that our happiness is event-driven. We depend on the whims of the world to provide our happiness for us, instead of creating our own and making it a natural part of our daily lives. Wouldn't it be wonderful if every day felt like it was a vacation day, and wouldn't it be a pleasant departure to live life stress free? Believe it or not, if you make a dedicated effort, both these things are not only possible, but absolutely attainable.

What I'm going to tell you is not a new concept. In fact, some of the most successful people, who I'll quote throughout, have been living this philosophy of life through the ages. Since happiness is one thing most people crave but is the one thing that can't be bought or bargained for, attaining it is something that is open to everyone who feels there is room for improvement in their lives. There is no equipment to buy or expensive lectures to attend. If the little things that once gave you pleasure no longer do, or life is getting to be more a chore than joy, it is time to figure out why and to do something to rectify the situation. **Just because that's the way it is now doesn't at all mean it has to stay that way.**

You might not be able to change the conditions of your life but you certainly can change your attitudes about them, and how you handle them. You'll find that is the one area you have complete control over, and discover attitude is the most important aspect of a happy life. There are ways of going about improving your life that are perfectly logical and easily understandable. This book is not a replacement for any religion. If you are devout, there is no reason to change. If you go to church or synagogue or mosque every week, there is no reason that this new lifestyle should have any bearing on that at all. This is not a religion. Organized religion is very important for many and the consolation it provides is irreplaceable.

I'm going to give you a little background on myself because I think it's very important that you understand the source of the information provided here. Whenever you study anything you always need to consider the origin so you can determine if what you're learning is valid or just an attempt to influence your thinking to the writer's point of view. Obviously, whenever a book is written the writer has a motive. You'll find the only thing I'm trying to influence is how you feel about things and your responses to them. It's important that you understand my motives and feel comfortable that your best interests are truly at heart, and not only mine. If there is an ulterior motive on my part, you should be aware of it. That's just honesty and one of the cornerstones of what you'll see emphasized here.

As you'll find, I have no ulterior motive nor am I trying to recruit members to follow me on the methods I espouse. It's entirely up to you to take them or leave them.

The last thing in the world I would want is to be considered some kind of guru. I'm not.

Anyone can claim honesty and integrity but the proof is in the writing. The more you read, the more comfortable you'll be with the fact that I do indeed want to help and through my experiences, make your life more the way you've only dreamed it could be.

My other motive is more mundane, and is the money I'll make if this book is successful. In all honesty, money is not the driving force and when you read further you'll see why. I do feel that the book is already successful because I've enjoyed the writing experience fully and in the process learned a lot about myself. It's also allowed me to reinforce everything I've learned and am teaching you and has actually increased my enjoyment of life even more. So, either way, this book has been a major success in my eyes whether it sells or doesn't. That is one of the concepts I'd like you to take away from this experience. Always do your best, no matter what you're doing, and then you can more readily accept the results, knowing you couldn't have done better or tried harder. In doing that, the image you hold of yourself will be allowed to grow in a positive fashion.

Fourteen years ago I was diagnosed with chronic lymphocytic leukemia and that in turn has caused other chronic conditions. In the last few years I've gone through some pretty tough times and on the whole haven't felt very good physically, and still don't, and probably never will. What I've found is that everything is much more difficult when I don't feel up to par. That's just a fact of my life and I've learned to accept it. Whatever I need to do to help control it, I'm more than willing to do.

Everybody has problems, and many much worse than mine, but I feel quite fortunate for the overall quality of my life. To give you some idea of what I've experienced and still am, in the last four years or so I've gone through chemotherapy twice; I've had cat scans, MRIs, colonoscopy, endoscopies, upper and lower GIs, IVP tests, and so many x-rays I'm surprised I don't glow in the dark. I also came close to having a bone marrow transplant. I was accepted into the City of Hope program only to find my chances of survival were too low for me to feel comfortable in going ahead with it. I have very severe allergies that never go away, and cause me to have a condition called Tension Fatigue Syndrome. That in turn makes my body speed and is quite uncomfortable, and has caused me to experience insomnia on a nightly basis. I have to sleep in a leather recliner so I can breathe. The allergies make me feel like I have a bad cold every day. All the medications I take make me very tired. After my last chemo I developed Irritable Bowel Syndrome which more than lives up to its name. Last year was particularly tough because while I was undergoing chemotherapy I contracted a very severe case of autoimmune hemolytic anemia, which led to the flu, which in turn led to pneumonia. I was out of work for eight straight months.

Still, with all that, I'm not complaining and I am a happy guy. I realize things could be much worse and that since I have a successful business, a wonderful family, good friends, and a nice place to live, I'm more fortunate than I could have ever hoped to be. As you can imagine, after hearing my litany of ailments, if I didn't lead my life with the attitude I have and follow my own advice, or if I ever felt sorry for myself even once, I'd be in big trouble. That's why when I tell you something or ask you to approach something in a particular way, you'll know it comes from personal experience, and from a person who's "been there."

This book is not a collection of theories or suppositions. Too many people are more than happy to write books or tell others how to live their lives when they themselves haven't experienced much adversity. Many self-help theories sound good on the surface but either are too time-consuming, too difficult to master, have too many rules to memorize, or are not practical for application by real people in their real lives. Or, as most of us have found out, they just don't work. A lot of what is written and espoused reminds me of fad diets. It seems like a new one comes along every week and most have one thing in common: their utter failure to deliver what is promoted.

I purposely wrote this book in a way that you don't have to memorize anything. Nor do I ask you to go to some mountaintop to "find yourself." You know where you are and you also know you're not completely satisfied with your life. If you were, I'd love to meet you because there aren't too many of you around.

Since every human being does have problems and always will, there's only so much we can do about that. But, what we *can* do is learn how to minimize them, keep them in perspective, and deal with them in a way that is constructive while keeping the stress level to an absolute minimum. I haven't experienced stress in such a long time I can't remember what it feels like. That took a lot of work and trial and error on my part. I'm a pretty average person and there is no reason that you can't get to the point I've reached and without the trial and error part of the equation. I've already done the legwork and I know from experience whether a particular way to approach something is really beneficial or just a waste of your time. As I've said, this is nothing new but I made it a point to make this book and the situations and examples in it relevant to your everyday life.

Many of the situations I use as examples are the same ones you encounter on a daily basis. Once you learn how to constructively handle the specific scenarios I've given, whenever you come upon that situation you can think back to what you've learned and apply that lesson in dealing with it. The true benefit is that other like situations that were a concern for you before and caused impatience, frustration, worry, or stress can be handled in the same way. Any specific example I relate here could easily be the answer for many similar situations. So, if I've given ten examples, that might cover forty or fifty similar, but distinct, everyday situations.

I wrote this book in a conversational style for a reason. I feel it is much easier to comprehend and retain information if the words flow as they would in a conversation with a friend than if I wrote in a way that made you stop and think to try to get at the real meaning. I'm not trying to impress you with my knowledge, because frankly, I'm probably no smarter than you. When you sit down to read this book there will be no need for you to keep a thesaurus or dictionary handy.

If you found yourself dropped off in the middle of a forest you would have no clue where to even begin to try to find your way out or even which direction you should go. You could walk twenty miles but if you don't know exactly which direction or at least have a good idea where the forest ends you might as well stay where you are. But, if you were given a compass and some clues to where help could be found, when you walked you'd have some direction and purpose. Instead of meandering about and wasting time, you'd be getting closer to your goal with each step. Without that knowledge all the effort you expend would amount to nothing and you'd be no closer to reaching the forest's end. You could easily make matters worse and with each step get further and further away from where you want to be. You'd be lost.

That's exactly how many of us feel when we try to find help

in making our lives more the way we'd like and our days more pleasant and the overall experience of every day happier. If given direction we can walk with renewed purpose and the tentative steps we might have taken will now have meaning. Because of that, maybe for the first time in our lives, the common goal we all have to attain -- serenity -- will come into sight. Think of this book as your guidebook out of the forest of confusion and uncertainty, to a path of direction and renewed purpose. When you take the first steps out of the thicket of confusion and muddled thinking, you'll do so with the knowledge that you truly are going in the right direction and each step is a positive one, and that in turn gets you closer to where you really want to be.

The concept that this book will teach you is how to live your life consciously. Basically, all that means is from now on before doing or saying anything or before you react to a person or situation, you stop and think before proceeding. You always need to remember what your goal is and that you are consciously working towards that every minute of every day. Since we all have thinking patterns that started developing when we were children, in most situations we don't stop to think before proceeding and pretty much live our lives on auto-pilot. We react to things the way we always did with no thought to whether there is a better way to go about it. You'll find there is almost always a better way. If we reacted poorly to a similar situation and have for our whole lives, we live with the fear that the next time that situation or a similar one occurs we'll automatically react badly and we might even dread the thought of the situation causing us to do just that. You'll learn that situations aren't the cause of your worry as much as you are. We don't so much dread the thought of what might happen as much as we dread the way we'll react when it does, or how much pain it might cause us again. That is projecting your fears into the future and causing yourself worry before anything has even happened. Not a good idea. This book will teach you basic ways to avoid those unnecessary fears you yourself cause and how not to be your own worst enemy.

There are five basic areas that we will concentrate on.

1. **Control:** There are many things in our lives that we have control over, but in reality the vast majority of things are those over which we have little or no control. If everything were in our power, life would be a piece of cake. When we encounter a situation that we have no control over, that often causes us frustration, anger, worry, or stress and our responses to those situations are colored by negative feelings. But, if we ever want to even come close to living a stress-free life, we have to learn to constructively deal with them. That means that previously disconcerting situations and our negative reactions to them need to be looked at and fine-tuned so that in the future those reactions will no longer occur. You'll learn to deal with situations that previously caused negative emotions to well up in you. They will no longer cause frustration and you'll learn to deal with them in ways that are actually constructive. If approached correctly, those situations will no longer cause the negative feelings that you easily could live without.

2. **Expectations:** One of the most important things you'll take from this book is how to keep expectations realistic without limiting your potential. When you go into any situation your chances of success are greatly enhanced and your chances of being disappointed and frustrated are greatly reduced if you have a realistic expectation of the outcome before you even begin. You'll find emphasized here the importance of being prepared for all things you embark on and you'll no longer be content just hoping something will work out the way you'd prefer.

If you make it a point to approach things in a realistic fashion with attainable goals you'll realize that more things will just naturally turn out the way that is beneficial to you. If you go to the trouble of expending the energy to do them, you might as well get the desired results. If you go in with unrealistic expectations from anything, you'll be frustrated and disappointed more often than not. We'll go over step by step how to avoid just those pitfalls, thereby increasing your success in things attempted, and at the same time limiting the negative effects of overblown expectations.

3. **Living In The Moment:** Much of the stress we cause ourselves comes from worrying about what's going to happen in the future. You'll learn that when life is lived in the very minute you're in, and not sometime in the future or past, the cause of a lot of the worry that seems to consume much of your time will be totally eliminated. You'll happily discover that result is absolutely possible and not at all an unrealistic expectation.

No longer will you develop scenarios in your mind of what might be and that only exist in your imagination, but in reality have nothing to do with anything that will actually happen. You'll see that when you allow your intellect to dictate to your emotions and not the other way around, by staying grounded in the present, you can achieve many positive results in whatever you endeavor to do, without fear or apprehension taking most of the joy out of it.

To get the most out of life you always need to live it in the very moment you are in. In that way you'll allow yourself the full enjoyment of whatever you are involved in, without worrying about what might happen next. You'll be amazed how much your stress level is reduced with that one simple thing, once you master it.

4. **Acceptance:** Since so many situations in our lives are out of our control we have to learn to accept many things we would really prefer not to. If we fight the inevitable, we're the ones who'll come out on the short end of the stick. You'll learn that acceptance in no way correlates to giving up or caving in. They are mutually exclusive things that some have a tendency to confuse.

When you learn to accept those things you'd prefer to be different, but no amount of effort or wishing will make them so, then your life will be much less frustrating and the ride will be a lot smoother. You should always try to do whatever is in your power that you feel needs doing or will be beneficial to you or others, and after doing your very best, accept the result. If you don't do the best job you can, then you'll be doing a lot of accepting of things you really shouldn't have to. You never want to go along just to go along, or give in for no good reason—there has to be a compelling reason to accept situations. Basically, once you've exhausted all avenues in finding a remedy, then acceptance is the final step.

5. **Fear:** Fear is the greatest obstacle we face that keeps us from reaching our potential. The fear factor limits our lives by keeping us from doing things that would be beneficial to our overall happiness, trying new things for fear of looking foolish, or keeping us from enjoying what we do have for fear of losing it. Fear also makes us do things that work against our own best interests in ways you might not even realize. Fear of the future keeps us from fully enjoying and engaging in the present. As you'll see, fear makes our lives uncomfortable when they shouldn't be, and is totally unnecessary and counterproductive to leading happy and stress free lives.

There is a huge difference between being fearful and being cautious. Caution in many aspects of our lives is beneficial and keeps us from making mistakes that are easily avoidable, whereas fear can lead us to make the wrong choices that are also easily avoidable. When we fear something, subtly or overtly, it changes how we view it, and never for the better, and, many times, causes us to make decisions we live to regret. You'll learn to step back from a situation to give yourself the time to view it from a more detached and more objective viewpoint so your choices won't go through the prism of distortion that fear can cause. When you learn to completely eliminate fear from your life, one of the major causes of anxiety that plagues us all is also eliminated and you'll enjoy a newfound freedom reminiscent of early childhood when you didn't know enough to have fear. There are no benefits to fear, only negatives. It's really not that difficult at all to completely eliminate that negative factor, just as with anything else, you only have to know how. I know how and now so will you.

As I've said, many of the examples I use will be very specific and can be utilized as a blueprint for you to follow when you encounter that specific situation. Others will be in more general terms which might or might not apply to situations you find yourself confronted with, but which give you an overall feel for an entire spectrum of situations as discussed. For example, I refer to the Israeli-Palestinian hostilities that are going on right now. That might not affect you directly but in a general way reflects overall problematic situations that can help you understand the ramifications of certain actions, and how they apply to your life specifically.

Much of what I've written concerns how I feel about certain social issues such as the homeless or equality to make certain points about attitudes, and how a person leading a conscious life responds to them in a way that allows them to continue living a flowing life, while at the same time being a positive influence by their example.

There are too many in our society who are more concerned with improving outwardly than inwardly. Billions of dollars a year are spent on surgeries lifting, tucking, suctioning, injecting, and implanting in an effort to become more attractive. In doing that, a person tries to improve the image they portray to the world, and at the same time bolster their self-image. When a person feels better about their appearance it helps boost their self-esteem. One of the problems with those who are attractive in relation to the rest of us is that they don't have to develop other qualities that, in the long run, would be beneficial to them.

When a person does, for example, have a face-lift, it's true that they feel better and have more confidence. The downside is that it can only take them so far. If the person goes into it with the expectation that it will be a life-changing event, then they're expecting too much from it. They are likely to be disappointed when that doesn't happen. If they find they do become more popular by say, increasing their bust line from a B-cup to a full C-cup, their sudden new popularity among a small segment of the population is for all the wrong reasons.

I personally don't see a problem with any of that as long as the person's expectations of the surgery are realistic. I don't find it admirable, though, and in the long run, I think it can cause more harm than good. The reason for that is since the person is more concerned with the external image, they are emphasizing the wrong thing, and many times at the expense of their true selves, which could use the work.

Anytime a person relies on an outside source, in this case their face or body, to provide their happiness, or at least boost it, they're taking a risky approach and are being short sighted. Cosmetic improvements only last so long. If it sagged before, it will sag again, and then what? Another surgery?

Since the foundation of a person's happiness is not at all maintainable if derived from the scalpel, instead of being on solid ground, they're more likely walking onto quicksand. Being attractive in no way correlates into being a quality person.

On the other hand, if the person spends as much time working on improving themselves inwardly as they do obsessing about their appearance and looking in the mirror, then, at least, their priorities aren't totally askew.

We'd all love to be attractive, it's just human nature to want to present the best possible face. But, as you're aware or will soon learn, when you do all the hard work it takes to really make yourself a "better person" by learning to live life on a moment-to-moment basis, and you build a strong foundation for a happy and tranquil life, you likely won't feel the need to tinker with what God provided you in the first place, and if you do you'll go in with realistic expectations. You'll learn that when you build a strong foundation for that happiness it is not a transitory thing and you won't ever have to worry about it sagging with age. On the contrary, with age and experience and effort, it only gets better and better.

Let's begin. We'll start with my awakening to a better life as I physically began to feel a bit better and proceed immediately to the heart of the matter. When I refer to my business I'm speaking of a small optical shop I run in Santa Monica.

PART I

MY OWN AWAKENING

As I progressively started to feel better physically, everything I had studied about conscious living over the previous years began to click. One negative emotion after another was shed until, one day, I woke up and felt strangely different—but I couldn't put a finger on it. Physically, that morning was difficult for a while (due to my severe allergies) but emotionally, I felt different—a little better but I wasn't quite certain. It was that new of a feeling.

Each day thereafter the feeling grew stronger and a lasted little longer. The transformation didn't take much time, just a matter of weeks. It snuck up on me and, to be honest, at first it felt strange. What I felt was happening to me I finally surmised, was a great sense of relief, as in having a heavy burden lifted from my shoulders. I soon realized that I wasn't worried a bit about what had been my two greatest concerns from many years: my health and security. Worrying about these issues and whatever other problems life would throw at me on a daily basis had for a long time given me a sinking feeling in the pit of my stomach, and I had spent much of my time in that mode for several years. I'm sure you've been there yourself, although maybe not the length of time I was. As you know, it's not a nice feeling, and you want it to go away as quickly as possible.

I was so relieved and I didn't at all miss the fear, worry, or anxieties that, for quite a while, had been running my life. Everything seemed to open up for me. It was an exciting, new, and wonderful feeling. I still had all of the same medical and financial woes you'll read about but all of a sudden I didn't care. It was amazing. Everything that used to worry and stress me no longer did. It's a great feeling, the freest feeling I've had since I was a child. But I had a lingering doubt that it wouldn't last. I've felt good before, only to be disappointed. But somehow I knew, after a few more weeks of steady improvement, that this time would be different. And, boy, was it ever!

There was a clarity of thought I had never before experienced. Gone was the muddled thinking brought on by years of low-level depression and powerful, mind-altering prescription drugs. I was instantly more dedicated than ever to saving my business, which had deteriorated along with my health, and I experienced an energy level I hadn't felt in 20 years. Life was fun again!

Having gone through physical and mental hell for the six previous years, I never imagined enjoying happiness again. I had felt so awful for so long I just didn't think it would or could be possible. It wasn't even a blip on my radar screen of imaginings. But, much to my surprise and delight, right then and there the seeds of a transformation were born. Suddenly and unexpectedly, my life was infused with meaning, it was starting to have direction and purpose again, and I wanted to live it to its fullest. Instead of dreading getting out of bed in the morning, I couldn't wait to get up to start a brand new day, fresh and alive. I now began to feel each day was a gift instead of a chore.

Everything was good again—the sun shone brighter, food tasted better, and my appreciation of everything, big and small was re-instilled. I finally came to realize again that life can be a beautiful thing! I had forgotten that in the confusion of everything that had been going on in my life. Gone were all of the ups and downs, and in their place was a levelness of feeling that I hitherto could only dream of, and could only vaguely remember from childhood.

No matter where you are right now—whatever your hopes, fears, attachments, longings, no matter how bad things seem at the moment—know this: **you too can be happy!** I know this for a fact because I picked myself out of the depths and, as I've said, I am in no way an extraordinary person. I'm a regular guy who has to go out every day, just like you, to make a living and try to do the best I can. Things don't always go my way, but that really doesn't matter. It's okay to lose some of life's daily battles. In fact, it's inevitable. What I would like you to take away from this is the ability to handle life's down moments in a better way than you're presently doing, and to consciously appreciate the up moments to maximize your enjoyment of them. As I've noted, as you read this you should relate the examples and my experiences to your own life.

If I were a guru or a deeply religious mystic and told you that you too could lead a happy, stress-free life, I wouldn't be surprised if you couldn't relate. Who has the time or inclination to spend their days in deep meditation or prayer? I'm guessing that you don't. Through personal experience I'm sure you realize that just wanting or craving happiness is not enough. As you're well aware, it doesn't work that way. It would be nice if it did, everybody would walk around with smiles on their faces, but it's just not realistic. What *is* realistic, however, is that with dedicated conscious effort on your part, it is more than possible for your life to turn around and happiness to be achieved. That's even if, at this very moment, you perceive that to be a remote possibility. Believe me, it can happen.

Stress will become like pain. I know that sounds odd, but what I mean is that, unless you're actually in pain, you can't feel it. You know you don't like it, but unless you're experiencing it at the moment, you can't recreate the actual feeling. As such, when you get to a certain point along your path, you'll remember stress as something unpleasant, but you won't be able to recreate the feeling. Not that you'd ever want to. Believe me, it's a great place to be and a whole lot better than the alternative. If eliminating stress is the only aspect of self-improvement you attempt to master, you'll be a much happier person for the effort.

Because I desperately craved serenity, I had read a number of books on how to find the elusive Holy Grail of happiness. Most of them were very good, because I was selective, and all contributed to my bank of knowledge on the subject. The one missing ingredient in nearly all of them was how to relate what I was studying to my own life. It's all well and good to tell someone to stop doing something negative, but how and why and when are just as important. If you know how and why and when to or not to employ something you've learned, it's a more relevant and easily-absorbed lesson than if you were to try to figure it out for yourself. A lot of times it helps just to see it in writing. I know it does for me.

This is especially true in the beginning. When learning anything new, it's best to begin with the basics and have object lessons to work from.

As I've stated preciously, I'm not a spiritual leader, so everything I relate is 100% from my experiences. I have a B.A. in history, so I'm not trying to pass myself off as something I'm not. The only thing I might know more than you is the year the Battle Hastings was fought. But the one thing I am certain of is that conscious dedication worked for me. Everything I'm relating I've done and am still doing. If you apply yourself, I can't imagine it not working for you, at least to some degree, and that's especially true if you really make a concerted effort.

It's all conscious effort. You learned at an early age to think about certain things in certain ways. But life is ever evolving. Something that might have been the answer ten years ago might not at all apply now. But chances are you're still thinking the same way you did then. You must learn to adapt to ever-changing life situations. Thus, in some respects, you have to change your thinking patterns. There's no way of getting around this (believe me, I tried and got nowhere). But I believe very strongly in what I tell you.

Part of the process involves eliminating negative emotions-not eliminating all emotions, just the harmful ones. We don't want to turn ourselves into unfeeling robots. Ask yourself this question: do fear and worry enrich your life in any way? No. Wouldn't you be infinitely better off without having to deal with anxiety, worry, stress, and fear on a daily basis? The ability to accomplish this is what this book will help you realize.

What's so rewarding is that, through practice, it becomes a way of life, and the best part is that, with conscious effort, no matter how good you start to feel, you'll only become better and better at handling life's situations which previously seemed overwhelming. You can learn to accept things that you found previously unacceptable. At every juncture, I would advise you to be patient with yourself and consider yourself an ever-evolving work in progress. With some effort, you should be able to make progress until the very end.

It's a very consoling feeling to know that, through conscious effort, you can be rewarded with happier life, a goal to which we all aspire but few ever achieve.

PART II

THE BASICS

CHAPTER ONE
CONTROL

There are very few things in our lives actually within our control. Things are what they are. This is one of the conditions that make life so frustrating. Events often don't happen as we want or when we want. That's life. How you react is entirely up to you, but many times this is where the problem lies. For example, if you're running late for an appointment and get onto the freeway only to find traffic is at a standstill, chances are you'll revert to your old, tired patterns of impatience and frustration. The later you get the more your anxiety level creeps up, your heart rate increases, and you start cursing under your breath (or out loud). You look repeatedly at the time, your blood pressure rises. Now, all that aggravation hasn't moved your car a foot forward, but it has certainly changed your mood for the worse. By the time you arrive at your destination, you're not in any mood to do what you went there for in the first place.

So your thinking goes, traffic has screwed up your day and put you in a foul mood. But, if you really think about it, it didn't—you did. *You alone are responsible for your mood.* You allowed something that you had no control over to get to you. It might sound harsh, but your foul mood is pretty much your own doing. It's like boredom. If you're bored, it's 100% your own fault. The world is chock-full of things to do, full of opportunities, if you take them. Say a couple of guys in the car next to you are joking and laughing.

If they don't have steam coming out of their ears as you do, it's possible that you overreacted to the traffic situation. So it wasn't the situation itself that was completely the problem. If others don't seem to view a situation as dire as you do, it could be that you're making more than necessary ado about it. You're the one that got yourself all worked up.

When it comes to things such as sitting in traffic, you have to consciously and emphatically tell yourself that allowing yourself to get upset is the worst thing you could do. Improvement won't happen unless conscious effort is applied. That means stopping and thinking first, then proceeding. Speaking of making more than necessary ado about something, it's very important that you don't ever do a "why me?" or see yourself as a "victim" in these situations. That *never* does you any good.

What I just related is an example of a minor but all-too-common occurrence. When a situation such as that arises, you must first tell yourself, "This is what is. This is what's happening in this moment of my life." It's just logic: you're stuck in traffic, you're late, but getting yourself all worked up is not going to change the circumstances. You must consciously and emphatically tell yourself that you accept the situation as it is, or you can try to fight it as you've always done—it's completely up to you.

Don't make the mistake of equating acceptance with passivity—they're very different things. A positive approach to this type of situation is to try to find an alternative route, or call the doctor's office to explain your situation and make a later appointment. Remember: explain, don't complain. Nobody wants to hear it, anyway. Accepting the situation in no way means you throw your hands up and surrender. As a matter of fact, when your mind is calm and not agitated, you will probably make better decisions to actually help yourself in getting to your destination faster, and if not, certainly with less stress.

One technique I use in that type of situation is to picture a beautiful place that I design in my mind, an ideal place where I'm alone and relaxing on a beautiful, secluded beach with lush green vegetation and sparkling blue water under a cloudless sky. It's not a real place but more my ideal place I make up. I stay there and simply enjoy the serenity and peace that such a place engenders. It makes the time pass faster and is much more pleasant than getting agitated. Hint: If you're driving, do this with your eyes open!

That's just one form of meditation and is very relaxing. There's any number of constructive things you could do, and this applies to all like situations: while you're waiting in a long line at the post office, if it rains on the day of the barbecue you planned weeks ago with people you are looking forward to spending time with, or when a big business deal you were counting on falls through, through no fault of your own. You must first accept that that's what is, and after that, start to deal with it—in an emotionally calm state of mind.

For the most part, things are what they are, and no amount of wishing will change them. If you're stuck in a long line, make it a point to notice how other people are handling it. Think of it as a show or a study in human nature. Some will not let it bother them, but many will. They may fidget, complain loudly, or generally make themselves and everyone around them miserable. *Who would you rather be like?*

It's pretty simple when you think about it that way. I spend a lot of time waiting in doctors' offices. What I've noticed is that the older people do most of the complaining. For the most part, it's not as if they have anywhere else to go, they're simply conditioned, through years of complaining, to automatically become agitated if things don't immediately go their way. They think it's unfair: Why did the doctor make all these appointments, knowing the patients would have to wait? I must have heard that exact sentiment expressed fifty times. But do they know all the facts? The doctor may have had an emergency, some patient visits take longer than anticipated, and so on. Life doesn't follow a schedule of anyone's making. But those who complain don't see that, they only see their own narrow view, making themselves and those around them suffer for it. I can almost guarantee they're feeling no worse than I am. However, I accept it for what it is: a minor inconvenience, and that's all. Life is made up of minor inconveniences, and it's your job, if given a lemon, to make lemonade. It really is that straight-forward and simple: make the best of whatever situation you're confronted with and accept it for exactly what it is without wishing it was something else—because it's not.

View things for what they really are and don't make situations into problems. Bring a good book to your appointments, bring some work with you, meditate, relax, watch others as if you were a fly on the wall, use the time to plan future events—there's always something constructive you can do. You will get better at it with practice, and in reality there are more than enough opportunities to practice on a daily basis. Do whatever it takes to take your mind off the situation, and use that time to your benefit. Since there is so much in our lives that we have no control over, a good way to go about existing with such things is to simply ignore them. Don't misunderstand me. You'll see what I mean. You're not denying the existence of such situations, but because you cannot control them, make them into non-events, at least as they pertain to you.

Here's an example. It's 7:00 a.m. on a Sunday, your only day to sleep in, and your next-door neighbors get into a loud, screaming argument. Your blissful sleep is shattered, and you're rightfully upset. It's not exactly what you had in mind when you went to bed late Saturday night. You're already up, so going next door to complain is a lot like closing the barn door behind the horse. It won't do you a bit of good and might cause future problems with your neighbors. What do you do? You might close your windows and ignore the noise, as much as possible. Remember, there's no law that says you must get upset in these types of situations. The argument will eventually die down, and if you can't fall back asleep, you have an opportunity to start your day off a little earlier than planned. It might be a blessing in disguise: you might get something accomplished you wouldn't have if you had slept in. The point is that you don't automatically allow yourself to get agitated. You slow yourself down and think first before any reaction.

By ignoring your inconsiderate neighbors, you don't start your day full of resentment and anger. We live in a society where we're right on top of each other, so it's inevitable that others' lives will intrude upon our own. I am very fortunate to live where I do, overlooking a park with a nice ocean view (when the trees are trimmed). But a freeway entrance is less than a mile away, resulting in a lot of street traffic. Sometimes the outside noise from my open window doesn't allow me to think, much less enjoy reading or watching television. Is this a problem? No, just a part of life. It only becomes a problem if I make it so.

If I wanted to live on a quiet street, I might not have my beautiful view. So it's a trade-off. I ignore the noise as much as possible and lead my life as if it didn't exist. Am I in denial? No, I realize what's going on, I simply choose to ignore it. In the beginning it's not easy, but as with all things, conscious effort will make it easier and easier. Don't think you're giving in. If getting upset would allow you to fall back asleep again or shut the noise out, I would expect you to do it. But it won't.

This applies to situations large and small. As I've stated, ignoring something is not denying its existence. You can be fully aware of whatever the situation might be, but you can also choose to go on with your day without letting it drag you down. In my own case, due to chemotherapy years ago, I have the stomach problems I've mentioned. Because much of the time my stomach is bothering me I take medications which certainly help, but don't eliminate the problem. So I learned to live with it and ignore it as much as possible, and allow it to affect me as little as possible. If I concentrated on it, it would only make the problem worse.

CHAPTER TWO
LIVING IN THE MOMENT

Many people waste precious time wanting to be somewhere else, doing something other than what they're doing (or so they think). If they're at work, they'd rather be home. If they're studying, they'd rather be shopping. What they are not doing is living in the moment. Big mistake!

We live life in a series of moments, one following another. If you're pining for something else, you might miss the opportunities of the moment you're actually living. The only reality is right now. It's important you convince yourself that where you are is where you should be, if for no other reason than that's the reality of the situation.

It only makes sense, since we can't be two places at once, you must make the best of whatever situation you are in—in the moment. Future events will happen when their time comes, and the past is no longer. Spending your time on either does you no good.

While there is nothing wrong with enjoying fond memories or looking forward to an upcoming event, the ideal is not to spend an inordinate amount of time in either of those places. As a matter of fact, as little time as possible is best. Consciously work to lessen the time spent out of the moment. Your living is being done right here and now. You're reading this book—that's where you are, and to get the most out of it, it's where your concentration should be.

If you're worried about a meeting you have scheduled for tomorrow, you are depriving yourself of the total involvement of read-

ing this book. The meeting will be there tomorrow. If you've prepared for it, forget about it until it happens. If you haven't, you should
get busy preparing for it and not procrastinate.

A major problem with dwelling on the future is that oftentimes
it causes worry, so I can't stress enough that if there is something
which needs to be taken care of, do it now (or at least get a good start
on it). Don't put things off. Unresolved issues tend to prey on the
mind, and worry and stress are the results.

*Try to think about it this way: the vast majority of things we
worry about never occur, and when they do, they're usually not as
bad as our minds built them up to be.* On the chance they do occur,
what good did fretting about them do you? It just made whatever the
situation is worse, and all that time spent worrying took away precious time you could have used to enjoy whatever you were doing at
the moment. You just double-whammied yourself by wasting the
present moment and magnifying the scope of the future problem.
You're already stressing about something that hasn't even happened
yet.

When something is over, it's just that: over, done, in the past.
Leave it there. If a hundred things go right for us in a day and one
thing goes wrong, that's the one thing we usually take home with us.
We have a tendency to replay the negative experience in our minds
and the hurtful feelings are continually relived. We can't get it out of
our mind, no matter how hard we try. Never mind that 90% of the
day went quite well—that's quickly forgotten. We have a tendency,
instead of dwelling on the positives, to recall only the most emotional and negative things. You're not alone, just about everybody
does it.

Knowing this is really no help. Misery loves company, but
when something bad happens we feel alone. But what we are doing
is allowing a past occurrence (even two hours ago is the past) to prey
on our present. We are taking a situation that is over and giving it a
life it really shouldn't have. We all make mistakes, we all have arguments, and sometimes confrontations we'd rather not, but we're not
living a few hours ago or a few hours in the future, we're living right

now. That's where our thought should be.

You have to consciously and thoughtfully approach everything you do or say or think. If you begin reliving a painful event of the day or week, you must consciously and firmly tell yourself that this is just a memory. Because that's all it is in reality. You are now firmly entrenched in the present. A helpful technique I've utilized over the years is to shut my eyes tightly for a few seconds and bring my thoughts back to the present. I'll tell myself: "Here and now, here and now, concentrate on here and now." It's as if I'm resetting my brain. If it doesn't take hold, I do it again. Every time the negative memory pops up, bring yourself back to the present immediately. Don't give it a chance to fester. That's one of the keys to success in making your life flow smoothly.

I just read a letter written to Dr. Joyce Brothers, where a family (the parents and two children) never enjoys their Sundays because they're worried about having to go to work or school on Monday. According to their letter that's all they can think about. Not including vacation, that's about 50 days out of every year they're guaranteed to feel crappy. That's just dumb! You wouldn't wish that on anyone else, so why do it to yourself?

One technique I utilized in the beginning to practice staying in the moment might sound unusual, but it was very helpful to me. I narrated what I was doing at the moment. Not all the time, just when I wasn't concentrating on something specific. On my walks to work I kept a running commentary in my mind.

I'd think things such as "Now I'm walking though the park and observing the deep blue sky and the waves of the ocean," or "I'm turning onto Main Street and it's a beautiful day." I'd do this all the way to work. It gave me practice at being in the moment and was also a nice way to start each day. You should try it. Through practice you'll be able to spend more and more time where you really are, and since it's not an all-or-nothing thing you will notice the progress you're making.

By staying in the moment you'll eventually build a supreme confidence that you can handle whatever you need to when the time comes. You won't be worrying about future events. When worry is taken out of the equation, all sorts of possibilities open up. You're no longer shackled by dread, and life will flow more smoothly.

Yesterday, I experienced a perfect example of how staying in the moment is supposed to work. I worked for nine hours in my store and lost money, a less than stellar performance. (I had more refunds than sales.) That's okay. The instant I walked out the door at the end of the day, I consciously made a point of enjoying each moment of my walk home. It was a beautiful and crisp fall evening, and I didn't let the day intrude on my thoughts even once. The day was over and as such it had no bearing on my evening.

I can always tell when one of my neighboring merchants is going through a rough patch. I just have to look at their faces. If I ask them how they're doing, their answer invariably has to do with how their business is doing. If their business is doing well, they're happy. If not, they're not. My answer when asked how I'm doing normally goes something like this: "Lately, I'm doing great, but I can't say the same for business." My happiness and the success or failure of my business are mutually exclusive things. How much I've done in sales has no bearing on my present happiness. Once the day is done, I'm outta there, physically and mentally.

This wasn't always the case, and for a long time my day-to-day happiness was linked to the vagaries of business. I no longer make the mistake of equating business success with happiness.

Oftentimes it's not only the fear of the future but also fear of how we're going to react when we get there. Your history will determine how you think you'll react. Through experience we can pretty much anticipate how we're going to act in an upcoming situation. If we've reacted positively in the past to a like circumstance, we feel confident we'll react the same way in the future. That feeling takes all the pressure off and worry becomes a non-issue.

However, if we've reacted negatively in the past, we have a certain dread that the upcoming situation might cause us similar reactions. This results in worry; we're projecting our future emotions. The situation hasn't even happened, and we're already anticipating a negative response. We're worrying about a future action as if it is something out of our control, treating past responses as a blueprint for future actions.

With conscious effort, the dread of future responses doesn't occur. What you did in the past has absolutely no bearing on your future. Keeping yourself in the moment allays all such fears. Every day is a fresh start and should never be clouded with even a hint of former negative emotions.

In one of my former jobs, I worried on almost a daily basis about dealing with my employer (the most anal-retentive person I've known). He would drive all of his employees crazy, and we all resented him completely for making our lives there unnecessarily difficult. I worried about overreacting to his provocations, and with good reason. I had responded very strongly a number of times to his "idiosyncrasies," and had on occasion given him hell, and I was afraid that as my enmity toward him grew so strong might actually cause me to physically harm him! So my fear didn't have as much to do with his actions but more on how I was going to react to them. I was glad to finally get a handle on the situation, and nothing physical ever occurred.

Over-committing oneself is another problem that complicates the task of living in the moment. A lot of times we make too many commitments, or the wrong commitments. I have a good friend who accepts invitations to parties or any number of events that she really doesn't want to attend. As soon as she accepts, she regrets, then castigates herself up to the moment she gets there. Instead of going about enjoying her present, she is stuck in the future regretting her decision of the past.

We all have occasional obligations (work, family, etc.) we'd rather not participate in. However, if you're really and truly averse to doing something, simply don't commit to it. If a friend needs your help, bite the bullet and be a good friend with a positive attitude. The point is that, once the commitment is made, forget about it until the time comes, but don't commit unless you are willing to go through with it. Life can be fully enjoyed only if we live it one moment at a time, and that's accomplished by not regretting past choices or future consequences of those choices.

CHAPTER THREE
LIMITING YOUR EXPECTATIONS

We all have expectations; in fact, life would be rudderless without them. We expect that, if we do a good job, we'll be rewarded. If we're driving, we expect others to stop at a red light and not plow into us. We expect a library to have books, a restaurant to have food, a building supply store to have paint. We expect bad people to be punished.

Sometimes our personal expectations become too high, and this can cause us unnecessary trouble. By having too lofty of an expectation, we put pressure on ourselves. Something that would be perfectly satisfying under normal conditions might not be fulfilling if we expect too much of it. For example, if you begin dating someone with whom you are infatuated, you might decide this person is "the one." Right away your mind races and you get ahead of yourself in the excitement. If the other person's approach is more casual, they may just want to see what develops (if anything). After a few months, if he/she decides to call it quits, you'll be very disappointed, having expected more out of the relationship. While the other person might be simply somewhat disappointed, you're disappointed to be point of being depressed. Your early expectations were way out of proportion to the circumstances, and you set yourself up for a fall. Much of the loss we feel when something like a relationship ends prematurely, is not so much the loss of companionship today but more our expectations of what might have been. We fear the loss of future happiness when we set up scenarios in our minds of the future we had planned to have with the other person; and now realize that will never be. But, what we're doing to ourselves is mourning something that's never been and only causing ourselves heartache by producing future scenarios in our minds that have nothing to do with reality.

The stock market is the perfect analogy for how expectations, when set too high, can cause more harm than good. Market analysts predict results that they expect a company to reach in a particular quarter. They predict gross sales, profit and earnings, net sales, sales as in comparison to last year, and so on. Out-of-whack expectations can turn something that is really good into something really bad.

For example, in the third quarter of 2000, Nortel Networks posted revenue up 42% over the same period last year. Net income shot up 83%, and sales rose an astounding 90% over the same period. You'd expect with results like that, the stock should have gotten a nice boost in after-hours and next-day trading. Instead, the stock plummeted. It lost 30% of its market capitalization in the next 24-hour period and devastated the entire sector the day after posting. Why? Because *some* analysts expected sales to rise 125%! Expectations were unreasonable, costing Nortel and its investors billions of dollars.

Keep the pressure off yourself, and if you're going to expect certain results, make sure you're being realistic. Unless you're crazy, you don't expect to win when playing the lottery. (Your chances are about 1 in 42 million in California, my home state.) Play if you want, but don't be disappointed if you don't win. Treat life as if it were a lottery. Do whatever is in your power to make whatever you want to have happen, buy the ticket, but don't live and die by the results. You can't expect to do better than your best, and this is exactly where your expectations should lie: in doing the very best you're capable of. That is the one expectation within your power to fulfill, and if something good comes of it, all the better.

When I began my business six years ago, I wrote up a detailed business plan and from that plan I had certain expectations. I projected what I thought were realistic revenue goals. I didn't want too many surprises, so (without low-balling it) I didn't make the mistake of setting my expectations too high. Realistic is the key word: goals and expectations go hand-in-hand. As long as they're reasonable and not outlandish, your chances of reaching them are greater. If you exceed them, all the better.

There's an old saying: "Happiness is achieved by fulfilling one's goals, if one sets them low enough, happiness is assured." That's the other thing you don't want to do. You don't want to set your goals so low that you shortchange yourself. This is as bad as or worse than setting them too high! You many not be disappointed, but you also won't reach your full potential. Think things through before jumping in to a situation with both feet. If you decide to proceed, give it your all and accept the results.

Just as you have expectations of others, others have certain expectations of you. This is trust. If a friend tells you something in confidence, they do so with the expectation that you'll keep it a secret. Without a second thought, they trust you implicitly, as long as you've built a good track record with them regarding such matters. They know they can depend on you and you on them. If they don't feel they can trust you, if they expect you to blab, you're left out of the loop. As friends they have every right to expect certain things of you. Strangers, on the other hand, can't realistically anticipate how you're going to behave. They don't know you and that trust has not been established.

When dealing with others you are sometimes at their mercy. If you take your car into a new garage for repairs, your expectations are mixed. You hope that you'll be treated fairly, but in the back of your mind, there's a lingering doubt, and unless you yourself are familiar with the workings of a car, you have no real way of knowing. If the mechanic tells you a new starter is needed, you go on faith that he's being honest. If your car won't start, you don't have time to ask for a second opinion, you just want it fixed.

In dealing with total strangers, you have a moral obligation to be honest and forthright, no matter what their expectations. If you're in business, it is incumbent upon you not to take advantage of others. My business is in an area that attracts tourists. Many come into our store in a buying mode; it's vacation time and the purse strings are looser than normal. We carry some unusual and hard-to-find eyewear. There's no chance they'll get the same thing where they live, so they're willing to pay top-dollar, and since they've never seen the same glasses elsewhere, they have nothing to compare our prices to. They would be easy to take advantage of. When business is down and its very survival is at stake, it's a tempting proposition for some. We could simply add $50 to the price of a frame and they'd never know any different.

However, I couldn't do that. I'm honest and have certain expectations of myself, that is to treat everyone, no matter whom, the same. If didn't live up to that expectation, my self-image would suffer. I just couldn't do it because it would be morally wrong and my business is built on trust. My customers can always expect fair treatment, as we've always provided in the past and which they have a right to expect in the future.

As long as others' expectations of you are reasonable, there is no reason you shouldn't live up to them.

One last point. Don't expect special treatment. You'll find that the further along you are on the road of conscious self-improvement, the better you'll be treated by others. It's not just slightly better, it will be very noticeably better. No matter how tempting, don't take advantage of it.

The reason you'll be treated better is because people will just be drawn to you, they'll like you more. It's natural. The more you are at peace with yourself, the more relaxed, happy, and patient you are, the more you will come across to others as a special person. In reality, you are (or will be). You're becoming what others only dream of being but have no concept of how to go about achieving. You may even start to feel a little special—not superior—big difference! But that will only happen after you've put in all the hard work. I've never had so many people genuinely happy to see me. When someone you see frequently asks how you're doing, and every day you give the same answer, "I'm doing great," they notice it. If they never see you stressed or in a foul mood, that's impressive, especially when done over a long period of time. It's as simple as people would prefer the company of a happy person than a not-so-happy person.

You make them feel more relaxed just being in your presence. They know they don't have to worry about you going off on them for any reason or acting in ways that makes them feel uncomfortable.

All too often, people have a surface veneer of civility, but scratch it a little and their true character emerges. Your true character is always out there for the world to see. What others expect in you is exactly what they can count on getting, and that's comforting to them.

CHAPTER FOUR
ACCEPTANCE

In a perfect world, everyone would act just as you'd like them to, and vice-versa. People would actually use their turn signals when changing lanes, bigots would stop hating, and inconsiderate people would become polite and civil.

As we know all too well, it's not a perfect world, not by a long shot. But, to paraphrase Rodney King, we all have to get along, there's no place else to go. Unless you become a hermit, daily interaction with others is inevitable, and to say that some people can be annoying is an understatement.

We all have certain pet peeves. Mine is noise. My business is on a busy street with buses, trucks, Harleys, and skateboards whizzing by incessantly. I've often wondered if it would be possible to make buses any noisier than they are (I don't think so). Even more than noise, my biggest cause of annoyance in loudmouthed people. You know the type: while everyone else is speaking at around fifty decibels, they'll clock in at around ninety. When they laugh, it reverberates the walls. As soon as they enter a room, the whole ambiance changes (for the worse).

I love to walk down to Peet's Coffee on Main Street in Santa Monica and just sit in their courtyard, enjoying my coffee and the L.A. Times. Plus it's fun to people-watch. I stopped going for a while because the same few boorish bigmouths would be there everyday, dominating the landscape and destroying what was once a very pleasurable experience for me.

I eventually decided I would not allow someone else to ruin

my morning ritual. Because I couldn't keep these people from being there, I decided to learn to co-exist with them. I realized they weren't going to change for me, so I had to do the changing. Unfortunately, people don't come equipped with a mute button. Either I learned to live with those people as they were, or drink my coffee elsewhere. So I adapted. I accepted the situation.

I would still *prefer* a lower volume level, but the probability is that that's not going to happen, and I've learned to live with it.

Acceptance applies to whatever bugs you most. As to others, you can't change them and any attempts at it could result in resentment. Trying to change people to more suit your taste is like trying to move a glacier—it isn't going to happen. So you're really not left with many options besides acceptance. A person will only change when they initiate the process themselves (and if they don't proceed in a conscious manner, they'll fail).

Because you are or will soon be the conscious one (since you're reading this book), it's up to you to make the necessary adjustments.

Accepting everyone as they are can be a hard pill to swallow. It takes time, a lot of effort, and patience with yourself. You might find it helpful to think of it this way: you can be pretty certain that whatever is getting under your skin is not specifically being done to bother you. If the other person realized it was, they probably would stop doing it. Then again, they might not.

If someone is doing something particularly irksome, think a moment. There's a good chance you've done that same thing, or something similar, at some point in the past, without deliberately trying to irritate someone else.

It's totally unrealistic to expect others to do things the way you would. A former co-worker of mine did everything "half-assed." He was as sloppy and lazy as they come, whereas I'm detail-oriented and believe one should always do your best. We didn't always work the same hours, so I'd leave my co-worker notes as to what was needed, and most of the time he ignored them. If he filled out paperwork, he'd leave out half of the necessary information, so I'd be lost.

And word filtered back to me that, on numerous occasions, he was very rude to clients. Our boss was aware of the situation but did nothing. I didn't outrank my co-worker and had already spoken to him a number of times about his attitude. Nothing ever came of it.

So, instead of banging my head against the wall or quitting, I just accepted him for what he is, a person with no pride in doing a good job. I made it a priority to work around how he did things and concentrated solely on my own job. It made my life a lot less stressful as I no longer concerned myself with what he did or didn't do, and eventually he lost his job. If you resent someone or how they go about things the only person you're hurting is yourself. They're probably content being who they are and acting like they do.

We all know people we would rather avoid for one reason or another. I've read in a couple of articles that, in a situation such as that, you should actually seek out those who most offend you. The thinking goes that a conscious person should be able to co-exist with these people, and it's good for you to learn to deal with them. After all, we're supposed to love everyone. My advice? If there is any way you can avoid them, do so. But only so long as it in no way interferes with or limits your path to a more conscious and happy life. You don't want to be inhibiting yourself just because you can't stand someone or something they do. For instance, you don't want to skip a wedding you're looking forward to because someone you don't care for will be there. You just wind up punishing yourself. But seek them out? No way! You can get more than enough practice in conscious acceptance on a daily basis without looking for someone irritating to practice on.

Because acceptance doesn't only mean dealing with others, if you want to reduce your stress level, acceptance will have to be a part of all facets of your life. As I've stated, acceptance has absolutely nothing to do with passivity. Passive people let the world dump on them and are too willing to accept less than desired results. Unfortunately, this includes things that are actually *in their control*. An accepting person understands that not everything is in their power and that fighting certain things is a losing battle.

If you can learn to accept things you cannot change, no matter how much you'd like them to, your life will follow a much smoother path.

I long ago came to terms with my illnesses. I've learned to view them as a fact of my life. It's no fun coming to grips with the realization that you're very sick. I used to say I turned from Superman into an old man in one day, that's how dramatic the change felt. The hardest part was that there's a very good chance I won't ever feel as good as I once did. The main problem in living with chronic conditions is how you feel on a daily basis. Take it from me, it's nearly impossible to accept how you feel when you feel so bad. It was unrelenting, every day and every night. Every one of the six past years I felt progressively worse. My feeling throughout the ordeal was that if I were to die tomorrow, so be it. I contemplated suicide, I think most in that situation would. Thank goodness I have a wonderful oncologist, Jerry Wada. His main concern is his patients' long-term health, but at all times he is conscious of how you feel in the short-term and how best to alleviate the symptoms. Because of some luck and because of Dr. Wada and his terrific nurses, *I'm now doing something I never though possible—living life—happily!* He treats me for everything, and I feel very comfortable with him doing that. I'm lucky that he's willing to do that because I know most doctors wouldn't.

I worked so hard to stay in the moment, stay positive, and accept things when I felt poorly. But for a long time it was too monumental a job for me to do on a consistent basis. I'm sure others would do much better than I under the same circumstances; hopefully you'll never have to find out.

Since a happy life is a flowing life, acceptance is one of the cornerstones of achieving your goal. In the beginning you might find it quite challenging; accepting what you once found unacceptable is not easy. But if you're committed to smoothing out the bumpy ride, it's essential that you dedicate yourself to the task. If you find the going difficult, I suggest starting with easy situations. Set your goals lower and don't allow yourself to be frustrated by the slowness of the process. Pick just a couple of things that, over a period of time, have consistently been a problem for you. Obviously, it must be things that are out of your control. Work strictly on them and don't concern yourself with anything else in this regard until you get the hang of it. If you do this, it should make it a much easier road to hoe.

Choosing a minor annoyance will also allow you to develop your own techniques, which will aid you in dealing with more important issues later on. I believe it was the Knights of the Roundtable who had a motto that is very appropriate for the study of conscious living. That is: "Adopt, Adapt, and Improve." You should adopt what I tell you, adapt it to your own daily life, and improve it by tailoring your approach to your own needs. If you try to do too much at the beginning, it might be a little overwhelming and cause you to doubt yourself. As with anything new, it's best to crawl before you walk. As you become better, and with practice you will, take on more, but *don't* put pressure on yourself. This isn't a race, and developing a solid foundation is the most important thing. Do that, and you'll find it's not just easier, it's really not that difficult after all.

If you lead your life consciously, and that includes not being lazy, the need to set deadlines to accomplish things also become a moot point. If you develop acceptance of yourself and your situation, through conscious living, you know you'll take care of whatever needs doing when the time comes, and before it needs to be done, and you'll act and do as you know you should without having to make arbitrary rules and deadlines to follow to insure that.

I used to do that myself, especially the deadline part. If there were something I had to do I would promise myself that by such and such a date I'd have this much work done on whatever it was. I was putting an arbitrary time frame on it. That was basically telling myself that I really didn't trust myself to do what I had to do in a timely manner, so I felt I had to set arbitrary parameters to ensure I did what I should. Through years of hard work and through experience I now have the confidence in myself with everything I do so there is no longer a need to pressure myself with artificial rules and deadlines. I just know I'll do whatever has to be done, and I've learned to accept the results. But, at the same time, I do it pressure-free.

At work, many times we can't avoid deadlines, we have to accept that's just part of job. Something "has to be done" by a certain date, and that's when the pressure comes in. The closer to the "due date" the greater the pressure we and others put on ourselves perform. There is something you can do about that and that is realized when you can teach yourself to "compartmentalize" and consciously prioritize what needs doing. You'll eliminate much of the stress you cause yourself. That's especially true if you have a lot to do, but little time to do it.

If you can consciously view each thing that you have to do as your only concern until that part is completed, and not worry about the whole picture, you greatly reduce the risk of being overwhelmed and your chances of getting depressed by the situation is greatly reduced. That's more easily accomplished when you train yourself to live moment to moment. Since we're the one's who put the greatest pressure on ourselves, how we go about our work is the one thing we have the power to change. We might not be able to change the amount of work, but by slowing down and concentrating on one small step at a time, can accomplish more with less stress.

It all comes down to slowing down, focusing on only one specific task at a time, consciously avoiding looking at the big picture once you've prioritized, accepting the fact that you indeed need to have the job done well and by a certain date, consciously relaxing and getting to work!

There is one more point I'd like to make regarding the unnecessary pressure we put on ourselves. If there is something you need to do, or even want to do, go to work on it and *don't* spend a lot of time talking about it! The more you talk to others about whatever it is you're going to do, the more you'll be asked about it and your progress. You might wind up with the same results, but the satisfaction won't be there because of the stress you've added by talking about it and now trying to live up to others' expectations when that was all unnecessary.

It's usually easier to accomplish things when no one is watching over your shoulder. A perfect example of that is the fact that I've been working on this book steadily for six months now and have a long way to go, but I've told only two members of my family what I'm doing. That was a conscious decision on my part that was made before I wrote the first word. It was done really to allow myself to write at a measured pace without having to take into consideration the expectations of others, and the added pressure that would bring.

Learning to accept what needs doing, formulating and carrying out a plan of action, and learning to take only one slice of the pie at a time, is not only beneficial in keeping stress at bay during the day, but at night time also. How many times have you been kept awake, or are jolted awake and can't return to sleep, because of worry about all that needs to be done tomorrow or all that you didn't accomplish today? If you're like most people that unfortunately isn't that uncommon an experience. That has a lot to do with not fully accepting the conditions of our lives. It's *always* harder to sleep if you're experiencing stress. As we know focusing on problems that you can't do anything about at the present moment, is totally counter-productive and again, that's why living only in the moment of your life you're actually in and accepting things you can't change at that very moment of your life, is so critical. If you can learn to not harass yourself, or beat yourself up over matters that need attending to, you're learning to live life consciously.

Say you have something unpleasant to do three days from now. It could be something as minor as getting your car smog checked, a dentist appointment, or something as major as a big business trip you'd rather not take, or a small operation. The conscious way, and therefore the stress-free, worry-free way, is to make all the arrangements ASAP, and then completely wipe all thoughts of it from your mind until the time comes to actually do it. Since you've probably done what most of us do, that is, anticipate and worry about something until it's finally comes time to do it, when you do start "accepting, planning, and then consciously forgetting," you're going about things in a way that causes you the least amount of stress. At first

you may even feel a bit guilty. You might get the feeling that somehow you're not putting in enough effort and planning, to do the job
correctly. You might think to yourself, "It really can't be this easy."
But, once you've done it a number of times you'll find that indeed it
really is that easy and you haven't sacrificed quality or efficiency at
all. The only thing that you've sacrificed is the dread that, for all
your life, preceded doing those types of things. The more you do it,
and just about every week something pops up that fits the bill, the
more you'll realize there was a simpler and better way all along.
Accept the fact of what needs to be done, prepare for it as much as
possible, forget it and enjoy whatever you're doing in the moment
you're in, and take care of whatever it is when the times comes. It
couldn't be more straightforward or easier.

        While learning to accept others and situations *not* within your
control, it's even more important to accept yourself just as you are.
Where you are right now really doesn't matter. This might be your
introduction to conscious self-improvement, or you might be well
along on your path. You're actively seeking a better life, and that
puts you one step up on 99% of the population.

        The very fact that you're seeking a better way means you're
not completely satisfied with the way your life is going. As noted, I
doubt very much if anyone is. But that in no way means that you
don't love yourself as much this very minute as you will tomorrow or
ten years from now. In order to consciously improve, don't get down
on yourself or judge yourself too harshly. I feel it's wonderful that
you're trying to improve your lot. You must accept yourself at all
times, and in all situations as you are, and not in a narcissistic way.

        If you're already happy, you just might find something here
to make you even happier. Progress will be made in increments and
results will be determined by both where you're starting from and
your dedication to the task ahead. This approach applies to all of the
basic principles and obviously takes a little longer if you're starting
from scratch. But that's okay! The more dissatisfied you are with
your life right now, the more improvement you will make, so it's
kind of a trade-off.

Work hard because every little improvement you make now will be one less that you'll have to make in the future, and it will make your later progress that much easier. But your task will be greatly complicated if you're not ready to look yourself in the mirror and accept yourself *exactly the way you are right now.* Don't just say it – mean it! The importance of this cannot be overstated.

Why would you be willing to learn to accept others if you don't give yourself the same consideration? We all have areas in which we are deficient, but dwelling on them is counter-productive. Since you are aware of your shortcomings keep them in the back of your mind. As you eliminate them one by one, your thinking will become clearer until that cluttered area becomes an empty shell.

Once you've begun leading a conscious life, instead of thinking how far you have to go, remind yourself how far you've come. Accentuate the positive aspects of your progress. Admit the setbacks, learn from them, but don't dwell on them.

Reading this book is a very positive first step, and I'm sure you feel a little better just for doing so. You're in the process of clearing the first hurdle, and you now have a definitive starting point. Since how long the journey takes is an individual matter, an important element is not jumping ahead and trying to do too much. That's one reason it's so important to keep everything in perspective and accept the good with the bad.

A very different form of acceptance is that of responsibility. All of us, at one time or another, have tried to lay the blame on someone else for something we've done. I'm sure we all know someone who always seems to do it: no matter what, it's someone else's fault. Children do it to avoid punishment. Governments do it to retain power. For some, it's a way of life.

That people reject responsibility is a basic, almost accepted, way, and it seems to me the trend is worsening with time. Obviously it's not the "right" thing to do, but because of insecurities, we are loath to admit mistakes. It runs counter to many people's self image to even admit they don't know something. They just cannot accept others seeing them as anything other than perfect. If those people believed in themselves more and had more confidence or a more realistic self-image, they would more readily admit their mistakes.

Conscious people *always* accept responsibility for their actions. Being conscious means being truthful, to yourself and to others. Part of being aware is thinking before you act or speak. You don't automatically try to think up excuses or reflexively lay the blame elsewhere. You'll find that consciously thinking before acting will make you less prone to holding yourself accountable for actions you may later regret. It only takes seconds to do before doing or speaking. The chance of having to accept the consequences for something you shouldn't have done is greatly reduced. That's all part of a flowing life.

One standard you should hold yourself to regards how you speak of others when they are not present. It can be embarrassing when word gets back to a person about whom you've spoken disparagingly. Then you really have no place to hide and must accept the fact that you really might be in for it – and you have it coming!
It's not necessary to speak glowingly of everyone all the time. But, as the saying goes, if you don't have anything nice to say, don't say anything at all. Negative speech adds nothing positive to your life; just the opposite. You wouldn't want anyone taking potshots at you behind your back, and neither does anyone else. Always remember how your words affect others. A very easy rule of thumb to always follow is to say only those things about someone who is absent which you would feel comfortable saying in their presence.

Follow this simple rule and people will come to recognize they can trust you and open up to you without fear of betrayal. You don't have to worry about repercussions of ill-thought-out words.

At one time or another, we all have trouble accepting others' points of view. This is especially true in the areas of religion and politics, two taboo topics if you want people to get along. In these areas, people have a tendency to see their views as the "right" view and others' as totally wrong. There's almost no room to compromise. Two events that perfectly illustrate this are taking place as I write: one is the Florida presidential election recount. Republicans see their Democratic counterparts as whiny losers who won't accept the fact that their man was defeated, while Democrats view their Republican brethren as having stolen the election through fraud and manipulation.

Positions harden and any chance of rational compromise is completely out of the question. When views are so polar opposite, any concession is seen as betrayal by the party stalwarts. But the way I choose to view this situation is as an opportunity to watch our democracy function and I see the entire episode as a lesson in civics and an important piece of history.

That's the best way to view things. Take an overall view of any situation and don't allow yourself to get caught up in the rhetoric and minutiae. We're living in an exciting time where things that used to take a hundred years to evolve now take a matter of months.

If you pay attention to the big picture and don't allow yourself to get bogged down in the details, then you allow yourself the enjoyment of watching events unfold, life is a lot more interesting and exciting, and you accomplish this without dredging up negative emotions that can only harm you. You don't have to open up a history book; history is being made every day—if you take the time to appreciate it.

A much nastier turn of events is occurring in the Middle East between the Israelis and Palestinians. The latter view the former as poachers on land they feel rightfully belongs to them, and the Israelis view this same land as their biblical heritage. The problem is as intractable as they come, and the hatred and mistrust are so ingrained, I can't imagine how it could ever be resolved.

For either to even consider the other side's point of view is out of the question. A very unfortunate consequence of this is the terrible bloodshed that is now an everyday occurrence there.

As conscious people, we learn to accept others' points of view. For the participants of the Arab-Palestinian crisis, given their history, that would be one monumental task, and to believe it could or would ever occur is almost unreasonable. In life, there are some problems that might be beyond resolution. It's unfortunate, but this is one of the reasons acceptance is so vital. We all have a tendency to take sides, but being a conscious individual, you have responsibility to yourself.

Part of that is to conduct yourself, especially with situations that stir passions, in such a way as not to be caught up in divisive rhetoric. This does not mean you shouldn't have opinions—I firmly believe that if you feel strongly about something, you should take a stand and not concern yourself with what others think. People will disagree, and that's their right. But one of your duties to yourself is standing up for what you believe if it matters to you, no matter what the consequences. That's even if those beliefs run counter to popular sentiment. You have to live with yourself and respect yourself, and that's a lot more important than what others may think in reaction to your beliefs.

I have always been an opponent of the death penalty. I think it's barbaric and an anachronism in the 21st century, or any century, for that matter. That goes counter to what most Americans feel. I've always had a difficult time accepting their beliefs because the consequences are so high, and it's a fact that innocent people have been put to death. My thinking goes that the state has no right to take someone's life, no matter what that person may have done. I also think that those who commit capital crimes should be severely punished, with no chance of parole and no country club living, no weight training, and limited opportunities to interact with others. The more heinous the crime, the harder the time.

If you really want to punish someone, the fact that they will spend the rest of their lives in prison is a lot stronger of a punishment. I think that prospect is a deterrent, if anything at all really is. When someone is put to death, their punishment is over. Forty to fifty years in the slammer is serious stuff. A perfect example is the case of Timothy McVeigh. What he wants more than anything is to be given a forum to espouse his perverted views and to end his suffering by being executed. Unfortunately, and unnecessarily, we are providing him with both of those things. The thought of spending fifty years in prison without the soapbox he has been given is what he fears more than anything else.

That my opinion may be unpopular is of no concern to me (although, because of mistakes that have recently come to light, public opinion is shifting). The point is that no matter how strongly you feel about something, you must accept the fact that other people have differing opinions, even on important matters such as this. You might disagree 100%, but the fact of life is that differences exist. That should in no way affect your beliefs. Don't be wishy-washy.

After reflection, you should believe what you say and say what you believe, and accept the fact that others feel contrary to your opinion. Accepting things like this keeps you on a more even keel and helps keep negative emotions at bay.

But it's important to go about it in the right way. A conscious person knows that you can disagree without being disagreeable. It's counter to a serene life to be confrontational. If you respect other points of view, and people cannot accept yours, so be it.

Perhaps you have noticed that, when criminals talk about their crimes, they almost never accept responsibility for their actions. I'm not talking about their protestations of innocence; I'm talking about how they go about apologizing to victims and their family members in court, usually in an effort to lighten their sentence. They might express remorse, although I have a feeling that that's tied more to their getting caught than to their actual feeling regret for their crimes.

In almost all of these circumstances the criminal will say, "I'm sorry for what happened," not, "I'm sorry for what I did." There's a big difference. They're apologizing but not accepting responsibility. They have probably done the same their entire lives and that attitude might have contributed to the predicament they find themselves in.

Then we have the case of the nuclear sub, the U.S.S. Greeneville and its skipper, Commander Scott Waddle. When he apologized for accidentally sinking the Japanese fishing trawler, the Ehime Maru, he accepted responsibility for his actions. In his apology to the captain of the fishing boat he said, "I apologize for causing so much sadness and suffering..." he didn't say, "I apologize for what happened". Big difference. That's the difference between an honorable man who made a big mistake and a person who can't admit his failings even to himself.

Some rabid sports fans go into a period of mourning if their team loses. They just can't accept defeat. To them, a loss is similar to a death of someone close to them, and they can't even look at the sports section of the paper the next day. Their happiness is closely tied to their team's fortunes, which is a seriously deficient way to go about life. They just can't come to terms with the fact that their team lost a game. It sounds silly but is a serious problem for some people.

"Fan" is short for "fanatic," and in these cases it truly applies. I've read about some fans that have, after a loss, done anything from kicking in their television screens to committing murder. If they cannot come to grips with such a trivial matter, it would be hard to imagine how they handle real life.

For example, when Nigeria recently failed in its attempt to defeat Ghana to qualify for the World Cup in 2002 one Nigerian fan became so distraught he committed suicide.

Before my discovery of conscious living, I also used to become upset when my favorite team lost, as most fans do, but most of us keep it in perspective. It takes all the enjoyment out of the game when you just can't accept the fact that your team isn't always going to win. In everyday life, we probably lose as many as we win, but common sense teaches us to get over it and move on.

How we react to something as insignificant as that tells us a lot about how we'll react when something of actual importance happens. If we find it difficult, even painful, to accept defeat, there's not much chance of accepting losses elsewhere with grace and with the proper attitude.

If more people practiced conscious living we'd see a great improvement in the overall treatment and opportunities offered to people who need some help. The reason conscious people are so effective is they can do whatever work needs to be done while not getting too emotionally involved. We feel empathy, but at the same time, we don't get emotionally caught up in the plight of the people we are trying to help. That's an important concept to understand. You can be much more effective if you stay on an even keel emotionally. Conscious people never take on the problems of others. We all should do everything in our power to lessen others' suffering, be it family, friends, or those in need, while at the same time staying focused on our core beliefs of acceptance of all situations and taking things as they come on a moment-to-moment basis.

Doctors, although they empathize with their patient's suffering, can't allow themselves to get emotionally upset or they wouldn't be able to do their job as they should. When you don't get emotional in helping others you're not at all being distant and cold, but centered and effective.

It's as with death. We realize it's just all a part of life, the last part, but a part nonetheless. Some lives are long, some are not, and death can occur at any time. If someone close to you dies, you need to stay focused and centered in order for others to derive their strength from you. You feel the loss as assuredly as everyone else, but at the same time we all realize death is inevitable, and if you stay strong, others, who at that point are working on sheer emotion, will have you to lean on. We all realize life is transitory and ever evolving, and eventually all of us must die. It's not a catastrophe but a natural progression that we need to accept as we accept all things. If you try to fight the reality you can't win, no matter how much you'd like it to be otherwise.

Part of acceptance is accepting other people. In our lives we only get glimpses of other people who aren't family or friends. We just see them in passing, or standing with us in line somewhere, or at the next table in a restaurant or while driving. We really don't know anything about them. You might never need to find out the details of their lives, but if you do, sometimes it's a real revelation. That usually only occurs when you're thrust into situations where you have to spend considerable time with those with completely different backgrounds than you or anyone else you've ever been close with. It could be a situation like being incarcerated or as in my case, Army basic training.

Those situations are not the same as say, living in a college dorm. There you are living with people with equivalent intellectual prowess and, for the most part, are the same age as you.

For the first time you're exposed for more than just a few minutes to people whose type you might not have even realized existed. Basic training was the first time I'd experienced that. You grow up with family and friends, classmates and have some basic expectations of other people's intelligence and abilities. You develop minimum expectations of how people act. It was the first time I'd ever spent any time with southerners, African Americans, Native Americans, people from all walks of life and from every region of the country – and people of all colors and economic backgrounds. It's also the first time I was exposed to some really dumb people. Truly dumb people. So dumb in fact, I've often wondered how they make it through life. Some of these trainees in my company were so clueless that even after the drill sergeants gave us every answer to our weekly Saturday multiple choice quiz on Friday nights, they still failed the tests miserably the next morning. That wasn't a good thing for the rest of us because all the failures made the drill sergeants look bad in our commander's eyes. They took their frustration out on all of us. Finally, it got so bad that the drill sergeants resorted to giving us the answer sheets during the tests. We were told to get a few wrong to make it look good. And, these questions were about as simple and basic as they come. Still, even with the answers provided, right front of them, a few still failed. I couldn't figure it out then and I still can't. I was in when there was the draft so our platoon was extremely diverse. We had people who were only semi-literate all the way up to Ivy League grads. Even with all the different backgrounds we got along remarkably well.

When you're in that type of situation you get attached to people more closely than you usually do, and that's not only in combat situations, something I never came close to. You tend to stick together in all circumstances. You're with each other for twenty-four hours a day and become a team, and are more willing to accommodate others' behavior. That's very important in the maturation process. Every night there was fire watch. You'd get one hour of duty basically just to stay awake and in the unlikely event of a fire, it was your job to sound the alarm. One night I was scheduled for a 3:00 - 4:00 a.m. shift, 4:00 a.m. being our wake up time. I hated that. To show you how close we became, the man who had the shift before me didn't bother to wake me up because he knew I wasn't feeling well, with the flu, so he just took my shift, as a favor I hadn't even asked for.

You also get to see others in every situation imaginable. When you get to basic training the first week or so you're in what's called Reception Station. It can last up to ten days and that's where you get all the paperwork, aptitude tests, physicals, uniforms, boots, underwear, and eye exams where they provide those thick framed indestructible nerd glasses. It's also the first time that most of the men had to do everything in a crowd. The initial major shock when you get to the reception station barracks is the latrine situation. You not only have to share it with the other men but with cockroaches the size of small mice. *But, by far the worst thing is the toilet situation.*

There are about six inches between them and facing you is another row of toilets no more than three feet in front of you. They also didn't have sides, or doors, and there were about sixteen of them in a little room. There was no privacy whatsoever. If you've ever had trouble with bowel movements in public restrooms, magnify the situation about a thousand times and you get the picture. Add that to the "unique" food you're now forced to eat and it's a real nasty combination. I remember my first Army meal. None of us could figure out what it was supposed to be, and tasting it was no help at all. Half the time guys would wait till the middle of the night to make an attempt, so they'd have some privacy. Stomachaches were the order of the day and one poor trainee didn't produce a bowel movement for the entire eight days he was in reception station. You also learn a lot more about others than you ever wanted to. In this case there was way too much information. For instance, I now know there are at least four ways to wipe your butt. I also now know that I'm glad I wasn't responsible for doing the laundry.

It would have helped me a great deal if I was living a conscious life at that time. I didn't want to be there. As a matter of fact, at the time, I would rather have been any place but there. That was the universal opinion in basic training, except for the few guys who actually joined. Misery loves company but it really doesn't help the situation. My first real taste of army life came the second day. I wasn't out of reception station yet but was already assigned K.P.

For someone like me, and this goes for most in my company, army life was a real shock to the system. A very unpleasant one. A conscious person would have been much more accepting and the adjustment would have been much smoother. We were all used to freedom to do and say as we pleased. But that immediately ended when we stepped off the bus. It was a gray and gloomy day, inside and out, and I had the worst hangover of my life. My friends had thrown me a going-away party the night before and it ended at 3:00 a.m., and I had to be at the airport at 5:00 a.m. For some reason I was placed in charge of all the recruits heading to basic from my point of departure, so already I had responsibility I didn't want. As soon as we stepped off the bus our drill sergeants were right in our faces, which took a little getting used to, although it wasn't as bad as I had heard. Sometimes it was kind of funny, though not intentionally. As long as you weren't a major screw-up you didn't get too much grief from them.

When we finally were allowed weekend passes everyone went into town and got drunk. Before you're allowed to leave on your weekend pass you get an hour class on what to watch out for. We were told the number of prostitutes that plied their trade in town, and were cautioned to walk in groups as everyone in the area knew when payday was. They knew it before we did. During our first escape in almost five weeks we were more than ready. When you hear the expression "hurry up and wait" pertaining to the army, that's exactly how it was. You spent probably twice as much time waiting to do things as you spent actually doing them. If waiting time were eliminated, basic training could easily be cut from eight weeks to four. That's another thing you had to adapt to, the boredom. You do so much sitting around, you start to feel like county road workers. You know the ones, one guy works half-heartedly, six guys stand around and watch him all day. Then, just so we wouldn't get too bored, they added a little terror to our lives. A week before my group arrived, a trainee was beaten and killed and his body was thrown into a dumpster. He was killed by some airborne troops who had just returned from Vietnam. We hadn't known this yet but trainees were for some reason despised by regular army troops. Normally, when you had guard duty at night, you were issued a baseball bat to defend yourself. Since that incident, all trainee guards were issued M-16 rifles with five rounds of ammunition. We were instructed to defend ourselves if attacked by shooting whoever attacked us, and we were told it probably would be regular army if it happened. They told us to shoot to kill. Now, that took a little getting used to. Only a few weeks before, I'd been sleeping in my own bed and hanging out with my friends. Now I'm instructed to defend my life. I wasn't very happy about that.

Another thing the army taught us was that individualism, which in America is prized above almost anything, is completely frowned upon and taken away from you. You're part of a unit now, and are taught to think that way, which was necessary if any kind of discipline was to be kept. When I got K.P., I had to report at 3:00 a.m., and we all came to believe that army cooks were more chosen for their sadistic bent than their culinary skills. I'd never been yelled at for nineteen straight hours before. No matter what you did or how hard you tried to do a good job, you got screamed at. After a while, I became somewhat immune to it and let it roll off my back. Some guys couldn't do that and the rest of us would do whatever we could to help them out.

The one great threat that was held over our heads was what the army called recycling. Not the kind we're all accustomed to. This was more of a do-over. If you didn't pass the basic requirements you'd be recycled—that is, you had to do basic all over again. That scared me more than guard duty. We spent three weeks becoming proficient with the M-16 rifle. You had to shoot well enough to pass three different tests at the shooting ranges, with pop up targets up to three hundred yards away. One of my new buddies was having trouble hitting the targets. If he didn't pass the third round of firing he was told he'd be recycled. He was fairly close to passing but almost needed a perfect score. The last test was conducted at night and for the first time we were to shoot from the hip on full automatic. Since it was night and the drill sergeants couldn't see too clearly, I decided to help my friend out. So, I shot at his target about half the time. I'd already passed the first two so it really didn't matter to me. If I'd only shot at mine I would have the rating of "expert," if not I'd only be a "sharpshooter." So, I was a sharpshooter and my friend passed. The way I saw it, they could have recycled this guy ten times and he still wouldn't be able to hit the target consistently.

When you're thrown in with such a diverse group, you really don't have any way of knowing how an individual will act in a stressful situation. A lot of guys who couldn't pass the weekly quizzes were the same ones who just didn't get it when it came time to learn various fundamentals of being an infantry soldier. In the army, no matter what your M.O.S. (military occupational specialty) you'll be assigned after basic, every soldier is considered an infantry soldier first. That's why you learn how to march, shoot, attack, bayonet, and so on, before you learn anything else.

We were on the hand grenade course for our lesson in the proper usage of that nasty little weapon. We've all seen them in old war movies but in real life they're much more impressive. The concussion and noise they make is pretty startling compared to what it's like in the movies. One by one we were called into a concrete pit that's floors sloped down to a concrete well below. It couldn't have been simpler: hold the handle down, pull the pin, throw the grenade like a baseball and duck. This one trainee didn't get it quite right. He pulled the pin and threw it, which left him holding a live grenade. Not exactly the way you'd want to do it if you expected to live. Our drill sergeant took the grenade out of his hands and threw it, at the same time covering the trainee with his body. It was quite impressive. On another occasion we were training to attack on fortified position using live fire. One of our platoon members became disoriented and turned around and began firing his M-16 at the rest of us. Having bullets whiz over your head was interesting to say the least, and again a drill sergeant saved the day by sneaking up on him and tackling him before he had a chance to kill someone. They hauled that trainee away never to be seen by us again.

I mention all this because, although I hated it at the time, I'm glad I experienced it. It taught me a lot about myself. I find it very interesting how we learn things about ourselves when we experience things. Even though you've been with yourself for your whole life, no one really knows how you'll react to any given situation until you're in it. For the most part we're usually pretty satisfied with the results, and that gives us the confidence to try more and more. That's why you should always try new things and enjoy as many experiences as you can without any fear. Either you'll be good at whatever or you won't, but I think you'll be pleasantly surprised when you do try.

What I found out about myself is that I was quite capable, at least as capable as the other men in my company. Even if I was unhappy (and it was a hundred percent my attitude that was causing that), I could still perform at top level, so that gave me confidence in other things. Besides, I needed to grow up and the army is a real good place to accomplish that. It also made me aware of how really diverse this country is, and that even with all our differences, we were really pretty much the same. It taught me to be much more accepting of others with different backgrounds, because, as you know, if you experience others that are different from yourself for enough time, you become more open to understanding them and accepting how they act. I truly believe that if everyone were given the same opportunity of spending time with others of different backgrounds, without having to resort to joining the military, we'd be a much less polarized nation.

In basic training, the one thing I would like to have changed was the one thing that was in my power to change: my attitude. I made the mistake of fighting the inevitable and since I wasn't mature enough or skilled in conscious living, I made things much harder on myself than they had to be. If it were today, I wouldn't be able to physically do it, although it really isn't that physically challenging if you're in any shape at all, but mentally, with what I now know, it would have been no problem.

Many times in our lives we are confronted with situations that we really want no part of, but due to circumstances, can't avoid. It could be any number of things, but the one thing that these situations have in common, is our distaste for them. That's all just part of life. If everything always went our way, there'd be no reason to live a conscious life. You wouldn't need it.

In situations that we'd rather avoid but can't, we need to try to change our perception of them through consciously telling ourselves that this is what is, it's the reality of the situation and for the most part is out of our control. If we did have control of whatever it is, we probably wouldn't be there. In that type of situation it's always best to just go with the flow, do what needs to be done, and move on when you can.

Along the lines of acceptance of people of different backgrounds, every once and a while some well-intentioned person or group comes up with a suggestion that is totally counterproductive to achieving that goal. If there were an award for truly bad ideas I think the Oakland School Board would stand in a category all its own, at the head of the pack. They are the group behind the idea of Ebonics. If you're not familiar with it, its main premise was to upgrade ghetto slang to a language that would be officially sanctioned and taught along with English in schools. When I first heard about the idea I thought it was a joke. But, they were very serious, and way off the mark. What's next, Brooklynese as a second language? It's not bad enough that the opportunities for a better life aren't there for many of our poorer citizens, now we should marginalize them even more by having them taught a "language" that almost no one outside the ghetto can speak or understand. What's the point? If you can't speak understandable English there's no way to compete, that is unless you decide to spend your whole life in the 'hood. And, even then, what kind of work could you get?

There was a great debate about Ebonics and many of its proponents still think it's the right thing to do. I thought about it and listened to the arguments and theories behind it, but it still comes out contrary to logic and reality, and in no way do I want something like this to be implemented. If their stated goal was to polarize the poor from the rest of society even more, that would make sense, because that's exactly what it would do.

Many people's perception of the poor as nothing more than "welfare queens" and lazy do-nothings would only be reinforced. If they're too lazy and unmotivated to learn the English language and especially if they have the gall to speak and learn another language in our country, the argument would go, why should our tax dollars go to supporting them? The one thing I'd like to make clear is that I kept an open mind until I heard all the facts. When I say "accept," that doesn't necessarily mean I agree, but I accept that their idea exists. If I do happen to disagree, even strongly, in no way does that have a negative effect on my emotions. That's acceptance, the emotional acceptance of all things out of our control. I won't change the school board member's opinions, but I accept them and disagree with them.

Fringe ideas that only give ammunition to social conservatives have no place in our society when we should be working on ideas that bring us together instead of those that widen the divide. As conscious individuals that's an obvious point. Our lives are spent seeing things the way they really are, and part of that is foreseeing the consequences of our actions. For every effect there is a cause. Anytime you do something or advocate a particular point of view, you need to analyze it from every angle, and consider all the potential ramifications. If you can't foresee where it might lead, then you'd better rethink your position.

All things happen for a reason. Nothing can be accomplished of any significance with a narrow point of view. Whatever good might be brought about by teaching Ebonics, although I fail to see any, there would be more harm in the long run. This is an example of un-conscious thinking. Just because something might sound good on casual observation doesn't mean it's worth the paper it's written on. As I've said before, you don't have to understand everything, but if you're going to get involved in a cause of any type, you really should understand what it stands for and how it will affect others. We need to comprehend others' points of view, or at least try to, so we can understand why they feel the way they do, and also to provide us with more information to enable us to make better choices.

Because we might not reject things out of hand doesn't in any way mean we agree with them. It's just the conscious and thoughtful way to approach everything. Even if, at first look, some ideas might seem outlandish, if we look closer there might be something we can learn from them. Even some bad ideas may have good aspects that aren't obvious without further investigation. We have a tendency when we hear something that sounds foolish, to reject it completely, even if we don't know all the details. Since part of being a conscious individual means trying to understand others' points of view, it behooves us to make an effort to dig a little deeper and be more open than most to the ideas and causes of others. Just because Ebonics seemed to be truly a bad idea, how would we ever know whether there was a valid point lying underneath all the rhetoric, if we rejected the idea out of hand?

CHAPTER FIVE
ELIMINATING FEAR

In order to be truly happy, you must try to eliminate fear. If you can achieve that, a major impediment to a flowing life will be removed. Fear takes various forms but is not a factor most people consider when they think of their personal happiness. That's because most of us don't associate fear with our everyday lives. But, in fact, fear is all around us. I'm not referring to the common fears we most associate with humankind: the fear of heights, of the dark, or of flying, to name some. But fear is such a pervasive force that it has a huge impact on how we live our day-to-day lives. It affects us on many levels, and keeps us from reaching our full potential.

We'll start with some of the basic fears that we're all familiar with and then go over the more pernicious types that can haunt our lives without us even understanding their impact. We're all familiar with the fear of failure. If it doesn't affect you personally you probably know someone who suffers from it. I use the term "suffers" because I consider it right up there with other chronic maladies that on a day-to-day basis alter our lives for the worse. I'll use my friend as an example. He's a prolific writer and calls me periodically to tell me of a new and exciting project he's working on. He's probably written ten books in the last few years on a variety of subjects, and on a number of occasions he's told me that by a certain date, after his latest book is published, he'll be a millionaire. Then he'll be able to pay me back the money I've loaned him over the years. I've always given him money with the expectation I'll never see it again (a very realistic expectation), and that still holds true. It's always a can't-miss project and in reality his ideas are pretty unique and interesting.

He'll spend untold hours in the library meticulously research-
ing subjects and his writing style is pretty good. I have a number of
his manuscripts at home and they're all well thought out and written.
He should be leading a very comfortable life—but he isn't. Instead
he lives in near squalor. When not in the library he spends his days
and nights in a tiny trailer that's no more than twelve feet long and
the ceiling is so low he can't even stand up straight. It's parked in
someone's back yard and his rent for the past twenty years has been
eighty dollars a month. It's crammed with computers and books, and
if he wants to cook or use the bathroom he has to go into the house.
Why does he live like this? It's all because he is afraid to fail. He's
never actually finished one book. He's written 90% of many but
when the time comes for him to pull the trigger and complete one, he
just can't do it. He spends as much time making excuses to himself
as he does on the actual writing. Every new book comes with a new
excuse. I've heard them all and over the years have encouraged him
to finish what he starts. And I know for a fact he'd love to lead a
more comfortable and normal existence, although he seems somewhat satisfied with his lot. That's a pretty extreme example of the
fear of failure but perfectly illustrates the waste a fear can engender.
He has so much talent and potential but because of that fear of failure
he'll never even come close to realizing it. His life is just a shell of
what it could be.

A fear doesn't have to necessarily be the magnitude of his to
cause problems. The following are some examples that limit our
lives.

If you're afraid of confined spaces you might not be able to
take an elevator. That eliminates working in a high rise office and if
the fear is bad enough even working in an office at all might be too
uncomfortable to do. That limits employment opportunities.

Many people are afraid of driving on highways, which limits
their mobility. Having the fear of growing old alone might cause one
to settle for less than their ideal partner. The fear of crime might keep
you in at night, the fear of losing what you've worked so hard to

achieve can prevent you from enjoying it, the fear of doctors might inhibit you from seeking treatment, the fear of losing a job can cause unnecessary worry everyday and affect your productivity. The fear of crowds can keep you from attending many events that you would have enjoyed, the fear of being inadequate at certain things keeps you from trying them—the list is endless. Either you accept the fact that you have certain fears and do whatever you can to help alleviate them—as best you can—or you don't, and tolerate constraints on your life.

Even if you can't eliminate a fear, if you consciously work at reducing it, at least you put the effort into trying to improve your lot, and that's something positive. You might accept that you have certain fears but that doesn't mean you necessarily have to take them lying down. If a fear is bad enough a person might want seek professional help once the fear becomes intolerable and causes one's life to become too narrow.

The point is, if there is anything you can do to help yourself, it's your responsibility to yourself to do it. If you don't, there are a lot of things you'll never do that would have added richness to your life.

Another familiar fear is the fear of rejection. We've all probably suffered from that at one time or another. Again, it limits our potential and is the root cause of much of our unhappiness. It's also interesting to note how another's fear can affect you. In order to be happy many of us need a partner in our lives to share the good with the bad. It's comforting to have someone who is strongly bonded to us and who knows our wants and needs as well as they know their own. Unique bonds are a form of strength.

Unfortunately, because we fear rejection there are millions of happy couples out there that will never be. It's a shame because there are so many wonderful people whose lives would be enriched immeasurably if someone were willing to take the chance and initiate contact. Instead, even though they might be leading satisfying lives there could be so much more, all for the lack of courage to take a chance. And the fact is their chances might have been good. They'll never know and their happiness is shortchanged without them ever realizing there was a potential interest on another's part. It's sad because instead of reaching for the stars we're content to settle for so much less. It's just safer that way and our egos won't be challenged. There are tens of thousands of actors living in Southern California. That profession is closely tied to rejection. If you can't develop a thick skin you might as well pack it in.

But stars aren't born. Until they're established, they have to go out and put themselves and their egos on the line time after time and accept rejection as a fact of life. For every part that is won there are untold rejections. I'm sure they never get completely used to it. But, you have to admire people who are willing to sublimate their egos for a chance to live their dream. And, the more they learn to reject rejection as an option the more the chance of success they'll have because their confidence will be higher. Losing fear will do that. That also goes for those artists, who instead of settling for a job in commercial art will take the chance of doing the art that truly makes them happy and fulfilled regardless of the likelihood that their work will not be accepted by the public. I'm not denigrating commercial artists but some people want different things. They're willing to forgo a steady paycheck to lead a life that will give them their best chance of finding true happiness. Take a lesson from these people. *Don't ever be afraid to try things or reach for the stars.*

Another fear we all have to contend with is the fear of letting go. It comes down to the fact that nothing is permanent and life itself is transitory. Whether it's relationships or work related, leisure activity or whatever, things are forever changing. Just when you learn the rules they seem to change. Most relationships don't last. Approximately fifty percent of the marriages in the U.S. end up in divorce and a large number of people who stay a couple are unhappy. Yet, many would rather stay with their partner and be unhappy then take a chance on the unknown and possible happiness. They are instead focusing on the possible short-term repercussions of their actions. In this case the person is not taking note of the overall picture. That's especially if your relationship is the root cause of your unhappiness. If you're just incompatible, you need to look at the overall to see what would be best for you in the long term.

Letting go is difficult when it comes to the death of a loved one, especially a child. Since we depend on others who are close to us for support, affection and companionship, the reality of never again enjoying those basic human needs provided by the loved one is almost too much to bear for many.

But we really don't have a choice in the matter. As difficult as it is, we must accept death as inevitable and move on with our lives. It's especially difficult with the death of a child because they didn't have a chance to live. We feel it's unfair, but life itself is unpredictable, there's no real rhyme or reason to it. Still, letting go of a child is one of the most difficult things we'll ever do in our lifetime, if it becomes a reality.

My sister Nikki lost her son Stephen at the age of fourteen. The poor kid suffered so much in his short life. He finally succumbed to a brain tumor, which had blinded him, after years of terrible deterioration. We used to sit him up at the dinner table so he could enjoy, even if just a little, what others take for granted. It was also important for us to spend as much time as we could with him because we knew that soon we wouldn't be able to. I remember the joy on his face on one occasion when I took him to a mini-car course where he could drive a little car around an oval track. I'd never seen him so excited. At the time he was wearing a helmet to protect his head after a surgery. The man in charge didn't want him to participate because he was afraid of liability should something go wrong. I could understand that. At that time I was a pretty tough cookie, and I wasn't above intimidation to get what I wanted. And there was no way that little Stephen wasn't going to get his ride. So, in this one instance I became a bully and he got to enjoy one of the few real pleasures that life would allow him. I would handle it differently now, but in any case, that little boy was riding that day no matter what.

Another time when he was nine or ten he was too sick to go trick or treating so he and I stayed home and Stephen got to pass out the candy for all the little kids that came by. He was such a nice little guy and was thrilled to be able to do it. He had a smile on his face all evening. He was also a brave little boy. I went to see him about 5:00 a.m. in the hospital on a day he was to undergo brain surgery. I couldn't sleep because I was worrying about him. He knew what was about to happen but there were no tears. As they lifted him off the bed and onto the gurney he actually gave us a little smile. Letting go of a special person as that was very difficult. It affected my sister for years after. Even though it's been years I still think about the little guy often.

It was much easier to let go when my parents and sister died. Each of them had been ill for quite a while, and when my mother passed away on her birthday in 1998, at the age of eighty-seven, we were more relieved than anything else. She suffered greatly with senile dementia and didn't recognize any of her children and spoke of dying often when she was rambling on incoherently. The passing of my sister Ronni 1995 was more difficult to accept because she was relatively young at age fifty-five. What was even harder to accept was the fact that she allowed it to happen. We used to call her the Queen of Denial because she could never face reality. She never accepted the fact that she was sick, and the fear of dealing with it led to her demise. The most galling thing is she should still be here with us right now. But, even if we can't understand how she allowed such a tragic thing to happen, we accept the fact that she indeed allowed it to happen and is no longer with us. My sister Nikki and I talk about it sometimes, how you think you know someone but you really don't. She had a long life ahead of her but since she made a conscious choice to ignore her disease we all suffered the consequences. I won't go into detail but it was such an awful situation that I believe some in our family were angry with her for allowing such a thing to happen. They always treated her with kindness no matter how they felt about it, and because my sister Nikki is such a giving person Ronni was allowed to die in the midst of family with dignity. I believe her last year was probably one of the happiest in her adult life.

Although each situation you encounter with a death of a loved one is terrible, it's like anything else: you learn to live with it. It's not that you want to, you have to. But, it's never easy.

In these cases you must consciously force yourself to accept what is. No amount of wishing will change it and no amount of effort on our part will make any difference. It's best to live in the present but when you reflect on a departed loved one, remember the happy times. Also consoling is the belief many of us have that the departed are in an infinitely better place. In my sister's Ronni's case her fears of reality did her in, and our fears of letting her go became reality.

As I've stated before, because of my medical problems, my greatest fears over the past few years were money and health. It was as if a dark cloud was perpetually over my head. My fear about health was that I would die before I had a chance to do a lot of the things I would have liked to. Although, when you get to a point of feeling so bad for so long, death no longer is such a scary thing. I frequently thought about the fact that I hadn't really accomplished anything of significance and my life would end on a low note. And it almost did.

I wanted to travel, something I'd never done much of, but most of all I just wanted to feel good again, I still do. I felt like I was trapped inside an uncooperative body. I wanted out of it, and unfortunately I frequently said so. Obviously, that's impossible and not accepting the fact for a long time made my life, and the lives of those who cared for me, miserable.

The money factor was also huge. I remember lying in bed day after day getting myself all worked up to a point of depression fearing I wouldn't have enough money to pay my doctor's bills, hospital bills, medical insurance, my mortgage, and the rent on my business. I'd already blown through much of my retirement account and my savings to the tune of a hundred thousand dollars starting the business and I wasn't making enough in the business to keep up. If I hadn't been so sick my fears would have been much less. But, I thought, since I can't work regular hours not knowing how I'd feel day to day, and if my business failed, what would I do? I was in my early fifties and I knew I wouldn't be an easy hire if I were forced to look for a job. Who would hire me? I'm a very good worker but because of my condition hiring me would have been a risky proposition. So, there I was, feeling miserable physically and becoming a basket case mentally. I read and re-read Ken Keyes' *Handbook to Higher Consciousness*: six times. It was a great help but for me it wasn't enough. My fears were becoming too ingrained and overwhelming. When I was at my sickest everyone did anything they could to help me. My partner Greg did a good job in keeping the store running. Family and friends and neighbors did all they could to help out. They called constantly to check up on me. They did my shopping and laundry and wouldn't accept a dime. That's a good thing because I didn't have one to spare. One of my neighboring merchants, Laura, who owns the dress shop, Gioia, two doors down from my business, organized all the restaurants on Main Street to provide me with lunches that she personally delivered.

Still, with all that, there was nothing anyone could do to lift my spirits. Intellectually I was gratified and at some points overwhelmed with the outpouring of true concern and affection. It's funny, you never know really what people truly feel about you until something extraordinary happens. Good people will rise to the top like cream in milk. People that came through the most weren't the ones who I expected anything of. One of those was my friend Marta, who I met through my business. She was incredibly helpful and supportive over a long period of time. When I was at my lowest there was nothing she wouldn't do and through her generosity and time, made everything much easier for me. But, I was the only one who could lift myself out of the terrible doldrums I had gotten myself into. I knew it was up to me. But, as we know, knowing something and doing something about it are two different things entirely. To add salt to the wounds in the midst of doing chemotherapy, my business got audited by the state franchise tax board. My accountant told me that auditors from this agency make IRS auditors look like pussycats in comparison. That's not what I wanted to hear just then. That threw me over the top. I now had to prepare for an audit when I had trouble just making it through a day.

At that point my consciousness was totally sublimated and I was running on sheer emotion. All negative. It felt like the world was crashing in around me and it seemed my worst fears would soon be realized. Even though we passed the audit with flying colors I was still in the dregs. After a while I finally got into the position where I could work part time. I didn't enjoy it. Then again, I didn't enjoy anything.

The turnaround came about when I took eight days and spent some time with my brother Joe at his beach house in Long Beach Island in New Jersey. I hadn't had a vacation in seven years. We hadn't spent much time together in the last twenty-five years, so for the first time in a long time I was actually looking forward to something. I went with no expectations, but Joe went out of his way to make me feel comfortable and he's such a good cook that my appetite returned and I ate like every meal was my last. I also had a lot of time to reflect. When I landed at Newark Airport I wasn't in a good mood. Then again, at the time, I never was. But, over the course of those eight days, relaxing on the beach and spending time with family and friends, a profound change swept over me. I read and re-read Epictitus' *Discourses*. I started to relax. My leukemia was in remission, the Tension Fatigue Syndrome that has a tendency to make my body speed wasn't causing me as much problems. My allergies had been so severe that they actually caused me the most trouble on a day-to-day basis, but they abated somewhat and my daily stomachaches lessened. That allowed me to think with more clarity. As you know, it's very difficult to think straight when you're battling some physical problem or problems.

I have a stomachache most of the time and my allergies never let up. That and all the medication I take daily, cause me to drag through most days and make it very difficult to concentrate on anything. But, I thought now that I had a chance to think more clearly, maybe everything wasn't so bad after all. I did have a lot to be thankful for if I thought about it. I have a wonderful family, good friends, I live in a place that before I could only dream of, and even if business was down, it was still viable. After a few days of relaxing on the beach at the Jersey shore my thinking started to turn around. What did I have to fear really? I have family and friends so if worse came to worse, I'd always have a place to live. My business could probably be turned around with hard work. For the first time in years I was feeling better physically so maybe things would be okay. By the time I left New Jersey I was feeling a whole lot better about myself.

The next morning when I woke up at home in California, I felt absolutely awful. The flight was delayed three hours in Newark and when I got to Phoenix to change planes that flight was cancelled. By the time I walked through the door I'd been traveling eleven hours and I was exhausted. My allergies were acting up so much I felt like I had the flu and for some reason, I've found the worse my allergies are, the worse my stomach aches. And, I had to go to work. It was our busiest day of the week. I thought I was back at square one but, since my muddled thinking was getting a bit clearer through conscious effort, my consciousness had a chance to take over from my emotions. **I soon realized to my great joy that sinking feeling that I'd carried around in the pit of my stomach for so long was no longer there.**

I attributed it mostly to the fact that, number one, I was feeling better physically. And two, there was no longer any fear. Zero, zip. That burden seemed to just lift off as I relaxed on the beach in New Jersey. Because there was no fear there was no stress, no anxiety, and absolutely no worry. I had never imagined I could reach that point and it all happened so quickly that I was taken aback. It was as if all my knowledge had been lying dormant all those years just waiting for a chance to rise to the surface and come alive. Everything I studied and studied about living life consciously was so ingrained that the first opportunity to get some clarity in my thinking brought it bubbling to the surface all at once. I haven't experienced a moment of stress since. *The effects of all my studying, all my reading, my meditation, my long walks on the beach, everything I'd worked on for the past six years came together perfectly.* I went back to work full time and started to fix my home up to where I felt very comfortable there. I was no longer being held back by fear and worry, and now with some luck I should be around for a long time to enjoy it. *I feel like a kid in a candy store.* When you make your emotions accountable to your intellect a world of possibilities opens up. It's truly a unique and wonderful feeling not having a care in the world. And, that's how I feel. With my illnesses I've gotten to the point that if I don't feel them too much I don't think about it. Unless it's really bad, I now ignore them.

Even when good things are happening in our lives there is still fear. If something good happens and we are truly enjoying it, our fear becomes the fear of losing it or not having it last. Right away scenarios develop in our minds that cause us not to fully engage in whatever is happening. In my case, whenever I felt uncommonly good physically, even for a few hours, I never fully allowed myself to enjoy it because in my mind I feared it wouldn't last. It hadn't before, at least for a number of years, so why should it now? Instead of just enjoying it I fretted about going back to my usual way of feeling crummy. The consequence of that was I basically squandered the good feelings. Instead of really allowing the good feeling to fully develop, I deprived myself of all the opportunities I had to take advantage of feeling better. My destructive fear of returning to how I felt overcame the good.

How you respond to others is a good indication of how you will respond to various situations. When people are asked how something they're doing is going, a lot of the time they'll answer: "It's going fine, so far." They've only gone "so far" but they're not really taking advantage of that, and just going with the flow and enjoying how well its going. Instead, the person is projecting a fear that the good will not continue. Something is bound to go wrong. Why assume such as thing? For all you know, everything could turn out perfectly fine. So, if someone asks you about something answer in the present. If it's going well, say so, don't assume the good times won't last, and don't allow yourself not to fully take advantage of it. That holds true for everything from relationships to material possessions. Fully allow yourself to reap the benefits without worrying about future happenings. You've got it right now and if you don't tomorrow, you'll deal with it then, but now is what truly matters.

To be truly free is to not fear. Your best possible future originates from the relaxed, non-expectant present. Anxiety is almost always caused by projecting of future events, worrying about what might happen next. That's something we're all guilty of. A good way to think about it is to remember that throughout your life you've handled whatever needed doing when the time came to actually do it. You've always taken care of business before, so have confidence in yourself that will remain the case.

Fear also inhibits us by keeping us from doing certain things because we're afraid others won't approve. It can be anything from the mundane to things that really matter to us. We might not take a job that our friends and family think we're overqualified for but we would really enjoy doing. If we fall in love with a person of a different race we might not act upon it because we fear being ostracized, or we're afraid of being singled out and hurt by strangers comments. In a conversation we might not express what we truly believe for fear of being criticized. The list is long and we might or might not realize fear is a factor in our judgments. You can't allow the fear of others' reactions to change what you do or say. They have a right to their opinions, but that's just what they are, opinions. As long as you're not doing something to deliberately upset others, their opinions, although taken into account, really don't matter that much in the end and shouldn't have a bearing on your actions. Conversely, you shouldn't try to run others' lives by showing disapproval of their actions. Give an opinion, but only if asked to do so. Others will resent your meddling in their lives as you would if they meddled in yours.

We all, at one time or another, don't attempt something for fear of looking foolish. In my hometown of Ridgefield, New Jersey, every winter, town officials would flood the little league field and transform it into a skating rink. It was situated lower than the surrounding land so it was perfect. I remember going down there with a couple of friends when I was around eight years old. None of us knew how to skate so we spent most of the afternoon on our butts.

Every afternoon thereafter my two friends would practice their skating and within a week they were spending a lot more time on their feet and a short while later they became pretty expert at it. I didn't. Only because I felt foolish that first day when a few people laughed at my efforts. I was afraid to go down there again because of the fear of looking foolish in others' eyes. What should have been a big part of my childhood wasn't because I allowed my fears of what others' thought to dictate my actions. It affected me so much that I never went skating again that winter.

It's obvious there are many ways we can damage ourselves with our fears. A conscious person does not allow any fear to affect any facet of their lives in any way or at any time. Believe it or not, as long as you see things as they truly are and don't magnify the scope of their threat to you, fear can be completely eliminated from your life. Only you cause yourself to be fearful. It doesn't have so much to do with bravery as it does with reality. Your perceptions shape your thinking process. If you perceive something to be a threat, realistically or not, it becomes a threat. You reap what you sow.

A particularly insidious form of fear is panic. On the battlefield it can make a brave soldier act in a cowardly fashion. People who are stricken with anxiety attacks in everyday life are as paralyzed in mind as a quadriplegic is in body. When a panic attack occurs, all reason and proportionality are out the window. A parallel is my allergies and how my immune system reacts to allergens. If even the slightest bit of dust is anywhere in my vicinity my immunity system over-reacts so dramatically and produces so strong of a defense that my physical reaction is immense. It's as if my body is its own worst enemy. If I sit in a chair with a fabric cover, within thirty seconds it starts to affect me and I have to stand. It's gotten to be totally out of control and is cumulative, which allergies are, feeding off themselves until I'm feeling miserable.

Panic begets more panic until it spirals out of control. That would be the case with combat fatigue. In everyday life it can build until it becomes intolerable. A good friend and I used to be managers for an electronics company. We had to attend a manager's meeting one day and five of us piled into his car early one morning for the meeting. It was being held at our company's headquarters. My friend had been spending a lot of time flirting over the phone with an exceptionally attractive secretary who worked there. He'd seen her once as she passed by during a previous meeting, but she didn't know him or what he looked like. She enjoyed their flirting as much as he did and was looking forward to finally meeting him face to face that day. It took us almost two hours in rush hour traffic to get there, and as we drove I could see him getting more and more agitated. No one else noticed, but I could tell something was wrong. All the other guys were good-naturedly ribbing him about his upcoming rendezvous. When we arrived, we all got out of the car except for him. He was in the midst of an anxiety attack. No amount of prodding could get him to set one foot out of the car. So, we all went in and he gathered himself and drove home—two more hours. Late in the afternoon he returned and waited in the parking lot for us. The meeting ran late and we didn't get through till 9:00 P.M. He'd been sitting in the parking lot for five hours.

All he had talked about for the previous week was how excited he was to meet her, and how he was thinking of asking her out. Instead, he missed an important meeting and spent a total of almost thirteen hours doing chauffer duty. He became completely overwhelmed with fear.

It's obvious that fear such as that is debilitating and all consuming. It is very difficult for the person afflicted to deal with it. And unfortunately, it's not that uncommon. You can't just pep talk yourself out of it, and might need some professional help. What you can do to try to alleviate some of the stress is to attempt to understand what situations cause such a response in you and to isolate it from the everyday problems that you have to deal with. When it's standing alone, and not surrounded by other problems that muddy your thinking, you might get a better handle on it. If you think clearly about just that, and why and when it happens, you'll understand the problem better. Understanding anything in life is a first step in dealing with it.

Because I spend so much time in my doctor's office, I see fear on the faces of people all the time. Especially with the newcomers. All the patients sitting with me in the waiting room have cancers of one type or another. Being very ill changes everything, and until people learn how to come to grips with their illnesses, it takes almost as much a toll as the disease itself. It also takes a major toll on loved ones. You're forced to live in a different environment than you're used to. You feel alone and at the mercy of medical science. You quickly realize there are a lot more diseases than you might have thought for which there are no solutions at present. The next unpleasant bit of news is that whatever the treatment, there are side effects, sometimes seemingly worse than the disease itself, and many times there is no guarantee of success. The overall environment causes fear.

In the beginning you feel as if you've been dropped into the Twilight Zone. Hospitals and doctor's offices are not comfortable places. The smell of disinfectant is not conducive to a relaxing atmosphere, and all hospitals have that very distinctive hospital smell. It takes a while to even get used to the fact that doctors and nurses are just like us. They joke, order in lunch, do everything other office's staff does except in an office with a lot of very sick people, nervously watching their every move. Everything is more difficult when you're not feeling well. It's much easier, for instance, to get stressed. There are concerns about what will become of your job, your family, and your bills should you have to go through long-term treatment. And besides, you just plain feel lousy. That's the worst part.

A friend I met through work has breast cancer and has gone through radiation and chemotherapy treatments. Unfortunately, she's still having problems and realistically the prognosis might not be good. She's resigned herself to that possibility. Because we share many of the same problems, we've grown close. I can always tell when she has a doctor's appointment coming up. She still gets so nervous that she has trouble eating and sleeping the week before. She knows that fear is the worst thing for her, but she's never been able to conquer it, and is depressed a lot. I don't blame her and fully

understand where she's coming from. Intellectually she realizes all
the worry and dread are counter-productive but she is incapable of
stopping it. Because of her cancer she doesn't feel as close to her
husband as she did. When you feel that isolated it's tough to dig
yourself out of the pit.

In reality, if you want to live your best possible life, you really need to make the effort. That goes for illness or anything else.
You have to adapt to the new situation. What choice do you have?
But how do you go about it? In the case of illness, you must first
accept the fact that your life will change, even if only temporarily.
When you might have been on the golf course or at work you're now
in the doctor's office or the hospital.

That's a big adjustment. You must undertake the difficult
task of convincing yourself that all your worry and fear is not helping, on the contrary, it's hurting your chances of recovery. Stressing
yourself out is bad for anyone, but is even more harmful for the very
ill. Just as you wouldn't start smoking if you were diagnosed with
something as serious as cancer, to panic and live in fear is almost as
deadly. Whatever you must go through will most likely be unpleasant, but it is necessary and vital that you approach it in a positive
frame of mind. At least as much positiveness as you can muster. You
need to realize that no matter how much friends and family want to
help, you're really in this alone to a certain degree. If it makes you
feel better, join a support group. They're very good because their
members are the only ones who really share your plight and it's nice
to talk with people who are experiencing what you are. In my case I
find no benefit discussing my disease with others in the same boat.

Try to keep as much of your normal life as possible. Enjoy
the holidays, go to a movie, and go to dinner with friends. Do whatever you would normally do as much as you can. Don't change your
routine any more than necessary. If you can do that you won't spend
as much time worrying and your life will not change as much as you
might fear. Do what the doctor tells you to. As long as you're comfortable with your doctor, there is no reason not to. If you're not

comfortable, find a different doctor. It's very important that you develop a rapport and feel he or she is doing the best they can for you, so that won't be a worry. Read all the information you can that's been written on your disease. Get on the Internet, read magazine articles or books on the subject. The more knowledge you have, the more chance you have to understand what's going on and the more comfortable you'll be with the situation. Keep a list of questions you have for your doctor. If you're anything like me you'll forget to ask once you're there.

If you have concerns between appointments, call your doctor's office. A nurse might be able to answer any questions. Don't ever feel you're being a pain in their butts—that's their job and most appreciate people who want to know more about their condition. At least, that's what I was told by a nurse. It's very important that you keep your thoughts in the present so you're not worrying about what might happen next. If you've never meditated, try it. It only takes twenty minutes a day and its benefits are truly worth the time. (Later you'll find detailed a very effective meditation technique.)

You can pray. Yoga is also extremely helpful. Anything you can do to help yourself relax and keep the fear at bay is good medicine. I did years of acupuncture and years of cooking up Chinese herbs in an effort to alleviate some of the symptoms. In my case neither worked. If you're in a lot of pain and medication is not helping as much as you'd like, try acupuncture, it might work for you. I know a lot of people who it's helped. Change your diet if you're not eating as well as you should. But, before doing anything new, talk to your doctor about it. He or she might have even more recommendations, and you don't want to do anything that could jeopardize or slow your recovery. **The most important thing is to accept your predicament and do everything in your power to help yourself recover.** Acceptance is the key here, because if you've got a running battle in your head or try to deny the existence of your illness, or any other predicament for that matter, you won't be nearly as effective in controlling your emotions. It's not denying the fear, worry, and anxiety exist but more not allowing them take over in such a trying time.

After that, whatever happens will happen but at least you know you've done everything possible.

PART III

BEYOND THE BASICS

CHAPTER ONE
ATTITUDE

It's interesting how our views of the world are colored by our hopes, fears, prejudices, and experiences. No two people see the same thing in the same way. Just as everyone who isn't colorblind sees the color red as red, no two people see it in the exactly same hue. Red might be red but is not perceived, due to physiological differences, in the same way by different people. Psychologically speaking, the differences can be subtle or great. If four people witness a car accident, there's bound to be four different points of view as to what occurred. When the scores are tallied after a prizefight it's not at all unusual that there are three different scores. One judge might even have one fighter winning whereas the other two judge the fight for his opponent. They watched the same thing but saw different things. How we view things shades all facets of our lives. Just as with everything we have a choice as to how we'll view them.

Since we do have a choice, why not pick the path of least frustration? For instance, if you're at home relaxing after a long day at work and are too tired to do anything else, you turn on the television to veg. You flip through the stations and lo and behold your favorite movie is on. You're thrilled. You sit back to relax, pour yourself a glass of wine, and get primed to be entertained. Unfortunately, you immediately realize the movie is three quarters over. You're disappointed. What lousy luck. Your all time favorite movie and you missed it. That's one way to look at it.

The way I would choose to view the situation is entirely different. Remember, you always have a choice. Consciously, I would remind myself how lucky I was to get to see the last half hour of the movie. I'd sit back and enjoy the ending with no thought at all as to what was missed. Why not enjoy what you have instead of focusing on what you missed? The importance of having the right attitude and ways of approaching things can't be overstated. Since a large component of happiness is attitude, the more positive yours is on all matters, no matter how big or trivial, will help determine the level of happiness you'll attain.

That even goes for something as everyday as people greeting you and asking how you're doing. Unless you're very close no one wants to hear your tale of woe. It's just a greeting after all. But, in reality whatever you say goes a long way in determining how you feel. If you say "Oh, I'm all right," that's really pretty neutral and the tone of your voice helps determine how others will feel about your answer. There's no ambiguity if your response is, "I'm doing great, never better." That helps you reinforce the good feeling as opposed to getting no benefit at all with the more neutral response. Say you're feeling so-so, and someone greets you. Why not say something like, "I'm doing very well," or "I'm enjoying the day," or "can't complain, everything's fine?" You're not lying because so-so isn't so bad, and you could feel a lot worse. And, you're also not contributing to a sour mood. You might find if you say it enough it can help elevate your mood. I know it does mine. I always feel better after giving a positive reply.

When I was feeling my worst, people would call to ask how I was doing all the time. If I answered exactly how I really felt I'd always regret it when I hung up. I made them worry and kept reinforcing the negative feeling in myself. I didn't want to do that anymore. Instead of a positive reinforcement by answering "I'm not feeling all that well, but that's just a temporary thing, I'm sure I'll be feeling a lot better soon," I made myself and the caller feel worse. Then I made a conscious decision. I decided to make a concerted effort to be more positive when asked how I'm doing, so my answers, and therefore my mood, no longer suffered. I wasn't going to lie, just put the best spin on my responses for my own self and theirs. It's true that physically I didn't feel any better but mentally I did. There was no more "why did I say that?" when I hung up.

Everyone has a different attitude toward money. I just read an article in the *Los Angeles Times* that perfectly illustrates that point. A husband and wife grew up in totally different environments. His was one where money was never a problem, the family was well off. Her experiences were completely different, and her family just got by. Those experiences still colored how they think about money to this day. In a telling quote the wife said: "Just thinking about money stresses me out. I could be making millions and it would never be enough to make me feel secure." In her mind, money and security go hand-in-hand and are a constant source of concern. His attitude is completely different. His thinking is: "It's always been there when you need, as long as you put out the effort for it to be there." Even though their finances were exactly the same, her perception allowed the situation to become stressful.

In my life I've lived both those attitudes, depending on where I was at the time in my thinking. Obviously, how you feel about money is an attitude just as most things in life are. I tend to like the husband's thinking more. He realizes the importance of having enough money to live his life, and is conscious of the fact that you need to put out the effort to get it. But he doesn't stress about it. He keeps it in perspective. In a letter to a friend Thomas Jefferson wrote: "It is neither wealth nor splendor, but tranquility....which gives happiness." You don't have to be rich or "successful" to be happy. You just have to have the right attitude.

As I've previously mentioned, in the last number of years, money was a huge concern for me. The stress, worry, and fear it provoked was almost overwhelming. A few days ago a good client came in to pay be back some money I had loaned her. It was bothering her enough that she wanted to at least make a start on repaying me. I could tell something was wrong the moment she walked in. She's unfortunately going through a lot of financial difficulties and has been for a while. The fact that she's struggling so much has caused her to become depressed. That's become the overriding thing that takes almost all the joy out of her life and negates any good that she's experiencing at the moment. The only thing that's saving her from complete despair is her fourteen-year-old son, who's a good kid.

In times such as this we, more than at other times, need the reassurances of someone close. When you get to the point she's at, you feel more vulnerable than before because you start to worry about such basic things as security, and providing for yourself and children. Things you always took for granted are now major concerns, and things that even recently seemed to be major problems now get pushed to the back, as the money worries take over. Right away you can see that maybe the things that were problems a short time ago, really aren't when we can afford to ignore them now. I listened to her litany of troubles and tried to reassure her that things would turn out just fine. I reminded her that she had seemingly overwhelming problems before and she came through them, and that she'd do it again this time. This is an important point. We all need to just have faith in our own abilities because that's what has gotten us this far. There's no reason to think any differently. Have confidence in yourself and your abilities. Try not to worry about tomorrow because that will do no good and tomorrow will be here soon enough. Then, if you don't like life consciously, you could start to worry about the next day. I think she felt a little better when she left, and no, I didn't allow her to pay me back the money.

In my own case it was a constant battle to sublimate my money fears. I absolutely realized it was foolish of me to worry because that wasn't going to solve the problem, just worsen it. But still, the fear was there. I even allowed it to affect the timing of treatments for my leukemia for fear I couldn't pay for them. I held off doing chemotherapy until I absolutely had to. My doctor was wonderful and was aware of my concerns. He would never do anything that would cause me harm, so I knew I could trust him to take the necessary steps when the time came. That was one thing I never had to worry about.

I finally got to the point where I felt so awful all the time I had to put my money concerns aside and just go for it. I remember one day while I was doing chemotherapy I could barely tolerate the terrible feelings in me. While doing chemo, all other physical problems magnify a great deal. I overheard Dr. Wada and Lisa, his head nurse, discussing what they could do to try to alleviate some of the stress on my body. They were both concerned for me, not because I was in any mortal danger, but because I was feeling so poorly. Both of them are very concerned about not only their patients' welfare, but also how they feel on a day-to-day basis. That's something a lot of doctors don't place great emphasis on. I know that for a fact. They decided to give me a couple of liters of gamma globulin intravenously in hopes of making me feel better. Their cost for that two-hour procedure was twenty-four hundred dollars and they knew my insurance would only cover eighteen hundred. Being good human beings first and medical people second, they decided to eat the difference in cost and went ahead with it. Lisa stayed the extra two hours to monitor the treatment, although she was due at their other office. My doctor's billing company billed me the six hundred dollar difference even though he'd asked them not to. I could have called him to have the charges taken off, but it felt unfair to him to do so. So, I paid it myself.

Unfortunately the extra treatment didn't have the desired effect and I felt just as awful after it. It mattered a lot to me that at least they were concerned enough to try to alleviate some of my symptoms. I was running lower on money and I knew if I didn't want to drive myself crazy, my attitude had to change. I knew I couldn't wait any longer and felt as if my back was against the wall. I knew if I could remove the stress I was causing myself, everything else would be a lot easier. Or so I hoped would be the case. It wasn't an easy thing to do, but so, I reasoned, was nothing else I was going through at the time. I began to change my thinking. If I was going to go broke at least I should leave no stone unturned to try to alleviate some of the problems.

I started to see a doctor of Chinese medicine and three times a week I went in for acupuncture and to pick up some herbs that I would cook up following the doctor's directions. This went on for two years. The only thing worse than the taste of the herbs was the smell. My house always stunk. But, I figured if it was going to help me I didn't care. Although my neighbors might have. It didn't have the desired effect and for that period I was shelling out two hundred and twenty-five dollars a week out of pocket because that treatment wasn't covered at all by my insurance. I also tried healing touch therapy and almost anything else people suggested hoping for some relief. My once healthy retirement account was now looking as wasted as me. I'm just so glad I had a sizable amount, as I wanted to retire young. Or at least that was the original plan. If you're trying to lead a conscious life you can learn a lesson from what happened to me. It's best to provide as much as you can for the future, but realize that since life doesn't follow a script you have to be ever willing to adapt to any new circumstances. You need to accept that fact and figure a way to work around it constructively. So, I won't be retiring early. I think it's a great trade off. I'll work more years but at least I'll be around to do it, with any luck.

If I had realized that sooner, I would have put myself through much less stress. Adaptability is a cornerstone of a flowing life. The world is not going to change to suit you. So that doesn't leave you much choice if you want to lead as happy and stress-free life as you can. If you can convince yourself to flow with the situation, no matter how distasteful or how much you'd rather the circumstances be different, you'll find that things which were so difficult before really don't have to be. If you fight it like I did, you'll come out on the losing end. Once you get the hang of it with one area of your life, you'll find that since you figured it out once you shouldn't have trouble replicating it when it comes to other things. It all begins with attitude.

On top of having to pay taxes on the funds I was withdrawing I also had to pay penalties for early withdrawal. It turned into a five-year-long vicious cycle. In order to pay for my insurance and treatments I had to close out some retirement accounts, and in order to pay the taxes and penalties on the withdrawals I had to close out more accounts. Instead of looking at the situation as: I'm getting older and my retirement account that I'd spent years building up is shrinking fast, I started thinking of it as a quality of life issue more and more. I look back now and see how really foolish I was, but at the time I didn't know how to get out of it. That's one of the things I want you to take from this book. There are always ways of handling things that can accomplish your goal and at the same time allow you to remain on an even keel. Since I wasn't sure if I was going to be around as long why not just go all out?

Unfortunately, at about that time I developed a severe case of anemia. I was starting to think the situation couldn't have gotten much worse. The anemia was causing my body to attack and kill the hemoglobulin as soon as it was manufactured. I wasn't getting enough oxygen. I had trouble with it for months, and I was put on some pretty heavy medication in an effort to combat it. My doctor and I had discussed removing my spleen in an effort to alleviate the problem but I was very fortunate it didn't come to that and the medicine worked. But I still didn't feel very good. I couldn't drive or work and was so weak I could barely speak. Friends and family were good enough to take me to the doctor's and pick up my prescription medicine, did my laundry, food shopping, and anything else I needed.

I also spoke to my doctor of the feasibility of a bone marrow transplant. He thought it might possibly help and there was no harm in looking into it. I went to the City of Hope hospital here in Southern California for an evaluation. That was an all-day thing and thank God I had my sister Nikki with me asking questions and taking notes. I was accepted immediately into the program. Usually, your doctor has to go before a panel of their peers to decide if you're right for the transplant, but in my case, they deemed the need to be so great I didn't have to wait. The doctor told me in my case the peer panel would just be a formality.

One of the problems was the basic transplant procedure cost two hundred thousand dollars minimum and probably would cost significantly more in the end. You're told to expect complications. My insurance would cover a major portion of it but still I'd be responsible for a pretty big amount, probably in the seventy-five thousand range. Still, if that's what had to be, I was now willing to bite the bullet to try to do whatever I could to at least feel better for a while. And I was willing to go into as much debt as necessary to do the job. Unfortunately, no one in my immediate family was a match, so the hospital went into their databank to see if one could be found. It turns out that worldwide there were seventeen possible matches. The fact that no blood relative could be found reduced my chances of a successful transplant. Everyone I knew, family, friends, and clients, wanted to help and I had dozens of offers from them to be tested to see if they would be a compatible match. The City of Hope provides potential transplant recipients with a thick notebook outlining the procedures and their side effects. That book was pretty frightening, and caused me to take a serious look to see if I would be willing to put up with the incredible problems and suffering a transplant would cause. If I thought I felt bad at the time, it was a walk in the park compared to the effects of the transplant. The hospital gives you the book so you go into the transplant fully aware of what you're getting yourself into. You really need to be mentally prepared for it. Still, with all that, since I felt so lousy all the time, I decided to go ahead with it. That was until while I was sitting in Dr. Wada's office one morning and I read what the City of Hope doctor had written regarding my prognosis.

They are very close-mouthed at City of Hope and really don't answer a lot of questions directly. They do that for a number of reasons, including the fact that there are no guarantees and basically so you won't get your hopes up too high. As I read the report my heart sank. My chances for survival for the first hundred days after the transplant were little more than fifty percent, and to survive three years the chances were closer to thirty percent. I'd sooner take my chances without the transplant than go with those odds. So, I called it off. Unfortunately, the hospital had spent time and money on me and now I owed for that. My insurance would pay the bulk of it, but again there was a sizable chunk left for me to pay. Now I was even deeper in debt and no further along on my recovery. My insurance paid most of my medical bills but still several times a year I'd get bills in the several thousands of dollars that I was responsible for. My insurance premiums were twelve thousand dollars a year (since raised) with a two thousand deductible. After that was met I still had to pay twenty percent of all bills, until I hit another deductible.

As I gradually started to regain some strength I started to feel a little better both physically and mentally. This was about four months after I contracted the anemia. I was at home in my recliner for the duration. At about that time I came down with the flu. I didn't realize I had it because I always felt like I had the flu. So now, I was back at square one but a little worse. I was by this time getting pretty fed up with the whole thing. That Christmas Eve at a family dinner I got the shakes so bad, I had to go home. The shakes lasted for eight days. That was a really strange experience, and nothing like that ever happened before. No matter what I did I couldn't stop them. What I finally did was drag myself into the shower and just stand under the hottest water I could handle for about two hours every day until the shakes stopped. I spent the rest of those days in the bathroom because I didn't have the strength to make it my recliner. Later on I found out that was exactly the wrong thing for me to do. The problem was the shakes are so debilitating that I was in danger of dying of exhaustion, and the showers didn't really help. Now I felt worse than ever. I didn't want to leave the house because of the way I felt. I had no strength at all and by that time all my muscles had totally withered and I could barely walk. I was taking 80 milligrams of Prednisone daily for four months, which was the equivalent of chemo every day. My doctor told me to expect some mental problems because of that, possibly hallucinations. Much of the time I couldn't even talk. People were getting very concerned. Everyone but me. My attitude had reached a point that if I were to die tomorrow, so be it. I definitely contemplated suicide at that point. I overdosed on medication just so I could sleep and forget everything. If I didn't wake up again, so be it.

That Sunday as a friend came by to deliver some food and check up on me, my sister Nikki called. She wanted me to go to the hospital but I wanted no part of that, besides I didn't think I had the strength to make it. She called back a couple of hours later and informed me I was going to the hospital and she was on her way to pick me up. Dr. Wada would meet me there. I had a temperature of 106 degrees when I arrived and they immediately started IVs. It turned out I had a very severe case of pneumonia. I was on a roll! I spent nine days in the hospital that time and another four months at home recovering. To this day I still have traces of the pneumonia. I take medication daily to prevent it from flaring up again, and I have to take this medication for the rest of my life. I have to stand up slowly or I'm gasping for breath. The hospital room was twenty-two thousand dollars for the stay not including the doctors and medicine. Again, my insurance paid the majority of the bill but I was again left with a significant chunk to pay.

At the same time I was seeing an allergist, when I could make it, and getting shots. I'd done it before and it didn't work but I was so desperate for any relief from anything, I decided to take a chance. My insurance was paying part of it but that still left me with payments. Right now I'm taking a lot less medicine but prescription drugs run me about eight hundred to a thousand dollars a month. My last visit to the hospital occurred about four months later and that was an expensive one. I was in the hospital only five days but the first day alone was forty-seven hundred dollars.

I relate this story not to elicit sympathy, but to let you know where I'm coming from in regards to my attitudes about money. At first I worried that I'd rack up all these bills and wouldn't be able to pay them. I never considered it an option not to pay what I owed, in good conscious. When people say whatever doesn't kill you makes you stronger, they could have been talking about me. Felix Frankfurter in *Reminisces* put it: "Old age and sickness bring out the essential characteristics of a man." I guess that applied to me. I came through that a much stronger person mentally, but certainly not physically. I can't do a lot of things I enjoyed and always took for granted like riding my bike along the beach for hours, walking a golf course, or doing strenuous yoga, but I don't really care. If I could return to those things that I loved, great. If not, there are a million other things I can do that are less taxing on my body. As a matter of fact, a few months ago I started water coloring, which I'm a lot better at than I might have imagined.

My attitudes about money have come full circle. My thinking is now razor sharp on the subject and my perceptions of money as a major concern in my life no longer exist. Nietzsche in *Beyond Good and Evil* put it well: "A matter that becomes clear ceases to concern us." It's not even a blip on the radar of everyday life. It just doesn't come up. Conscious effort over a prolonged period of time works for even problems that at one time seemed all consuming and intractable. I'm literally to the point that I don't believe I could worry about it even if I tried.

I grew up in a family that didn't have much money. But, I had the most wonderful childhood imaginable and never even realized how difficult it must have been for my parents to make ends meet. I never had money so I didn't worry about it. When I started working, money still wasn't an issue. Years ago I quit a job I had managing retail stores after five years with the company. I had only a few thousand dollars saved but felt absolutely no pressure to find another job. I was enjoying myself too much being unemployed. Even though I had no income I'd go to breakfast with friends every morning, play golf all the time, and just had a wonderful vacation. That's even though I wasn't collecting unemployment. During one stretch I played golf nine days straight. This occurred when I was in my late twenties and later when I was very concerned about money, I always looked back to that time to see if I could recreate that carefree feeling. Recreating that attitude I found wasn't something I could do. It's like trying to relive your youth, it's a once in a lifetime thing, and it can't be duplicated. Heraclitus touched on just that idea in *Fragments* when he said: "You cannot step twice into the same river, for other waters are continually flowing in." That's why it's so important to keep on top of it. If you have been able to keep a good attitude regarding something you've found troubling in the past, you can in the future, as long as you're willing to consciously work on it.

Once I let go of the money worries I was set free.

Since money was my biggest concern after (and because of) my health, letting go of it, by changing by my perception, I was now able to be stress free. The situation hasn't changed, but it's no longer a problem at all because the most important thing had: my attitude. All my other worries were minor in comparison, and quickly began taking care of themselves to a certain degree. Whatever troubles you most is what you should direct most of your energies to re-thinking. If it would be helpful, make a list of all the things that cause you the most worry, and rank them according to severity. This way you'll know what to focus on first.

It's also important that you always realize that whatever you're going through is not unique to you. Whatever it is millions of people before you and millions of people after you have gone and will go through the same thing. They've survived and so will you. Once you are underway resolving the most thorny issues but only after you've made significant progress, you'll find the rest of the list that much easier to conquer, as you take on more. It's like a person wanting to quit smoking. It might aid that person if they think of the millions of people who've conquered the addiction. It can help them to realize that it is indeed possible no matter how rough the going. All self-improvement is, is a re-setting of your thinking patterns on particularly troubling aspects of your life. It's that straightforward. You tweak a little here, a little there, and before you know it, problems that seemed almost impossible to get a grip on, no longer are of great concern. The trick is sticking with it. You need to consciously approach everything you do or say, all the time.

That is an adjustment. Thinking before acting on a consistent basis is not an easy thing to do. It takes a lot of practice. The good and bad thing is that every day, all day is practice.

CHAPTER TWO
PERCEPTION

Being an optician, it's a part of my job to be familiar with colors. I'm also somewhat knowledgeable on how perceptions of colors can influence our thinking. I think colors and how we perceive them is a good analogy for how we see things in our lives. That's because as in taste and hearing, color is a sensation and each person experiences it differently. If a number of people looked at a group of tomatoes, there would be no consensus as to which tomato was the reddest or even how they would rank as to redness. Each individual would see the redness but after that physiological differences would color their perception. As with many things in our lives, the perception of color is subjective. Each person's experience is unique to his or her self. There are a number of factors that go into how we perceive color. Since it is such a subjective thing we need to take into account such factors as the environment in which we are viewing it, the actual mechanism of our eyes, the emotional effects that are invoked by the color, and the effects on that color by its surrounding colors. As such, our moods are affected by our environment, the company we keep, our outlook, and where we are on our path, etc. Colors can have an effect on our moods just as surely as outside influences affect our outlook on life.

The mere mention of a favorite color or colors can evoke a warm feeling. Others will evoke just the opposite reaction. The mention of certain colors can immediately bring an image sharply into focus. When most Americans speak of the colors red, white, and blue, that brings into focus our flag and might even engender a feeling of patriotism. We associate red with aggression but also with warmth and fire, as opposed to blue, which we associate with water and coolness. That's illustrated by the fact that many faucets are labeled red for hot and blue for cold.

When we view art we tend to describe a picture as being warm if the predominant colors are oranges, reds, and yellows, and cool if they are greens, blues, and violets. Messages can be conveyed by color, as well. Traffic is regulated by red, green, and amber lights. Since many of us associate red with aggression, police have a tendency to stop red cars more often than other colors because red gives the officer the perception of aggressive driving. I can attest to that. I own a red Toyota Supra and once as I was driving down the 5 freeway from San Francisco to Los Angeles, I was pulled over and ticketed for speeding by a Highway Patrol officer. The limit was 65 M.P.H. and I was cruising at around 85. I was going no faster than the traffic around me, but because of the color of my car and the feelings associated with it, I was singled out for the ticket, which I deserved. The officer said that since I obviously chose red to be noticed that he obliged and noticed me. His perception of me was prejudiced by my car's color. I told him that was not at all why I chose red, it was because I thought the color was the most flattering for the lines of my car. He didn't know me but made an incorrect assumption because of his own view of the color red.

I'm sure you've noticed while driving if one car is pulled over by the police, traffic tends to pick up and everyone else feels a bit relieved. I call it the Wildebeest Effect. It's analogous to lions stalking and killing their prey. Once that happens the herd can relax and go back to migrating and grazing. Once one of us is pulled over we can go back to our usual driving habits. It's as if one of us was sacrificed for the good of the herd.

Being relieved in that type of situation is just human nature and although we might feel a little sorry for the unfortunate   herd member, we tend to get over that real fast. We might view it as their turn and realize sooner or later it will be ours. The statistic is for every four hundred moving violations each one of us commits we get ticketed once. That's like anything else in our lives. Eventually we have to pay the piper for our transgressions. The more conscious and honest our view of what transpires in our lives the longer it is between tickets, until the time comes when we are no longer singled out from the herd. If we learn to play the game of life correctly, the more we view things the way they really are, the less time spent distorting our image of events through our prejudicial filters, the less we misinterpret what is really happening, the smoother the ride will be.

We also create associations between color and language. A person can be "blue" (sad), "green" (inexperienced, envious), or "yellow" (afraid). We associate yellow with sunny moods, or exciting and uplifting feelings. Green is associated with pastoral scenes and nature, and can symbolize fertility. Purple is traditionally associated with royalty. We also tend to have favorite colors and are biased towards them. Many times those colors are linked to fond memories.[*]

If your favorite color is blue, for instance, you might wear blue more often than other colors. But, what does blue have that green doesn't? Nothing that I can figure. It's only how you view it that causes it to be your preference. How you view it is ultimately how you feel about it. Everything we experience is seen through our refractive lens of bias toward or against a particular event or person. Things that might really be pretty neutral aren't after we get through with them. That's because we all have a particular attitude, our own way of viewing things that has a lot to do with our experiences.

Unfortunately we tend to look at things and compare them to previous life experiences. We are not looking at things with fresh eyes, thus twisting them to fit into our pre-conceived notions. Peter Weiss once said: "The important thing is to pull yourself up by your own hair, to turn yourself inside out, and see the whole world with fresh eyes." When you were a child everything was exciting and new. We weren't comparing today's events to past experiences. But looking at things with fresh eyes is the to way conscious living. **Don't**

make the mistake of comparing today with yesterday. Every day is a new beginning and, to enjoy it to the maximum, every minute of every day should be lived as a unique experience. I believe that has a lot to do with how time seems to whiz by faster and faster as we get older. There aren't as many new and exciting experiences and when there are, we tend to compare them with past experiences, thus diluting their effect.

Our lives tend to get into ruts, and we have to go looking for ways to enliven them. George Gissing in *The Private Papers of Henry Ryecroft* says it well: "It is familiarity with life that makes time speed quickly. When every day is a step in the unknown, as for children, the days are long gathering of experience."

Let's take a look at how our perceptions affect our daily lives. If you view work as a chore, a chore it becomes. The ideal would be to enjoy your work as much as your leisure. But many of us view work as a necessary evil, a way to pay our bills. A means to provide us with the money to live what we consider our real lives—leisure, activities, or anything other than work. Whether it be reading, fishing, golfing, knitting, attending spectator sports, watching our favorite shows, whatever, that's where many of us feel our true life is lived. But, what a waste.

The average person working full time puts in about two thousand hours a year. When you deduct time spent sleeping, then our lives tend to become narrower and narrower. Instead of a week having one hundred sixty-eight hours, we've effectively sliced it to around seventy-two hours. If we deduct commuting time to and from work we're now at around only sixty hours. There's not much we can do about the sleep part, but there is everything we can do about the rest. Most of our attitudes about commuting tend to be negative. Sitting in traffic behind a huge truck that's belching diesel fumes is not anyone's idea of a good time. And, getting stuck by the omnipresent SUV where we can't see anything in front of us can get to be a real pain. The average commute is only going to get longer. In L.A., the projected speed of the rush hour commute will be down from the mid-thirties of today to the low-twenties in the next ten years or so.

So, if our commutes are pretty much guaranteed to get longer and therefore more stressful, we'd better change how we view the situation right now. If we can't get a job closer to home we'll have to adapt, basically to keep ourselves from going crazy. For years I commuted from Glendale to the west side of Los Angeles. It was only fourteen miles but took forty-five to fifty minutes. By the time I got to work I was already stressed. That was the result of sitting in stop-and-go traffic the whole way. In later years, it got to be more like stop-and-stop traffic. There wasn't much *go* going on. I put up with it, but just putting up with something unpleasant is no way to go about life if we want to enjoy all facets of it. I wasn't smart enough or conscious enough at the time to figure a better way to use that hour and a half to my benefit or at least not to allow it to stress me out.

I'm extremely fortunate now that my commute consists of walking five blocks to my business. I'm one of only 3% of Americans who are fortunate enough to be able to walk to their jobs. Obviously, there's no stress involved there. To the contrary, I get to view the ocean, meet friends, and just generally enjoy the entire experience. On the occasions when I take a slight detour and walk on the sand, I'm often greeted with the sight of dolphins. But, the fact that I walk to work wasn't an accident. I consciously considered the commute when deciding where to locate my shop. So, it was a very conscious decision made to uncomplicate my life. We only looked on Main Street and Montana Avenue, both in Santa Monica, when deciding where to locate the business. I never wanted to commute again and it was in my power to do something about it. That was something in my control so I took advantage of it. Most of us aren't so lucky. We don't often get to pick where our work is located. Commuting becomes part of the daily grind. And, that's exactly how most of us look at it.

Perception becomes reality. The phenomenon of road rage didn't just happen. It was born out of frustration and that frustration is now boiling over with greater frequency. While driving, there are a few things in particular that really drive most of us up the wall. I'm sure you have your own list but I think you'd agree that people driving forty miles an hour in the fast lane, tailgaters, people who cut us off or change lanes without signaling, distracted cell phone yakkers, and those who constantly apply their brakes for no apparent reason right in front of us, are right up there. We tend to view these people as incompetents or worse who shouldn't be allowed to drive. At least during rush hour. But, most of them aren't going anywhere, both literally and figuratively. So, we must view them for what they really are—road hazards, an all too common fact of life. We curse them, honk our horns, flip them off and give them as nasty a look as we can scare up when we pass them. That's where it normally ends. But, sometimes, it doesn't. Instead of allowing yourself to get upset by these boneheads, what I've found effective for quite a while is at the first safe opportunity, look away for a second and re-set your brain. In that split second think of consciously not allowing yourself to get angry or upset in any way. If you do it with the right attitude, it effectively calms you down and then you move on from there. It's important that once you reset, you consciously make it a point to forget. Wipe whatever just occurred from your mind. And, never, ever try to get someone back. Remember, you're not out there trying to teach someone a lesson . It's very important to always remember if someone cuts you off or does anything else unsafe or rude, *don't take it personally*! They don't know you and to them you're just another car.

A woman from Alabama was the first female convicted of manslaughter in a road rage murder recently. She was being tailgated by another woman, and they got into that ridiculous game of cat and mouse. You tailgate me and I'll show you by slamming on my brakes. Well, if you have the nerve to do that I'll get right on your bumper. All this was being done at highway speeds. The up-shot is that the tailgater, who relatives admitted was aggressive and had a bad temper, was shot in the face and died instantly. The killer was sentenced to thirteen years. I'm sure out of frustration we've all played that silly game of tit for tat to some extent. But I'm sure we'll all agree that is not the right thing to do. No matter how much we resent the incompetence or arrogance of another, that in no way should affect you or how you feel.

So, since commuting is a daily fact of life for most of us, and is a major source of our daily stress, the best thing we can do for ourselves is to consciously learn to perceive it as something other than a chore. No matter if the person in front of you is talking on the phone (my personal favorite), putting on makeup, sightseeing, reading, or whatever, that's no reason for you to get upset. View them for what they are and don't allow their inattention to frustrate you. There is no rule in the driver's manual that says you need to get angry when provoked while driving. You can and should choose not to. The one thing you have to be is more vigilant. If some of these people aren't going to pay attention, you have to even more so. Take the overall view. Your objective is to get from point A to point B, while putting as little pressure on yourself as possible. Always try to flow with the situation and not fight it, because that will only increase your anxiety level.

You might want to think of commuting as no more than part of your job. You wouldn't be working if you couldn't get there.

Use the same methods you employ to cope in your work as you would driving your car. If you normally wouldn't be impatient at your job, don't be while driving. Whatever works outside the car, there is no reason to change once you get behind the wheel. It could be that annoying things seem to happen with greater frequency when you're behind the wheel. If you can't see yourself giving someone the finger at the grocery store for knocking into your cart, they why would you see it as acceptable behavior while driving? It's true that sometimes the meek become lions when behind the wheel of a three thousand pound vehicle but the best thing to do is just stay out of their way. Driving should never become an ego contest and your personality shouldn't all of a sudden take on a hard edge. Do whatever you need to stay on an even keel. It makes the trip a lot more pleasant when you're not carrying anger and frustration with you. Just because others do a Dr. Jekyll and Mr. Hyde, make doubly sure you consciously don't. If it takes relaxation tapes or singing at the top of your lungs, go for it. Make a conscious effort to view driving as a seamless part of your everyday life.

Oftentimes we have pre-conceived notions about people or things. A lot of those times we're way off the mark in our initial judgments. It's happened to me more times than I can remember. I've seen someone for the first time and they immediately seem like a particularly annoying type. They appear to have many of the qualities I don't find attractive. Whether I happened to overhear a conversation they had, see them at an event, or have them as a neighbor they just seemed to rub me the wrong way. A lot of it has to do with how they carry themselves, or their voice, or they just might have reminded me of someone I didn't like. Somewhere along the line you've probably experienced the same thing. Most of the time, after meeting them, I realized I was dead wrong.

I don't know if this ever happened to you, but it's an interesting phenomenon. Someone is doing something that annoys you, maybe making a lot of noise or anything that irks you. But, then, you see who it is and realize it's someone you know. All of a sudden it's not so bad anymore, the person can't be the insensitive jerk you thought they were. You know that they really have a lot of fine qualities. The conclusion you initially made was incorrect. Obviously, if you can suddenly change your perception of the matter, you have more control over your responses than you might have thought.

Many times, what I initially perceived as glaring deficiencies were in reality minor personality traits. I think we all have a tendency to judge things before we know much about them. The first impression phenomenon is real but is usually wrong and normally quickly dispelled upon further examination. Off the top of my head I can think of numerous examples where my perception of someone and the reality of that person were not even close. In these cases perception wasn't reality. I now make it a point not to judge anyone, not only on first impression, but at any time.

That's just part of accepting everyone as they are. In the first place, it's unfair to them, and second, I wouldn't want them to do it to me. Since I'm pretty quiet I realize that many people have an erroneous impression of me. People have a tendency to warm up to me after some interaction but I'd never be mistaken for the life of the party. Your perception of an individual or a group should never even be formulated until all the facts are in. There seems to be a rush to judgment when in fact there usually is no real need for urgency at all. It's not as if we're the police who have to make snap judgments as part of their everyday work. I would suggest you get into the good habit of not judging anyone. Although there are certain times you must make a judgment and have to rely somewhat on how you perceive a person almost immediately. For instance, if you have a child who needs daycare, no matter how many references are provided by the caregiver, your gut reaction as to that person's character is at least as important. It could be Mother Teresa but if you're not comfortable with the individual, you'll probably pass, and I would consider that the right thing to do in this circumstance. In making that decision you could very well be making a mistake and it might even be unfair to that person, but with something as important as your child's care, you have to be comfortable that they're safe and happy and also so you're not worried all day and can concentrate on your work.

For some reason we also have a tendency to perceive others as being happier than ourselves. We see people laughing and joking with friends and we think of how lucky they are and how carefree and stress-free their lives are, unlike our own. For the most part that impression is also erroneous. Everybody has problems. Some people have big problems but treat them more casually than some with small problems, who tend to magnify them. We also make the same assumptions when we see people who have a lot of money. Right away we're viewing their lives as being fuller, more interesting, and a lot more fun than our drab existences. We see the wealthy as being happier and more attractive than ourselves. The more attractive part maybe, as rich men seem to have no trouble attracting women whose looks are a cut above most. The happier part I'm not so sure of.

Although money does make some things in life easier, I'm sure it has its drawbacks too. I've never had too much so I can't talk from experience on that. But, I do know when I was making twice as much as do now, and I was doing pretty well, it had no effect on my level of happiness. As a matter of fact, years ago when a friend and I were living together we both made very little money and had to sometimes borrow to make ends meet. We'd save what little we could and when we had enough we'd go to dinner at a nice restaurant. Instead of just being a dinner, since we had to save so long for it, it became more of an event. It's amazing how much more you appreciate something like that when you have to save for it and it becomes a special occasion when you finally do. You should consciously appreciate *all* the good things that happen in your life. I even remember what I had for dinner twenty years ago. That was a very happy time in my life and if I had ten times more money I doubt if I'd been any happier. I think the same goes for my friend. It was a very happy time in her life, too. The one thing I do know about wealth is that it doesn't count for anything if you're not happy.

I know this is totally out of the question and would never happen, but I think we'd be as a people much wiser to have happiness, in place of money, a luxury car, and a house in the country as the American dream. We view wealth as the ultimate American goal when, in the perfect society, happiness should be the recognized sign of success. Ideally, it would work that the happier the person, the more at peace they are, the more esteemed that person would be in society's eyes. It would become a self-fulfilling prophecy. If people realized they could truly be happy simply by working at it, no matter how rich or poor, that would become everyone's top priority. And if you were to achieve happiness, it would be totally irrelevant if you had money or not. That, to me, would be ideal.

Unless we're exceptional or very lucky, most of us won't ever be wealthy. It's a very difficult goal to reach even in the Internet age. That's partly because you need to rely somewhat on sources outside of your control to make it happen. Achieving happiness can be accomplished all by yourself. Most people just need some guidance such as this book supplies. It's much like getting a mental shove in the right direction. A conscious person perceives happiness as the main goal and after that is achieved, the rest is just icing on the cake.

As to the supposedly happy people mentioned before. In my line of work I get to meet a lot of people and since it's such a personal business I get to know them pretty well. Some people are truly happy—they're blessed with it as their nature. They have a tendency not to take situations too seriously and their perceptions of events are closer to reality than most. But, believe me, they are the exception. Most people are neither very happy nor very unhappy. Most of us fall in the middle area where events help to determine our day-to-day happiness. If you have a good day at work you're happy, if you have a bad day, you're not. If things are generally going well we might feel pretty good, but in the back of our minds we know it won't last. That's because our day-to-day happiness doesn't have a strong foundation but is event-driven. The vast majority of as fall into that category. If I get to know a particular person well, there are always problems and day-to-day stresses in their lives no matter how they come across on casual observation. The more you get to know someone the more you realize the vast majority are really just like yourself in regards to the every day ups and downs. So, if it seems everyone is having a much better time in life than you—that's really not the case. You just could be more reserved and quiet, less outgoing, or maybe you're just not as much a people person as others are. Maybe you are but just don't realize it. That has absolutely nothing to do with happiness. Being loud and outgoing in no way correlates to successful living. You have as much chance of reaching your goal of being happy as the person who always seems to be joking and having and good time.

Remember, a lot has to do with your perception of things as they really are. The less you try to bend events to fit into your preconceived patterns of thinking, the easier it will be to stay on an even keel. And, many people do have a misconception of what happiness is since they've never been there long enough to know for sure. Happiness is the opposite of a manic-depressive state with its high highs and low lows. Instead of riding the rapids of the Colorado River, you're more on a raft peacefully floating down the Mississippi. Happy people don't necessarily walk around with a perpetual smile on their faces. If there were a line-up, you might have no chance in picking the truly happy person out. That's because happiness is mostly an attitude, and unlike some people's emotions, happiness is not worn on the sleeve for the world to see.

Always remember this fact when you start feeling a little down on yourself. We are living like kings and queens compared to the vast majority of the world's population, and those who've gone before us. Our lives are not a struggle. We have enough to eat, a place to go home to at night, laws that protect us from exploitation, all the modern conveniences, and just everything we could possibly need to live an easy life. It might not always seem like that when troubles strike, but we're not just getting by and troubles can be resolved. We live in a beautiful country and most people would give their right arm to be in the position we're in. But, most of us never think of things that way. We get so caught up in our petty problems that aren't problems at all. We take for granted everything that people before us didn't have access to or could even dream of. Never ever forget how good you really have it and when you start to feel sorry for yourself, make it a point to remember how very blessed you really are.

Again, using the latest crisis in the Middle East as an example, perceptions of right and wrong, good and evil, fair and unfair are at polar opposites. Abraham Lincoln, in *Meditation and Divine Will*, wrote: "The will of God prevails. In great contests each party claims to act in accordance with the will of God. Both may be, and one must be, wrong. God cannot be for and against the same thing at the same time."

He was referring to the American Civil War but the same holds true today, and down through history. And, it's not only religious fervor, or actually the perversion of religion, that causes problems. It's all kinds of ideologies— democracy versus communism, contests that pitted monarchy against republicanism ideals, rich versus poor, apartheid versus integration and fairness, the list is endless. In each case, the perception that their position was right, or ordained by God, and that their enemies were nothing more than heathens who needed to be defeated, is the same as good versus evil. In every war or conflict, leaders pound into their constituency that very notion. In World War Two our propaganda machine worked overtime to demonize the Japanese and Germans, as did theirs to demonize us. Americans were taught that the enemy was less-than-human barbarians who needed to be annihilated so the forces of God and good could reign again. We were defending our democracy. If the masses' perceptions could be hardened the war effort would be made that much easier. Recruitment would be more successful and fervor in battle would be assured. If your enemy were to be perceived as less than evil, it would be that much harder to produce victory. That's why today's conflict between the Israelis and the Palestinians is only going to get worse before it is resolved. It will be resolved to some degree in some fashion eventually, but not until the combatants stop demonizing their enemy. As long as the perception exists of unfairness and prejudice, walls will stay up.

I've always found it fascinating how our perceptions of people change according to how in favor they are at the moment. When things are going well, say you're in a relationship, the faults and mannerisms you would normally find unattractive in another are glossed over when we speak or think of that person. But, when the relationship is on the rocks, the rosy picture changes noticeably. Every little thing that's ever annoyed us about them, even to the tiniest degree, is enlarged till the picture we paint of them doesn't at all resemble the previous one. We tend to demonize those out of favor. We can't look hard enough to find faults and we tend to leave no stone unturned as if to rationalize to ourselves that the person wasn't really worthy of our attentions in the first place.

Obviously, that's not at all the way we should act if we want to lead a peaceful and consciously flowing life. Our perceptions needn't change because the situation does. He or she is exactly the same person as before, even if our perception of the person changes, and we should approach them in the same way. If they want to make you out as some kind of devil to their friends, let them. It really doesn't matter much how you are viewed by others because you don't really have a lot of control over that. Let people think and say what they want since you know what type of person you really are, and if their perception of you is erroneous, you can live with it.

When we're young we think of things in terms of black and white, right or wrong, good or evil. We don't take into account the gray areas. As we get older our perceptions become somewhat more complicated as we learn that gray areas are the predominant areas. (That's another example of how a color can evoke meaning.) The more conscious we are, the more we develop the ability to see both sides of the coin. To try to see things as another gives us a more complete understanding of what is really going on. We also appreciate it if others try to understand where we're coming from. You must always, if you truly want to understand why others act or react the way they do, try to see things from the other person's perspective. That doesn't mean you have to agree with them, just consider their point of view. It gives life more sense and gives you the ability to make more informed judgments. Sometimes, though, no amount of effort on your part will allow you to fathom some people's actions. For example, if you're honest, it's almost impossible to understand why some people shoplift if they're not in need. It just doesn't compute. Even if they explain it away as thrill seeking, you just can't understand how someone can justify taking another's property. And I don't think that's necessarily a bad thing. In some cases no explanation suffices or even makes sense.

As we've seen, sometimes people's perceptions are such that they cause harm to another. Erroneous perceptions almost always do that. That's one reason you should always take care to be as realistic as you can in evaluating another or something they are involved in.

One of Jeffrey Dahmer's victims actually escaped from Dahmer's deadly clutches. He ran down the street, still naked, right into two Milwaukee policemen's arms. He thought he was saved from a horrible fate. But he wasn't. And only because of those officers' misbegotten perceptions of him as a promiscuous homosexual. They totally discounted the fact that he was a human being in big trouble, and ascribed the situation to a queer's spat. He wasn't taken seriously and the cops actually had a good laugh about it.

Because of who he was they placed less value on him than they would have had for another. If a beautiful blonde came running naked into their arms, instead of an Asian-looking homosexual, do you think they would have done the same thing and so casually handled the situation? I rather doubt it. That had to be a nightmare of Stephen King proportions for that poor young man. Can you imagine being terrorized to that point and your "saviors" not take you seriously, only because of their prejudice? The fact that the police judged someone and the fact that he was a homosexual in this case amounted to a death warrant. As I've said, if it were a like situation and if he'd been white and not Asian, heterosexual not homosexual, he'd most likely be alive today. This is an extreme case but illustrates how pre-conceived perceptions can cause harm. Everyone should at least at first be given the benefit of the doubt. Because it costs you nothing to have an open mind, there is no reason that you shouldn't.

We also have certain perceptions of places that are shaped, not through our own experiences, but from others. My favorite place in the world is the island of Kauai. I've spent time there and because I thoroughly enjoyed myself, even the mention of it makes me feel good and evokes happy memories. Mention Paris and most Americans think of a beautiful, historic city where some of the world's best restaurants and museums can be found. We also tend to think of Parisians as being unfriendly and condescending to Americans. That's the reputation.

My own experiences have been just the opposite. Next to my shop is a restaurant owned by a few young French guys. They've been very gracious and are a pleasure to be around but I do remember I had an experience with a French tourist years ago in my shop, and in speaking to him got the impression he thought he knew more about my job than I did. He was what we used to call as kids, a "know it all." He really didn't know what he was talking about but you'd never convince him of that. As he was leaving I wished him a pleasant trip, although I don't know how he'd have one considering his attitude of Americans and the country in general. I can't even imagine why he came. But, I just couldn't hold myself back any longer, and when he made another disparaging remark about Americans, I said to him, "Even if you don't think much of us, I hope you enjoy your stay, and by the way, it's nice to know that Frenchmen can be at least as obnoxious outside their country as they are in it." I obviously wasn't leading a conscious life at the time. He confirmed the stereotype I my mind with his behavior. But, as conscious individuals hearsay doesn't matter at all. Let others say what they will. In the first place, we don't judge and in the second, if we don't have the facts, how can we have an informed opinion? Others' attitudes and opinions don't constitute fact.

There are certain places that come to mind as the continual butt of jokes, two of them bring: Cleveland and New Jersey. I grew up in New Jersey and the perception of it as being dirty, crowded, and crumbling, couldn't be further from the truth. For the most part, New Jersey is a beautiful, lush, green place that I'm proud to be from. I've never taken the jokes seriously anyway. I spent the first twenty-four years of my life there. People tend to think of the Turnpike and Newark when thinking of New Jersey. I've only driven through Cleveland but I'm sure it's not what it's said to be. No place can be that bad. I used to be as guilty as anyone when talking about places with which I had no experience. When the Raiders were in L.A., I attended a game against the Cleveland Browns, where the Raiders lost. My friends and I joked that even if we lost the game, we won, since we didn't have to go home to Cleveland afterwards. I've since learned not judge places I haven't been or really didn't know too much about. What is one person's heaven is another person's hell.

Since we're not judging others we shouldn't judge others' homes or lifestyles. On the west side of L.A., there is an air of superiority about the quality of life and the quality of air, compared to the San Fernando Valley, just a few miles away. If you have an 818 area code it's really not very cool at all. It almost sounds like people are apologizing when they tell you their phone numbers. (818 is the area code for the Valley). If you have a 310 area code, you can give you number out with pride and not have to worry about people looking down on you. (310 being the area code on the Westside—including West L.A., Pacific Palisades, Malibu, Brentwood, Santa Monica, and Beverly Hills.) I always hear people bragging that it's been (fill in the time in months, and the longer the better) since they stepped outside Santa Monica. On a number of occasions, people have bragged to me how they haven't been across Lincoln Boulevard in "x" amount time, there's how far they've broken it down. Lincoln Boulevard passes through Santa Monica about eight or nine blocks from the beach. I always found that kind of talk to be just silly, but it's something some people take pride in.

People in San Francisco love to make fun of Los Angeles. It's so ingrained I think it must be taught in their schools. The late Herb Caen made a living out of it in his newspaper column there. The funny part is most Angelenos like San Francisco and take their jokes with a grain of salt. But, the truth is belittling others' homes or accomplishments or whatever is just a way to make ourselves feel superior. An ancient Hindu proverb puts it in proper context: "There is nothing noble about being superior to some other....the true nobility is in being superior to your previous self."

If you're trying to feel better about yourself or your circumstances, belittling another is no way to go about it. As the proverb says, the only thing you might ever feel superior to is your less conscious former self, and since that's past, you really shouldn't do that either. And, what you say gives the outside world a glimpse of what you're really about. If someone doesn't know you, as soon as you start talking, opinions start to form. As I've noted, we can't, for the most part, control people's perceptions of us. But, it's also true with that being the case, we do have certain obligations to ourselves. And, in this case, that is to always present yourself in a positive fashion in speaking with others. That's for a lot of reasons. Our perception of ourselves is extremely important as it has much to do with how we approach others and other things. You have to like yourself first, if for no other reason than you can't get away from yourself. You're

with yourself more than any other. You wouldn't have a best friend
you didn't like, that wouldn't make sense. You need to be your own
best friend first in order to be a friend to others. That's just as you
can't give money to charity unless you make the money first.

PART IV

APPLYING THE BASICS TO OUR THOUGHTS

CHAPTER ONE
VANITY AND EGO

Many people want to be perceived as being important. Their whole self worth revolves around just that. I'm sure it happens everywhere but where I live in the Los Angeles area it's almost at epidemic proportions. I don't know how many people live in houses they can't really afford and drive cars that are too expensive for their pocketbooks, but I know it's all too common.

Cosmetic surgery is a huge industry and if this were baseball L.A. would win the M.V.P. award, but in this case instead of standing for Most Valuable Player it would symbolize the Most Vain People. To be fair, the vast majority of L.A. residents aren't at all like that. But, it's more common here than in most places. I've often joked that in L.A. it's more important to look good than to feel good. That's the vibe you get. I've had clients who could hardly smile, their faces have been pulled so tight, because of one too many cosmetic surgeries. I also have clients who are plastic surgeons and they all do quite well, and have more patients than they can handle. This all sounds silly on the face of it but it's deadly serious stuff around here.

It's somewhat understandable, especially with actresses, as once they lose their youth the prospects for getting work diminish. It's not as bad for men. We get more distinguished as opposed to women who just get old. You see that in the movies all the time. We have middle-aged actors and some past middle-aged starring in pictures where their love interest is half their age. You almost never see a middle-aged actress starring in a movie and if you did there's not much chance she'd be paired with a young actor as her love interest.

It's amazing how there are double standards with just about everything. It's certainly not fair, but then again what in life is? In most places being a narcissist would be a problem, but here it's an accepted way of life. If you've ever read the entertainment newspaper *Daily Variety*, the trade paper for the movie industry, it's not at all uncommon to see self-congratulatory ads prominently displayed. People actually have the nerve to laud themselves and congratulate themselves for a certain performance. But people here don't give a second thought to it. When I first saw that I was blown away, until I came to realize that in Hollywood vanity rules the roost.

You can see that in all the awards there are for actors. It seems not a week goes by without some awards ceremony being televised. It's gotten to the point where if you're an actor and you don't win some award sometime during the year you really can't be trying too hard.

Everybody wants to be "recognized" for their achievements as if nobody actually notices what they do. It's gotten to the point where much of this is just another massage for over-sized egos.

Can you picture a farmer in Iowa taking out an ad in the local paper congratulating himself for coming in with a bumper crop? He wouldn't be able to show his face in town. People would think he had psychiatric problems. But, here as in other places, modesty is not high on the list of virtues for a small segment of the population.

It reminds me of people who name their businesses after themselves and whose picture accompanies their ads. They become "stars" and are recognized on the street. It's a great boost for their egos, but in reality, no one else really cares.

I've compiled a list culled from local newspaper real estate ads. This might sound like a joke but it's taken very seriously and this is the basis for many real estate transactions. For some, they can't just live in a nice home. It has to be in a prestigious area as well, or they won't even consider it. Prices reflect that and here on the Westside million dollar homes are a dime a dozen. There are little shacks in the area I live that go for half a million dollars. In some ads there are features for homes advertised where I don't even know what they're talking about. How about having a "trumbled travertine" in your bathroom? I don't know about you but I find that I can no longer live without one, although I have no idea what it is.

Here's the list (with my comments, and remember I'm not making this up):

1. Prestigious Street: That's interesting how even a street can be prestigious. It's not enough to live in an exclusive area, now you have to live on a particular street.
2. Gated Compound: This way you can keep the riff-raff out.
3. Beverly Center: They're talking about a shopping mall, which, by the way, is not in Beverly Hills.
4. Beverly Hills P.O. (or adjacent): For those unfortunates who actually can't afford to live in Beverly Hills you can impress people with your zip code.
5. Beverlywood Adjacent: In reality it's not Beverly Hills or Hollywood, just plain, old L.A.
6. Hancock Park Adjacent: L.A. again.
7. Gated Enclave: See #2. If you can't separate yourself from the unwashed masses, how exclusive can your area be?
8. Guard Gated Enclave: Even better.
9. Walled and Gated: For those who want to keep the riff-raff *and* their relatives out.
10. Private Promontory: I had to look this one up.
11. Prestigious: Sound pretty tame after the rest.
12. Villa: Anything larger than a breadbox that is even remotely Spanish.
13. Hedonist Heaven: Now, doesn't that sound like someplace you'd want to live?
14. Emotional Family Home: I never realized houses have emotions.

Then we have the "Perfect Starter Home" that was listed for $350,000. I guess something like that could be considered a "starter home" if you're a member of the Hearst or Rockefeller family. I always wonder if the people writing this copy can keep a straight face when their claims are so outlandish.

But, my favorite "starter home" was recently listed in Santa Monica. The agent had the audacity to call a small home a few blocks from me, "the perfect starter" that sported a price of $569,000. What are these people thinking? I guess that's not too bad because the house listed actually comes in one piece. A home in the Los Feliz section of L.A. was listed on the same page as the "perfect starter" for only $789,000. You get such a great deal because it's a fixer upper. For that kind of money you'd think it would already be fixed.

My personal favorite though is <u>Trophy Property</u>: For middle-aged men to house their trophy wives or girlfriends.

And for those who can't afford to move, no problem, just change the name of the town you live in, or even better yet, just the section you inhabit. That's how we get places here in Southern California such as West Hills, formerly part of not-so-cool Canoga Park; North Hills, which used to be Sepulveda, and there are no hills; Valley Village, formerly part of un-hip North Hollywood. I'm sure the list is much longer. Many of those who've pressed for those changes argue that the name change enhances their real estate value, although the snooty factor is primarily behind all this nonsense.

As conscious people we realize that trying to impress others is no way to go about life. What we see as just silliness is to others a way they approach many facets of their life. Everything some people do has an eye towards how others will perceive it. Their perception of everything is totally askew. Who really cares what Joe Blow thinks? I've always told people the only way I'd do things with an eye to impress them is if they'd pay my bills. It's funny but there have been no takers on that. These people might not see the other person again or have seen them before but that doesn't stop them from trying to make an impression. This type of person will even push for credit even though it might not be due them. That's why movies nowadays have so many producers, at least in the closing credits. Everybody and their brother is listed, even if they had nothing to do with the production. But it's very important to them and gives them bragging rights and makes them feel like big shots. It also allows them to get better seats at this week's hippest restaurant. You wouldn't be caught eating at some eatery that wasn't on the "A" list. Many times people will go to certain restaurants not to enjoy the food but to be seen. And to break it down further, where you sit in the restaurant is as important as being there. For example, if you had scored the #5 table at Wolfgang Puck's Spago in West Hollywood (since closed), you got a prestigious spot. What's next, eating a particular menu item? It must take a lot of time keeping up with what happens to be this week's status symbol. I guess in Hollywood if you snooze you lose. Last week's watering hole is just so passé and if regular folk have no problem getting in, how hip or desirable could it be? That's even if anyone who is anyone just had to be there two weeks ago. If you're not "cool" you can forget about getting into a trendy nightclub. If you're not one of the "beautiful people" you might as well stay home. That's the point to these people—if you can gain admittance to the coolest places, you are now separated from the unwashed masses.

That also goes for the homes people have built. Aaron Spelling, the television producer, had a mansion built that is around fifty-six hundred square feet. That's way past being a home and is more a monument. Who on earth would ever need such a large house? You could easily house thirty-five families comfortably in it with plenty of room to spare. It's Mr. Spelling's money so he has every right to do what he wants with it. He is known for his generosity so I wouldn't ever begrudge him anything. But, to many the most important thing is that others recognize their success and power. Instead of walking around with their net worth glued to their forehead for all to see and admire, they build homes that others couldn't possibly match.

It's not at all uncommon around here that some of the larger homes have eight or ten bathrooms. Either the homeowner has one of the world's worst incontinence problems or they have six of seven more bathrooms than they'd ever need. But it's a status symbol. There was a home recently put up for sale in Beverly Hills that had, and I'm not making this up, twenty-seven bathrooms. Can you imagine what it cost just to buy towels for all those bathrooms?

In Santa Monica where I live, the most fashionable area of town is north of Montana Avenue. In the San Fernando Valley a few miles away it's south of Ventura Boulevard. Of course, in real estate ads it's played up to the hilt. I'm one of the poorer folk so I have to live south of Montana, but even so, I manage to scrape by. Due to neighbors' complaints our town council recently passed a law limiting the size of the homes that could be built north of Montana. The trend is to buy a house, north of Montana, of course, tear it down, and build something two or three times the size on the same lot. It doesn't matter that the house that originally occupied the land was perfectly good, if you can't impress everyone that goes by, why bother?

This is the same type of person that feels a sense of entitlement. It goes along the same lines. Some people actually strongly believe they are due special treatment because they are who they are. Their whole self worth is wrapped up in just that. If their obvious superiority isn't apparent, they make it a point to make it so. Just in case you missed it. It's a lot like some ballplayers who have contracts stipulating if another player is given a contract for more than theirs, their contract has to be amended so they make more—even if it's just a dollar. And it's always the same thing: respect. The one thing it's never about is money. How these people can say that with a straight face is beyond me. But, that's the line they always try to give us. In reality, it's all about the money. That and feeding their oversized egos.

Here's an example of that type if silliness. One year, the Seattle Mariners finished a weekend series in Milwaukee and had another series coming up in Chicago 90 miles away. Normally that meant the team would take a bus for the short trip, not a Greyhound, but, a luxury bus. But, Ken Griffey, Jr. decided that riding a bus wasn't good enough for him. So, he had the clubhouse manager arrange for a limo to take him the 90 miles. When some other players learned of this they too decided that the bus wasn't good enough and all got their wish, and the topper is, none of them wanted to share. They wound up in nine limos. One each. And they wonder why people think they're more like spoiled children than adults.

We also have the world's lamest excuse when a ballplayer demands to renegotiate his contract in the middle of it. I've heard this one a number of times: "I have to provide for my family so I have to make as much as I can while I can," without honoring his end of the contract, of course. It's almost as if there's some kind of competition amongst some of them to see who can tell biggest whopper. When the demands become too ridiculous even for the team to bear, some General Managers have been known to leak the most outlandish ones to the media.

Immediately after their ridiculous demands become known to the public, the ball player, seeing how he is being perceived by the fans as arrogant, greedy, and in general, just a jerk, claim that they never asked for those things in the first place, or they were misunderstood. They didn't give fans much credit and compounded the negative image by lying about it. Most of the ones doing this demanding have already earned tens of millions of dollars playing ball so "providing for the family" isn't an issue—just an excuse to justify their greediness. That is, unless, of course, their family's size is roughly the same as Idaho's population.

I don't begrudge them their salaries at all. They're just getting what the market will bear. The only problem is that if a family of four wants to see a game, between the parking, tickets, and overpriced food they might have to take out a second mortgage to do it.

Getting huge salaries is just the tip of the iceberg. They also demand special perks, another way to set them apart from the crowd. I'll give you another example. Los Angeles Dodgers pitcher Kevin Brown's contract is for over one hundred million dollars. This is not at all unusual today. Alex Rodriguez just signed a ten-year contract for the sum of two hundred and fifty-two million. Both of these players, and any others that command such exorbitant salaries, expect, for example, the use of a private jet, luxury accommodations, sky boxes, separate accommodations on the road, and anything else they can wrangle out of the owners. The funny part is (and this is just my opinion—I don't know these guys or whatever other talents they may have) that these guys would be driving a UPS truck for a living if it weren't for baseball. The fact is that with his salary Kevin Brown could afford to buy three private jets a year and have enough left over to feed a small country. But, that wouldn't separate him from the other players. He just wouldn't be special. And, that's really what it's all about, after the money of course.

This type of wrong-headed thinking permeates society. From the need to have the most expensive car, the largest SUV, the most toys, or the corner office, everywhere you turn people's lives revolve around one-upmanship.

This silliness also extends to fads. Some of us need to be perceived as being hip. I have a few names for that, one being the Sheep Syndrome. We had a series of fads going at the same time a couple of years ago that made for some interesting viewing. If you're a guy, or in this case a human lemming, this is what you needed if you wanted to be considered cool by other lemmings in L.A. at the time: a goatee, a tattoo or tattoos, a Harley, an SUV, and a cigar, not a White Owl, that just wouldn't do, but an expensive Cuban. That, and a trophy girlfriend and you were set. There's not much funnier than a twenty-year-old kid trying to look mature by puffing on a cigar half his size. The only thing better, and this would really set you apart, would be if you could finagle a royal title to complete the picture.

It's hard for me to take these kinds of things seriously. How anyone could stake their happiness on such vacuous and irrelevant things is really pretty sad. Obviously, to a conscious person all of these trappings don't mean a thing. Since we realize that happiness is not achieved by how outsiders perceive us, we can take them or leave them. Conversely, don't not do something because it is a fad. If you buy an SUV, for example, because your family needs the space, that's a valid reason. You're not doing it to impress others or be hip. There's a big difference. One time when Shaquille O'Neal came into my store, I saw him drive up in a humungous SUV. That makes sense because of his size. I can't imagine him trying to squeeze into a Toyota Corolla, it just wouldn't work. If you view things as you should and not as a status symbol or because everyone who's anyone has one, then you're doing it for the right reason, and impressing others is never the right reason. I can see you trying to make a good impression if you're meeting the in-laws for the first time, or you're interviewing for a job. That makes sense. In the case of the SUV, some people just like to be seated higher because it affords them a better view of the road. You might buy a luxury car because you like the style. That also makes sense.

Things people do to change people's perceptions of them are almost limitless. Some will go so far as to change their name to seem less ethnic. And, it's not just actors and actresses, but anyone whose esteem is tied to their carefully crafted self-image.

Years ago I was friends with a man who served with me in the military, that is, until he pulled some strings and got an early out. He was from a wealthy family and was of Polish descent. Before he married he decided to change his name to a very Anglo sounding one. I was invited to his wedding at the Bel Air Hotel in L.A. When his father was introduced at the reception the man who was emcee-ing the event didn't realize my friend had changed his name and introduced his father as Mr. "Ashley," the new name my friend had taken. His poor father couldn't have been more embarrassed. Here, before his entire family he was being called a name that had nothing to do with his heritage. It was bad enough that the son didn't think enough of his lineage to keep his name, but, having his father intro-duced with the new Anglo name just poured salt on the wounds. The name change was done with an eye toward how people would per-ceive him and for no other reason. He already had a well-paying job, had just married a beautiful wife, and had a nice home, all accom-plished with his old name. It's his right, no doubt, but if it wasn't necessary to do to, say, further his career, his reasons were as shal-low as he evidently was. That's a very un-conscious thing to do. If you're determined to impress others, which is something you should never do, it's better to do it with accomplishments.

If you have cable TV, you probably get the local access chan-nel. If you don't, you're missing some of the weirdest television on the air. If you're not familiar with it, the way it works is, a person pays a nominal fee and gets a half an hour airtime to do with as they please. Some of these people have had weekly time slots for years. I don't know how many times I've sat in front of the TV with my mouth open for the whole half hour in disbelief as to what I'm seeing. To say it gets interesting is an understatement. There is no way to reference it to anything you've seen before. It's truly like entering the Bizarro World.

Although ninety percent of the shows on the access channel are as boring as anything you'll see on network television, there are some that are truly memorable, and not for the reason the people putting them on envisioned. A few hosts who've had the shows on for a while literally think they're stars, even if only nine people are watching. There are some, and these are the ones who are truly memorable, where the person on stage is terribly and embarrassingly off the mark on how they are being perceived. There are a dozen examples I could give but a couple will do. As I've said, you really shouldn't concern yourself with outsiders' perceptions of you as long as you're trying to live a conscious life and are comfortable with yourself. But, there are a few who are way too comfortable with themselves. (Of course, again, this is my personal observation and opinion.) Usually the show is named after the "star".

One show has a middle-aged woman who is overweight by about sixty pounds dancing, disco style to "music" that's she's written and recorded. She sings and plays the harmonica. Unfortunately for the viewers she does this wearing a bikini and frilly accessories. You can tell she feels really sexy as she flirts with the camera. The "music" is absolutely atrocious, only matched by her voice, and the one time she had a guest the poor guy looked so shell shocked you knew he didn't have a clue as to what he was getting into. I don't think I've ever seen a person so uncomfortable especially when the woman, twice his age, directed her attention toward him. The first time I saw the show I watched the whole half hour waiting for some kind of disclaimer telling us the whole thing was really just a goof. When she attempted a split I almost lost it. She gyrates her hips provocatively as she bats her eyelashes. Then she started with the tricky camera work, something many of these shows have in common. I guess they figure since the camera is capable of it, they'll use it. In this case she had two images of herself super-imposed, so instead of having two hundred pounds gyrating and vamping for the camera, we had four hundred filling the screen. If you can picture this: an overweight middle-aged woman with bleach blonde hair squeezed into a bikini three sizes too small trying to come off as Marilyn Monroe, that pretty much sums up the show. In describing it I haven't come close to the actual bizarreness of it all, but you get the picture.

I would love to watch some of these shows with a psychiatrist just so I'd have some inkling as to these people's motivations. I would love to know what a psychiatrist thinks when someone has such a gross misinterpretation of how they actually come off. It would be interesting to hear how the person feels about their show and what they think people's reactions are to it. I'd like to know what's going through their mind when they're doing their act. Do they see themselves as professional entertainers trying to get a break in hopes of being spotted by a Hollywood talent scout or is it all just a big joke? If it is, they're doing a helluva job.

Our bikini clad go-go dancer obviously doesn't see herself at all realistically. When she looks in the mirror she must see a young, beautiful, talented, and very sexy woman as opposed to the rest of us who see a completely different picture. (Or is it just me?) Or else why would she expose so much of herself? She's not hurting anyone so there's really no problem, but if her perception of herself is so far off, you have to wonder about how she sees other things. To me it's like someone with a filthy car inside and out. Whenever I see that the first thing that comes to mind is: how must their house look? If this is the face they show to the public I can only imagine what kind of pigsty is not out there for others to see. When you see surreal things such as this lady and since it is so far off the wall, you can only conclude she must have a very unique perception of life. The world is certainly a more interesting place when some people who inhabit it have such a unique perspective. This woman seems to be having a real good time even if she appears to be living in a world of her own.

Then we have the lesbian whose entire show is a monologue. This one I still haven't been able to figure out. I find it so confusing as to what she's trying to accomplish I keep watching to see if it starts to make some sense. That's one thing about many of these shows, they're so "unique," they just don't compute. In one half hour she goes through every emotion in the book and then some. She exhibits emotions where not only have I never seen them before I didn't even know human beings were capable of producing them. There's more drama squeezed into that short period than was exhibited during the invasion of Normandy. She laughs, she cries, she hits highs and lows, and everything in between. If there is an emotion available she uses it. I can never tell if she makes it up as she goes along of is working from a script.

The monologue usually has to do with a lover who she's lost, found, misplaced, she's had a falling out with (for some reason this is something she can never understand, although I have some clues), who's betrayed her, made love to her, is uncommunicative, beautiful, lusty, unforgettable, irreplaceable, sexy, withdrawn, happy, unhappy, fun-loving, dour, mischievous, all that within a half hour. We also get to hear intimate details of her love life, and what she would do if the other woman were there. That's a little too much information. I have to think she leads a pretty busy life. The emotion is so thick you can cut it with a knife. Every emotion is carried to such a degree that I'm not sure what she's trying to do. But, it's weird enough to be a truly unique experience and it's not easily forgotten. Maybe that's the idea. Again, she isn't hurting anyone, but it makes me wonder what this woman perceives herself to be.

The point is that when we look in the mirror we might not see what's really there. As a conscious person it is your responsibility to yourself to be as realistic as possible in viewing yourself as you do others.

Men have a tendency to see themselves as more attractive than they really are, and women's tendency is to underrate their appearance. Until I was in the eighth grade I thought myself quite a stud. Reality hit when I was on a class trip to Washington D.C. I just happened to glance up as I walked by a full-length mirror, and for the first time noticed I had a big nose and not much of a chin. That came as quite a shock and took a while to get adjusted to. But, I'm glad it happened when I was young. A dose of reality is not such a bad thing no matter your age. It taught me at a young age that appearance doesn't matter that much because even though I'm pretty average looking at best, I still had a lot of friends and people even then who treated me with respect.

If you want to consciously live a happy life even your appearance counts. I'd say that there's no more than five or six percent of us that we'd all think are very attractive. The rest of us are pretty unremarkable looking, although there's a wide range in that area. Most of us accept the way we are; we might not be thrilled with our looks, but it's a good thing that we can accept it. My father was a very handsome man and I've often wondered what happened to my brother and me, who aren't. I've joked that he must have had a couple of off nights, and wondered on many occasions what it would be like to be handsome. There is a bias towards good-looking people in everything from getting a job to how one's treated by salesclerks. Most of us do it, unconsciously or not.

The one thing in your power is to look as good as you can, as much as you can. I don't mean you have to dress as if you're going to the prom every day, but take care to be clean and dressed as if you care. That means don't go around in wrinkled shirts or due-for-a-wash pants. Even if you prefer jeans and a tee shirt just make sure you're not walking around like some kind of slob. It's not for others so much as it is for your own self.

There's a man who gets coffee at Peet's where I do. Every day he shows up looking as if he just went through the car wash. His hair is going in all different directions, his tee shirt has holes and his pants are dirty. He's obviously not poor because he lives in walking distance to the coffee shop and this is not an inexpensive area. He projects a terrible image for the world to see. It's basically I don't give a crap and I don't care who knows it. How can he feel good about himself when he doesn't take five minutes to look even presentable?

Even if this seems like an insignificant thing, it's not. It's a part of the whole picture and just one little thing you can do to achieve an all-around happy and caring life. As I've said, everything good you do, no matter how small, is a positive step in the right direction. As Thomas Fuller, in *Gnomologia* put it: "By the husk you can guess the nut." Or as he also said: "A good presence is a letter of recommendation."

On the other hand, some people have a tendency to strut around like peacocks. Their egos are quite a bit larger than their accomplishments will ever be. But, the fact doesn't seem to disturb them. If you watch professional football you'll see there's more preening and strutting over the smallest things. If a lineman sacks the quarterback, he's into his routine of "see what I did," before the quarterback has even gotten up. But, isn't he being paid millions of dollars to do just that? That's his job, but in case you should miss it, he wants the world to know he's the one who did it. And, it's not spontaneous excitement, it's all planned and practiced. They seem to forget it's a team sport. If that attitude carried over into our everyday lives, every time I made a big sale, I'd immediately go into my victory dance. I'd want to make sure any client, who might not have seen me make the sale, was thoroughly impressed with my sales skills.

Modesty doesn't seem to be a high priority for many. Their perception of themselves doesn't take into account the facts. And, I find, the more accomplished the individual, the less need for them to bring attention to themselves. People like Albert Einstein or Mother Teresa, though not perfect by any means, actually accomplished great things that benefited mankind, and what they did was important. If anyone ever had a right to do a "see what I did," it would be them. But could you imagine something like that occurring? I'd rather doubt it. Their importance to the advancement and comfort of civilization certainly had nothing to do with self-importance.

I've noticed it more in young men than in young women.

Women seem to be more grounded and realistic in their self-assessment at an earlier age. Although as a nation we seem to be in denial when in comes to certain issues. That goes for men as well as women. One of those areas is the issue of weight. New government statistics state that an astounding sixty-one percent of Americans are overweight (15-30 lbs. plus above the standard). But, only 38% of the population acknowledges being overweight. To see that for yourself, just go for a walk, or better yet, wait in line at the DMV, and you'll come to the conclusion that the government survey was being conservative. Both men and women are guilty of not facing reality when in comes to this issue. We're a bunch of fatties, but if you asked people, many think the problem only belongs to others.

Many young men are a lot like I was, although I never reached the point of arrogance, which is something I detect more and more. They have a tendency to see themselves as more accomplished, smarter, better looking, and more desirable than the reality might be. They also tend to think themselves more the center of things and take less responsibility for their actions. This obviously doesn't apply to all young men, but what I'm talking about is not at all uncommon. The old attitude of "boys will be boys" is indicative of society's attitudes. Because they're naturally more aggressive than females, some of their actions are more accepted. Women are expected to toe the line more and if they do some of the same things as young men they're treated more harshly by society. It's still not "ladylike" to act aggressively and instead of explaining it away as youthful exuberance as with boys, it's considered pushy and not at all a desirable trait in a woman. If anything, young women don't consider themselves as good as they really are. As I've said, they tend to be much more modest in their appraisals of themselves. A lot of that has to do with society's attitudes that reward aggressiveness in men, but condemn it in women. Women have to work that much harder to be accorded the same respect as their male counterparts. If young women had the same attitudes about themselves as young men, society would be much worse off. We need the counter balance of femininity to offset the aggression of the young males. Ideally, women, even if they

didn't exhibit aggressive tendencies, would be given the same opportunities without having to resort to being self-centered and conceited as some in the male domain.

Overall, I've always considered women far better human beings than men. For the most part they're more giving, more willing
to listen and learn, less self involved, more modest, more sympathetic to the plight of others, and overall, more caring. As I've said,
this is a general appraisal and there are many men that exhibit caring
characteristics, just as there are aggressive women. Women tend to
keep things together when it comes to family and personal responsibility, and if I had to choose, I'd rather be stranded on a desert island
with females, and not only for the obvious reasons. They seem to me
to take relationships more seriously and are more willing to try to
work things out, as opposed to many men who might look for the
exit at the first sign of trouble. If there is a conflict, women are much
more willing to try to talk it through, whereas men just want the
problem to go away. Because of women's nature, for the most part,
it's easier for them to get going on their journey to conscious living.
Although, men who look to conscious self-improvement are usually
those who aren't self-centered and ego-driven, but tend to be more
centered and sympathetic in their nature.

When you begin to live life consciously, by that I mean accepting life on its terms and staying centered in the moment, you'll
find your ego comes into play less and less. When you get to a certain point you'll realize that your ego was a major impediment to a
flowing, peaceful life, and without it interfering you can accept things,
especially those that others do, much more readily. You'll no longer
be involved in petty ego contests that you might not have even realized you were part of; but over the years took their toll in lost happiness and the elusive goal of serenity.

When I first got into the optical field, I worked with a man
who let his ego run the show. If I'd chosen a pair of eyeglasses for a
client and they asked me to put them aside for a few days, so they
could think about it, invariably, when they came in to purchase them,
and this only happened when I wasn't there, this man would tell them

that the pair was not at all right for them, and he would choose a more appropriate one for their face. It didn't matter to him that the sale was already made and the client, after deliberation, thought enough of their and my choice to buy it. It was important to him to feel superior to me so he could feel that much better about himself. Since he was highly opinionated and really quite forceful about this, and it turns out, just about everything else, many times my client would be cowed into buying this man's choice. And oftentimes the client would not be happy with the final product. I can't count the times people told me they wished they'd stuck with their first choice. It didn't seem to matter if the client specifically asked for plastic frames, especially if that's what I'd chosen for them. Just to prove his superior dispensing skills he'd show them only metal ones and tell the client plastic was all wrong for them.

Since the idea of business is to give people what they want, not what you think they should have, or what you're trying to get rid of, you could expect problems. I'd take back the glasses, and then make new lenses for the frame they originally chose, not because I had to, but because I feel people should wear glasses that they're comfortable with and happy with, and besides, it's just good business. I brought it up to this man, about how he was subverting the business but as I knew he would, and is customary in this type of situation, he'd denied ever doing such a thing.

When you're no longer ego-driven, you'll approach situations in a different way and with a different attitude. A strong ego makes many people immodest. They may feel the need to be perceived by others as being smarter, wiser, or more capable than they really are, and to achieve that, they spend a lot of time tooting their own horn. There is a huge difference between loving and accepting oneself and having a big ego. You should absolutely love yourself, accept who you are, and be glad about being you. And, if you actually do accomplish something special, you'll find there is no need to talk yourself up. People *do* notice. As a conscious person, you never do things with an eye toward impressing others. Too many of us go through life as if it were a continuous job interview. There's a tendency to embellish and to try to make an impression. With any short-comings we might just fill in the gaps in a way that, although there might be a kernel of truth to it, it's colored to put us in a more favorable light in the eyes of others.

Large egos have to be continually fed. It's not enough to do the best you can and be satisfied with the results as with conscious people. The actual accomplishment is secondary to the adoration large egos crave. I'm going to use James Cameron, the very successful movie director as an example. The reason I'm using him is that he is so well-known, and even if the impression he gives is erroneous, and he's not really the way he comes off, we've all gotten a certain image of him from his own words. He made the most successful movie of all time in *Titanic,* a creative and box office success, and made millions of dollars from it. But, when he declared himself "King of the World" he didn't seem to be kidding all that much. If the impression he leaves is true he has the ego the size of Mount Everest. What's truly amazing is he has a reputation as being egotistical in a town where egomania is a cottage industry. I'm surprised anyone in the industry noticed.

If he and people like him would just give it a rest, they'd actually be much more revered than they presently are. He would be much wiser letting his work speak for him and letting others speak glowingly about him. If true, his reputation of being an egotistical taskmaster does not as all serve him well, at least in the eyes of the public. Pretension never serves anyone well. If you're that good, people will be quite aware of the fact, without you having to go to lengths to prove it.

There are so many ways to approach situations that you should always step back, analyze what's happening, push your ego to the back, and proceed in the most open, honest, and loving way. When I say "loving" I don't mean you fall in love with every person you have contact with. I only mean that you accept everyone as they are with no pre-conditions or thoughts of molding them to fit your model of how you think they should be. Since every situation you encounter has a myriad of potential responses by you, you should always do what you think is the right thing, the moral thing according to your own code. Ego should never play a part in your conscious decision-making, as long as whatever you do is for the right reasons, and that's for you to decide. Remember, it's far more important that your actions have substance than it is how they play to others.

One of the problems encountered by ego-driven people is that they attach so much importance to being self-centered they leave themselves open for a bruising. It's like a fighter who leads with his chin. If he exposes his chin instead of tucking it in, there's a much greater likelihood of his lights getting punched out. If you constantly lead with your ego there's a far greater chance that it'll wind up being bruised. Egoism leads to pettiness. Even the smallest thing can lead to an overreaction for a conceited person. If you take the most innocent happenstance and make it personal, that's exactly what it becomes. Something as minor as how an envelope is addressed can cause chagrin. If it's addressed to two people, and the person with the large ego is not listed first, that will certainly not go unnoticed. If a large ego is walking down the street and is innocently bumped by someone, right away they feel disrespected.

If a large ego is cut off in traffic, the attitude is "how dare they," as if the other person were specifically targeting them. If there is a conversation and for whatever reason they're not included, or they're included but feel their words aren't getting the attention they deserve, they might withdraw and sulk. If they're talking too loudly in the library and are asked to please tone it down, their feelings are wounded because they were singled out. If they get seated at a restaurant and at the same time someone else gets what they consider a better spot, they feel it's unfair to them. If they're passed over for a promotion, asked to leave a place where they might not even have a right to be, are involved in a minor argument, or are not treated with the personal attention they feel due them, in all these everyday situations, instead of consciously accepting the fact of what is happening is what is, and for the most part out of their control, they have a tendency to personalize it. Don't personalize things that aren't personable! You need to be careful not to assign meaning to something or try to read something into a situation that really isn't there.

Most of our lives are pretty straightforward and only get complicated when we search for answers to questions that don't exist in the first place. If you want your life to flow smoothly only go by what you know to be fact and leave the conjecturing of motives to others. If you find yourself being singled out as described above or something similar occurs, first realize the situation for exactly what it is and try to learn from it so in the future you'll either not put yourself in that situation again or at least if you do, you'll take it in the right way; second, accept the fact that whatever occurred is now past and it's already time to move on, no matter if you're feelings were hurt or not, and third, once you've forgotten, forgive. Don't hold a grudge. Remember, as the conscious person you expect more of yourself than you do of others.

For example, if someone is walking on the left side, or the wrong side, of the sidewalk, coming right at you consciously make it a point not to allow yourself to get perturbed. Just move over and move on. Don't get into a chicken contest to see who will move out of the way first. It really doesn't matter who's right or wrong, you're the one who's consciously trying to reach the goal of serenity and tranquility, and you can consider this situation a learning experience and a small step forward on your path. That used to bother me quite a bit. I always had the same thought when someone was coming at me in the "wrong" side of the sidewalk: "There's a reason why it's customary for people to walk on the right side of the sidewalk—so we don't have the situation we're experiencing right now—you idiot."

Make it a point not to let your ego intervene and cloud your judgment. Every time you consciously think first and act second, especially if taking that few seconds to think altered the way you responded for the better, the closer to your ideal you get, and the easier to act in the best way possible the next time.

When I was younger, just past my wild stage, I had an ego disproportionate to my experience. Like many young people, I thought I knew a lot more than I really did. Despite everything we learn from experience, the older we get, the more we realize how

little we really know. There is just so much information and there's
getting to be more and more all the time. You couldn't possibly know
even a billionth of a billionth of all that is out there. I couldn't name
every genus of insects, all the stars in our galaxy alone, or even the
Prime Minister of Canada. That's one reason you should understand
your limitations without limiting yourself, and try to maximize the
knowledge of information in your realm. It's far wiser to be expert at
a few things than being a dabbler in many, and the master of none.

I used to dispense advice as if I were a guru. This was when
I was I my twenties. Since, as I've said, I've always looked the part
of being intelligent, and always was very logical in my approach to
things, people felt I knew what I was talking about. If you look at
things logically, sometimes you don't really have to know that much
to seem to make sense to others. Even if I didn't know something I'd
bluff my way through because I was afraid to look less than perfect
in the eyes of others, who I felt counted on me. I now realize it was
no more than an ego trip of major proportions. I'm just very glad I
didn't do any damage with my advice, at least I don't think I did. At
the time my ego was ten steps ahead of my knowledge.

I was enjoying life immensely. I had a beautiful girlfriend
who made me very happy. I had a good job managing a hi-fi store
and all the managers who worked for the same company were a tight
knit group, and we did a lot of partying. But there was one area of
my life that wasn't so perfect. I still had a bad temper. People who
worked for me would sometimes get a nasty dose of it. But still, for
some reason, I was quite popular with my salespeople and they were
very loyal to me. When I was transferred to a larger store, the employees I couldn't take along all quit, even though I urged them not
to.

That temper of mine could be quite intimidating and I often
used it to my advantage. On one occasion I'd gotten a call from a
very angry customer who was upset about the stereo system he had
just bought. At the time, being cocky, I didn't think customer relations were a high priority. The customer told me he was bringing the
stereo back and he was in no mood to take any guff from me. I'd

never met him but he wanted me to give him a refund, no ifs, ands or buts. Our company policy stated there were to be no refunds, just exchanges. Since I was naturally quite muscular I'd also think nothing of using my muscles in my arsenal of intimidation. I was waiting for him. My office was three steps up and open to the showroom. As he entered carrying the stereo, I could see how angry he was. So I went into my act. My poor assistant manager was standing next to me so he became my designated whipping boy for that little show. I just went berserk on him, calling him every name in the book and threatening that if he ever did that again I'd personally remove his head from his body. He hadn't done a thing. Thank goodness he caught on to what I was doing so he played along and didn't resent the fact I was using him. I also made sure the customer got a good look at my muscles. A muscular body can be quite intimidating to some men in a confrontational situation. That was all part of the routine. As he reached the counter I came charging down the stairs at him with my eyes narrowed. The message was delivered before I even opened my mouth. Just in case he wasn't sufficiently cowed, the first words out of my mouth were: "What the hell do you want?" it was said in a tone that was unmistakable—I was in no mood to take any crap from him. Needless to say this poor man wanted no part of me. I think he thought I was nuts. There was no talk of a refund and a few minutes later he left the store feeling lucky to have made it out alive—still clutching the stereo.

The intimidation worked like it always had. I got what I wanted but didn't feel good about what I'd just done. I was beginning to realize I didn't like myself when I acted like that. I was in my late twenties at the time. I still didn't realize that if I worked at it, I could change my ways.

That Christmas selling period was very good and the company I worked for made a lot of money from my store. I was given a bonus because of that and shared it equally with all my salespeople. The one thing that bothered me about the situation was that my company paid commissions to my salespeople on only a few items. For each sale that was made I had to look it up and see if there was commission and then submit that to company headquarters for them to pay it. For some reason a lot of the commissions that were listed were being kicked back to me unpaid. That, plus the small size of the commissions was bad enough, but as I looked there seemed to be less and less merchandise commissions were paid on. I'd get memos every week deleting more and more commissionable items. It was not at all unusual that a five hundred dollar sale would generate no commission at all or if it did, it might have been five dollars. I thought that unfair because my people depended on that money to make ends meet, because their pay was supposed to be salary plus commission. So, I called my district manager and told him of my concerns. He told me there was nothing he could do about it.

I decided to take matters into my own hands and started submitting requests for commissions on items where none was supposed to be paid. I knew that at such a busy time the company wouldn't check, or at least I hoped not, and so they began issuing checks to my people for more than the company felt they were entitled. They never realized I was doing it, not the company or my salespeople. I could have easily gotten away with it except that temper of mine got the best of me. Right after Christmas a manager's meeting was held to go over our strategy for the upcoming year. For some reason I brought up the commission thing again and how it was unfair to the salespeople. My district manager didn't like that because he thought the issue was resolved and didn't want the other managers to get any ideas. He was already angry at me for talking about it.

When you're not in control of your emotions but allow them to take over you tend to do and say things you shouldn't and normally wouldn't. I was already annoyed with my boss for being angry at me. Obviously, it wasn't hard to annoy me those days. One thing I said frequently at the time if someone was getting on my nerves was: "If your intention is to get me angry that won't be hard to do. But if you do, you'll have to suffer the consequences". And I used to mean it.

So, I just blurted out what I'd done and told him exactly what I'd been up to. As I've said, I looked intelligent. I didn't always act that way. This was one of those occasions.

My boss was shocked and let me have it with both barrels. Instead of being smart and keeping my mouth shut for once, I totally lost it and went back at him with a vengeance. It was an incredible fifteen minutes. We yelled and cursed at each other at the top of our lungs and when another manager tried to intervene on my behalf, my boss told him to "shut the #@$ up!" I was a good manager but why I didn't get fired I can only guess. You don't normally get to curse your boss out as I did and still keep your job. I found out later that the entire office had heard the argument and the secretaries got as far away as possible from the meeting room. I was such a contentious argument they were actually afraid.

After that I knew I had to do something to get control of myself. But, I didn't know how to go about it. I was at the point where I felt worse and worse about myself with each outburst. I had already decided to quit smoking and drinking in the new year so I just added eliminating my temper to the list. I'd always said I'd get rid of my bad habits before my thirtieth birthday. Quitting drinking and smoking was a piece of cake. I was so determined to get my act together that after around eleven years of smoking, as much as two packs a day, I didn't have one craving after I quit. But, I still didn't know how to get rid of my temper. I tried, but as you're well aware, if you want to be successful in self-improvement or anything, you need some kind of blueprint so you have an idea as to how to proceed. Then I read a flyer offering night classes in meditation and an introduction to conscious living. I was intrigued.

Taking that class was one of the best things I ever did. I knew nothing about conscious living so it all was a revelation to me. I was excited by what I'd heard. I'd decided I needed a complete overhaul, so I paid close attention to what my teacher had to say. It was like someone turning on a light bulb in my head. I never realized you could think differently than you always had. It was such a revolutionary concept for me (you have to remember it wasn't a hot topic at the time) that I started meditating and trying to live a conscious life immediately.

We were assigned two books to read, one of them was Ken Keyes' *Handbook to Higher Consciousness*. That became my main source of information on the subject for years. His basic premise is to raise all addictions (that being negative emotions) to a preference. Your expectations are kept in check by preferring something to happen or some outcome to be the way you'd like, instead of wanting or needing it to be that way. You can enjoy any positive outcome that does occur just as much by preferring, and if it doesn't work out as you'd hoped since you didn't need to have the outcome come out your way, then you shouldn't be disappointed as you would if you depended on it.

I absolutely ate this stuff up. I previously briefly described the meditation technique that was taught. Now I'll fill in the details. We'd first take a number of deep breaths to loosen any tension, then we relaxed every set of muscles in our bodies one by one, starting from the top of the head on down. As we did this, environmental tapes were played and the lights were lowered. It was usually the sound of a babbling brook or the Amazon Rain Forest, both very soothing. By this time we were feeling quite a bit relaxed already. The actual meditation began when our teacher told us to picture a place in our minds where we would be the happiest. It could be a real place or something we invented that has all the ideal characteristics of where we'd like to be. If you do try this, which is something I recommend you do, sit in a chair with a firm back in a quiet room that is candlelit. Play environmental tapes if you'd like. In your ideal place you should be alone, although in case, for example, you're a horse lover, you can have a horse accompanying you, but no other humans. There should be vibrant colors, especially the deep blues of the sky and water, bright greens of vegetation and grasses and the most colorful flowers your mind can devise. All the colors except red, and I can't remember the reason for that. But, we were told to concentrate on the vivid blues and greens predominantly. Our eyes were closed for the duration of the meditation—twenty minutes.

What I loved about it was the wonderful feeling in my stomach area, taking the place of the mild twinge of anxiety that usually resided there. It was a totally relaxing and mentally refreshing experience. Right away I was hooked on the whole concept. But, what I remember most, the most vivid memories, are those of the few examples given by our teacher of real life situations and how to go about living them as a conscious person. The one lesson that stands out most and also the one I used most frequently was a situation involving driving.

Since I never realized I could actually change my attitude, I used to get as frustrated as the next person behind the wheel. Since I had a fairly quick wit, riding with me was an unusual experience to say the least. Nothing ever happened in my vicinity that I didn't comment on. Sometimes it was pretty funny and a lot of people at the time told me I should charge admission because my running commentary was funnier than any stand up comedian's routine. If we were going somewhere my friends always wanted me to drive so they could enjoy the show.

But other times I could be downright nasty if I felt provoked. It was that ego thing again. If I got cut off my blood would start to boil and I might try to retaliate in some way. Or, I'd get upset if someone didn't use their turn signal when pulling in front of me. I wasn't any worse than the average driver who experiences frustration with careless or unskilled drivers. But, since I was now learning a better way to deal with it, and it was the easiest way for me to practice what I was being taught, I started driving consciously for the first time. It was so important to be given a very specific lesson in how to consciously deal with something that one has to encounter every day. That's why I remember what I was taught twenty-five years ago. Too many times lessons, whether in school or elsewhere, are taught but are not related to actual experience. Abstract lessons don't stick. If there aren't relevant examples for the student to go by, the lessons are quickly forgotten.

It didn't take long before the practice started. After leaving class my girlfriend and I got on the freeway and within five minutes were being tailgated. In L.A. it almost never takes long for someone to do something boneheaded on the road. But, instead of doing what

I usually did under that circumstance, applying the brakes and slowing down to annoy the tailgater, I put my signal on and moved over—and, much to my relief, the world didn't end! I actually was a little proud of myself for consciously deciding to do the safe thing instead of going by instinct and habit, and doing the usual thing. *I thought to myself: "You know, this stuff might actually work." I was encouraged because I could easily understand and apply the lessons I was just taught.*

The only problem was, that was only one of the few concrete examples given by my teacher. I needed more because although I started to understand the theory behind conscious living, I had no idea how to apply it when I most needed it. That's why I include as many examples as I can in this book. I want you to be able to apply whatever you learn without having to try to figure out how. I want you to be encouraged with the progress you are making so you'll want to use what I tell you more and more. I have no desire for you to have to try to figure out what you should do, but, in that moment, when you think before acting or speaking, to remember what you read regarding the type of situation you're experiencing. I basically filled in the gaps of my knowledge of conscious living through study and trial and error, and I don't want you to have to do it that way.

You can see the importance of living without your ego intervening in your decision-making process. I jotted down and kept what Frank Leahy said years ago in "Look" magazine on the subject of ego: "Egotism is the anesthetic that dulls the pain of stupidity." Or, at least, it makes us do stupid things that go contrary to our own best interests.

CHAPTER TWO
SUCCESS

Some people's lives revolve around their work. Their perception of themselves is closely tied to their jobs. It's very evident in professions dealing with the arts where the artist's whole being goes into whatever project they are currently working on. It's not something that many artists can just walk away from when their day is over. Since art is such an intellectual process, the work is closely tied to their lifestyles, and is never far from their minds. Another group whose work is closely tied to their lifestyles is business executives, with early meetings, business lunches, dinners with clients, lots of travel, etc. Many of their friends are business associates, so even when they're off, business is never far from their minds. As I've said, that's just the opposite of my life. When I leave work, that's it. Even with it being my own business I make it a point to leaving my work at the shop. It took me quite a while to train myself to do that, but that's my preference.

The problem with tying one's self image and many times happiness to work is pretty self-evident. It's an external force that you really don't have all that much control over. If, on the other hand, your life revolves around work and you enjoy it and don't stress too much about it and you take care to lead a conscious and varied life, then you have the best of both worlds. But with many executives their responsibilities are so vast that they're always in a hurry, stressed, and their workday is tightly scheduled.

One of my good clients was a television producer. At one time he had six shows on. That's a huge amount of work for one person. I'd get a call from his secretary letting me know almost to the minute when he'd arrive and how long he could stay. If he was in my shop more than fifteen minutes he'd get several phone calls. He was a wonderful person and had tons of money and fame, but at the same time he paid for it in stress and worry. People like him who have "made it" have usually worked extremely hard to where they are, and even with all the money and fame, I'd much rather be me, running a little shop, making a modest salary, worry-free. People such as that producer aren't necessarily unhappy but I don't know any who aren't overworked and overstressed. It's true I don't have a home like he does, the private chef, or the getaway house on the beach, but that couldn't be more irrelevant. If you're willing to put in all the hard work and your dream is to get rich I really can't see a problem in that, although I might disagree with your priorities. One note, that old saying, "It's just business" shouldn't be an excuse to act any differently. That's how many businessmen justify changing their behavior and their personality to do things they wouldn't find acceptable outside the office. You should consciously make it a point to act the same, at a high level, whether you're at work or not. You should stay the same person no matter what you're doing.

One point I would like to make, and this is important: you should never begrudge another's success. People who have made it have usually put in a major effort and countless hours to get where they are. If anything, they should be admired for their tenacity. Your time will come, as long as you put out the effort to make it so. Resentment and jealousy *never* serve you well.

Years ago, I worked for a man and his personality would change for the worse when he stepped foot in his office. He was aware of it but never did a thing about it, much to his employees' chagrin. He even referred to himself as Dr. Jekyll and Mr. Hyde on one occasion. Unfortunately, we always got the Mr. Hyde part. I remember when he came back from vacation once and he was so relaxed he was like a totally different person. That usually lasted an hour, but I remember him telling me that he wished he could be that way all the time at work. Not nearly as much as we did. But, he was acting as if making that change was completely out of his control. When in reality we know it's a hundred percent in his control, as a matter of fact he's the only one who could have done it. He'd do things at work that would make his employees cringe on a daily basis and, as with others, he'd justify his actions by telling us it was only business and we would do the same thing if it were our business. He was attempting to bring us down to his level and if he really believed that's how we'd be, he'd feel better about himself.

A big problem with people investing so much of themselves in their work is obvious: they can lose their jobs. Whereas many people would easily move on and find another one, people's whose perception of themselves is so closely tied to what they do will take it as a huge loss. In fact, it can be as devastating as a death in the family. Since all aspects of their life are so intricately woven into that particular job, losing it would be so crushing that their self-esteem would take a huge hit. It's important that whatever your line of work that you always do the best job you're capable of, but keep it in context. A job, no matter how important, is still a job. It doesn't matter if you're president of a large corporation, leading a one-dimensional life, no matter how much you enjoy it, is not a healthy situation. And you'll never know what you're missing since you don't have the time to find out. Putting all your eggs in one basket is risky and an invitation to trouble.

Being so busy, there are always trade offs. Since there are only twenty-four hours in a day, you might not have time to give your family the attention they need and deserve, or participate in leisure activities you enjoy. Leading a balanced life that includes various activities is the healthiest way of going about it. On the other extreme are those who go to work but really don't have a vested interest in it. That's the majority of people. Their self worth is not derived from their work, and they either put a lot of stock in their daily efforts or just show up to collect a paycheck. Unfortunately, many of those people also lead a pretty one-dimensional existence. Their routine might be to get up, go to work, come home and plop themselves in front of the television. Truly conscious people realize that's no way to go about things, especially since we want to lead a full life. It's always, "Yeah, yeah, I'll do it tomorrow." We have a tendency to put things off even if it's something we might benefit from. It's easier just to sit there with remote in hand and be entertained. But, is that living or only existing? Edgar Lee Masters in *Spoon River Anthology* said it well when he wrote: "It takes life to love life."

Life is meant to be lived. It's not meant to be day-to-day existence. There is no sense of urgency about it because we learn to take each moment as it comes. But we realize we only have one chance at this. There are no do-overs. Does that mean you should cram as much as you can into every day? Not necessarily. I'd say a well-balanced life that includes work and leisure and possibly some kind of activity in which you help others would be pretty ideal. When you do for others, you feel that much better about yourself.

As Americans we're spoiled. We have a tendency to take much of what we have for granted. Even today a quarter of the world's population exists on less than a dollar a day. Every day we should wake up and make a point to give thanks for everything that we have. Too many of us are always wanting more. We're so wrapped up in trying to get more and more we forget to be thankful for everything we have. Aldous Huxley in *Variations on a Philosopher* said: "Most human beings have an almost infinite capacity for taking things for granted."

If you can learn to be satisfied with what you have, you won't spend so much time always want something else. Anything more is just icing on the cake once you learn to become content with what you already have. The more conscious you become the less you'll feel the need for more material possessions. Ideally, you should be just as happy with the bare necessities of food, clothing, and shelter, as you would with a mansion in Beverly Hills. That's not to mean that having nice possessions is wrong, but that shouldn't be the focus of your life. If you can be just as happy without them, you're way ahead of everyone else.

It's much more important that you be way ahead of where

you formerly were. If we feel the need to make comparisons, that's where your comparisons should lie. When you get to the point of not having your day-to-day happiness tied to the events of the day, things that you formerly depended on to provide you that happiness will no longer be as important. Instead of providing you with happiness, these outside sources of enjoyment won't constitute your reasons for being happy any longer. That's a huge difference. Since you no longer depend on external sources to provide your happiness, it becomes something you consciously carry with you wherever you go or whatever you do. It becomes broader and not as situational. Now you really don't need the same things to assure that at least you'll be happy while you're doing whatever it is, since your happiness is totally internal and not dependent on outside activities. You still do the things that you used to count on to provide your happiness, but now you go in with no expectations that this will be the source of your happiness. You no longer "need" these things and with that attitude you can actually enjoy them more, because there is no pressure to have a good time while you can. You know that happiness will follow wherever you go.

But work is important when it comes to being a conscious person. You should strive to make your life's work more on improving within. The ultimate goal is tranquility, and that's only reachable through conscious living—that means every minute of every day you need to remember what you're trying to accomplish.

Being conscious means always living in the moment, accepting things you can't change, eliminating all fear by not projecting your thoughts into the future, accepting all people as they are, and consciously thinking before doing or saying anything. The more you practice, and all day every day is practice, the more you'll get out of it. When you've mastered the art of living, then tranquility will be yours to enjoy, all the time. If you don't stay on top of it, it'll never happen. The good thing is you're only relying on yourself to accomplish this so you're not dependent on the whims of others. You don't need any equipment, or have to buy anything outside of this book. In the beginning, think of it as a challenge. Just as you would anything that's not easy to accomplish, but well worth the effort.

When you went to school the way you mastered math was to go over it until it became second nature. Think of it the same way, although, in trying to lead a conscious life there are no crutches as with calculators, although you always have this book to refer back to. Just as you learned to add, subtract, multiply, and divide by memorizing the tables, you learn to live consciously by remembering and utilizing the some simple points. It's really not that difficult at all and it certainly isn't complicated. *Through hard work, and some pretty easy steps that sinking feeling you carry around in the pit of your stomach will be just a memory. It will fade faster than you can now imagine.*

CHAPTER THREE
RESPONSIBILITY AND MATURITY

Did you ever watch a single ant out on its own foraging for food? To get from point one place to another seemingly takes forever. Unless they're following a chemical trail laid down by other ants they're all over the place, there seems to be no rhyme or reason for their actions. When we're young we have certain expectations. Everything is pretty regimented, there seems to be a pattern. When our parents went out, we usually tagged along. Meals were normally prepared at set times as were our wake up and bed times. When we got to school we were on an organized schedule. For a long time everything seemed to be planned for us and we followed that plan in our everyday lives. So, as we grew, our expectations were that that's how life is really lived. And at that time, that's exactly how it was lived. We didn't know any other way. You went along not following a chemical trail but a schedule others laid down for you. I think in the beginning that's how it should be. Having something you can count on is a very stabilizing factor and gives children a constancy that is reassuring and comforting.

Our perception of life as a seamless, flowing entity begins to change as we get older. That realization comes to different people at different times depending on the circumstances of their lives. If one lives in a stable environment surrounded by family, the change usually comes more gradually and at a later time. Some people are thrust in to more mature situations at an earlier age due to any number of circumstances, sometimes out of their control. They may have to make a living to help support their family, or they might be more mature than their counterparts, or just have an adventurous streak in them.

Whatever the reason and however long it takes, our perceptions of what life is all about, change. For most of us the change is underway before we even realize it's occurring. When we're young we feel everyone we know and love will always be around us. Family gatherings with aunts, uncles, and cousins are usually festive affairs and with times like that we have a tendency to feel they'll never end. As we mature we begin to realize there's no master plan and our lives more resemble the lone ant's journey. People we thought would always be around are no longer. Getting from point A to point B, which now isn't laid out for us by others, is uncharted territory. Our perception of a smooth ride suddenly seems to get a little choppy.

For most of us that's exciting but also a big adjustment. The safety net of familiarity and reassurance is taken away to a certain extent, and we're more on our own than ever before. Sometimes it's scary and sometimes it's fun. For the first time we get to test our wings. We're not quite as sure about the nature of life as we once were. As our perceptions change our attitudes about things change along with them. That just means we're maturing and starting to understand the world around us a little better even though it does get confusing at times. How well we learn the lessons we're taught early will have an impact on how we conduct ourselves the rest of our lives. Although, those lessons can be expanded upon or even changed later in life through conscious effort. As we soon learn, things in our lives are transitory and changes are made sometimes for the better and sometimes not. Sometimes change is brought about by ourselves and sometimes it happens when we wish it wouldn't. The stability we all crave to give our lives meaning is now up to us to create. We now begin to determine basic things such as when we get up, where we spend our time, and where we live. These are reasons many of us look so fondly back on our childhood. It was a very comforting and stable environment and we didn't have to worry about things. Most of the deciding was done for us.

As we realize we're more on our own and now more responsible for our conduct, we have to concern ourselves with little things that make up our daily life. What was once simple now often isn't. Some people react better to this than others, who have a more difficult time adapting to their new responsibilities. That was me. To say I was slow on the draw when it came to living up to my responsibilities is being very kind to myself. If you look at me now and then, when I was a young adult, you wouldn't recognize me as the same person. I wanted all the freedom accorded to adults but I wanted nothing to do with the responsibilities. Although my parents never said anything I must have been a great disappointment to them for a long time. I was pretty wild and never considered the consequences of my actions. I've often said I'm surprised I lived past my twenty-fourth birthday.

I was about as far as one could be from living a conscious, responsible life. No one, including myself, knew if I'd show up at home or not. While still living with my parents it wasn't at all unusual for me to go out, telling them I'd be home a little later, and thinking I would, and then not show up for two or three days. At that time if something felt good or sounded like fun, I was definitely up for it. I'd think nothing of dating two girls at one time, and often on the same day, without them knowing it, although I wasn't very good at it. I think if I had referred to Nancy as Mary one more time, she would have killed me. I'd break off relationships for no good reason, just because I felt like it. I had a lot of friends who were much like I was. We were young adults but acted like spoiled children. Everything we did, we did to excess. I lived life without a care in the world, but not in the same way as today. I must admit though, I had a good time. But that's different from being happy.

As I've stated, at the time I also had a pretty bad temper. That was some combination and because of my attitude and temper I was never far from trouble. The only thing I can figure to account for my reckless lifestyle is I was reluctant to grow up. Being the fourth and last child I'd always had it easy. I was never pushed to excel and I wasn't the type to push myself. So, I grew up with a cavalier attitude about just about everything. It wasn't my parents' fault, but 100% my own doing. I was fairly intelligent but always did just enough to get by in school. I was popular so I thought it was okay and that's how life really was, and since no one challenged me I just kept it up. I don't think it would have made a bit of difference to me if they did. I was self-assured almost to the point of being cocky and thought I knew a lot more than I really did. If this sounds familiar that's because it's not all that uncommon.

Still, with all that, I was basically a nice guy who usually got along with everyone. I know that sounds odd but I was never one to push myself on others or be disrespectful to my elders. Some guys never grow out of that stage and think themselves to be much more than they really are. At a certain age that attitude changes from being childish to buffoonery. Two examples I can think of who exemplify that childish attitude and lifestyle are Joey Buttafuoco and Howard Stern. Two very different people but with their own brand of absurdity. If I needed to point out some examples of how not to be, I'd point to them.

Buttafuoco comes off as a preening, vain, self-centered, and immature individual, who thinks he's accomplished something, but really hasn't. I think Howard Stern is childish to the point of ridiculousness, and who thinks the world revolves around him. What I think his worst character trait is his cruelty, especially to his adoring sycophants, who treasure his every word. To me, Stern and Buttafuoco are no better than the buffoons of the professional wrestling world. They all strut about as if they're the center of the universe. Buttafuoco cheats on his wife with an underage girl, does a little jail time, and now has an agent. He wants an acting career. What I think is kind of sad is we have this guy, plucked from obscurity, who breaks the law in a particularly vile way and because of that is now famous. What kind of message does that send?   Do anything you have to, no matter how odious, and you'll not only achieve fame, but also make a lot more money than you would have if you hadn't?

I could never figure the attraction to Howard Stern. Here we have a developmentally stunted narcissist who panders to the lowest common denominator of the human psyche. He's childish, callow, and a role model from hell and yet is paid a ridiculous salary to act the way he does. There is something wrong with our society when we reward people who act like this and accord them fame.

That kind of skewed thinking and rewarding of aberrant behavior seems to be getting worse and worse as communication becomes instantaneous. Everyone is becoming a "star," no matter how odious they are or the values they keep. For the "castaways" on the show "Survivor," characteristics most people feel are negative in real life actually help you win on TV. Normally scheming, lying, and backstabbing aren't traits that serve a person well, but on this particular show, they are encouraged and in fact the formula for not getting "voted off." That's pretty sad when that type of behavior is rewarded. Basically, the worse the person is, the greater the chance that they win the grand prize.

Did you ever know someone who perpetually walked around with a cloud over their head? Such people spend their lives lurching from one catastrophe to another. A week doesn't go by without something bad happening to them. You could be leading basically the same life they do, have an equivalent job, and live in the same neighborhood, but you don't have the litany of problems they seem to. Problems don't just happen. There is always a cause, and if the person seems unusually "cursed," they've more than likely brought it on themselves. That's especially true if you see a pattern develop. These people tend to be the ones who habitually cut corners, who feel the rules are for everyone else but them. And, when the problem does strike, it's usually someone else's fault. Just ask them. It becomes a way of life, and for some reason, and they can't imagine why this is, they get singled out and picked on. They might be guilty of a number of things including but not limited to: cheating on their taxes, not studying for exams, lying, or cheating on their spouse. Or maybe they're lazy and don't do their jobs as they should, or spread rumors, or treat others with disrespect, blame others for their shortcomings or show absolutely no initiative, or collect parking tickets like they were autographs, or cheat people in business, or are physically or verbally abusive, or are always trying to get something for nothing, or drink to excess, or are loud and inconsiderate, make promises they have no intention of keeping, or are always trying to get away with stuff, big and small – the list is endless. What all of these people have in common is their distorted attitude about everything and their inability to accept responsibility for their actions. Another thing these people have in common is the level of stress they cause themselves when the time comes to deal with the consequences of their actions or inactions. They get stressed about it, and that in turn, affects all those around them. And when their actions come back to haunt them they lash out or find it incomprehensible. They are 100% responsible for making their own lives, and the lives they come in contact with much more difficult than they should be. There are too many Ralph Kramdens in the world; people who are big shots in their own mind. People who always have the big deal or major score right around the corner. They want the world, even feel they're entitled to it, but don't want to put out the effort it takes to improve enough to reach their goals.

They're so busy scheming that they don't take the time to do the little things that could improve their lives immeasurably, and that actually would increase their chances of improving their lot. If a person has a "something for nothing" attitude about life that's basically what good they will receive for their misdirected efforts–nothing.

A farmer can't expect to yield a crop if he doesn't plant the seeds. Good things don't just happen—there's always a cause, conversely, if bad things seem to happen consistently, there's also a cause. You alone are responsible through your own actions, of determining which way your life will be: hard working and honest, and therefore pretty straightforward, or lazy and manipulative, and therefore stressful and problem strewn.

For the most part, people aren't lucky or unlucky. If good things seem to constantly happen to a particular person, they've more than likely put in a great effort to make it so, and are to be admired for their good work ethic. If you sit back and expect good things, and you want certain results, but are not inclined to do the work it takes to attain them, if they do happen, it's pure coincidence and not sustainable, because it has no foundation.

A builder can't build a house without a solid foundation, and if he does, the house won't be there for long. If you are willing to lay the foundation through hard work and honest effort, good things will happen for you, and you'll wind up achieving your goals more often, than if you just wished them so, and it will be accomplished with a lot less stress and with a lot more satisfaction.

Too many people who cause totally unnecessary and totally avoidable problems have a lax morality where the only regret they ever have is the regret of getting caught. That usually occurs when some activity of theirs catches up with them. They may in no way regret the actions that got them in hot water in the first place, just the getting caught part. That's the attitude shared by many, that as long as you don't get caught, then it's all right. Some people are so self-forgiving that they truly feel that the ends justify the means instead of the means justifying and creating the end result.

That's just another way to excuse lax moral behavior. According to how this works, if you don't actually get caught, for example, knowingly keeping more change then you were entitled to due to a cashier's mistake, (you gave her a five and she mistakenly gave you change for a ten) it's fine to keep it. Or if you claim three dependents on your taxes and in reality only have one, it's okay to accept the larger refund, as long as you don't get caught, besides when you rip off the government or large multi-national corporations it's not really stealing.

What many of these people have in common, is their ability to rationalize their behavior. That's one of the ways the get in trouble. They have an infinite ability to excuse themselves and make excuses to themselves and make excuses to others about themselves. That kind of "my dog ate my homework" lifestyle, always using alibies, is a pretty lame way to go about life.

In reality either you're responsible for something of you're not. There's no "I did it but let me tell you why I'm not actually responsible" for it. You can't honestly have it both ways. As a conscious person since we readily accept responsibilities for our actions and take the time to think before acting, in order to help us determine if something is the "right" thing to do or not, there should never be a time when we have to "justify" our actions.

The 20th century has rediscovered the word karma. I strongly believe in it because it is a concept that takes into account the responsibility we have for any actions that we do. Karma is simply taking responsibility for consequences. It puts the responsibility of being accountable for your actions squarely on you. That also includes the concept of "what goes around, comes around." If you do everything on the up and up and treat everyone you come in contact with exactly how you'd like to be treated, you'll find that the more good that flows from you, the more will be returned to you and many times over. If you do ten kindnesses in a day for ten different people, even small seemingly inconsequential things, you'll find that the good you've put out will be returned to you in many ways, subtle and overt.

Conversely, if you treat others with disrespect or in an offhand manner, that too will come back to you many times over, but not in the way you'd like. People might not say anything but that doesn't mean they don't notice. Most people are just like you in that they're basically good people and all they ask of others is to be treated fairly and honestly. We don't expect others to solve our problems just as sure as we don't expect others to cause our problems. Those expectations of others, who lead their own lives are realistic. Putting out only good and fair vibes in dealing with them is totally in our power. That's positive karma. If you make it a priority to treat others as you wish to be treated, then you have a basic understanding of what conscious living is all about. As long as you consciously make it a point to do just that. No matter who they are or what station they have in life, even it the person is down on their luck and living in the street, if treated with dignity and respect, you'll enrich their lives and let them know you believe their lives have value. The homeless don't get much in positive reinforcement, but a lot of negative. A few kind words, which cost you nothing can make a huge difference to a homeless person and will go a long way in making them feel better about themselves in that moment.

In the old Honeymooners show, Ralph Kramden had a line: "Be kind to people you meet on the way up, because you're going to meet the same people on the way down."

CHAPTER FOUR
FRIENDSHIP

Another important thing that makes a person more than just an acquaintance, is your personal concern for their well-being. It's important to you that friends are happy and you'll usually go the extra mile to try to insure that. That concern is one thing that distinguishes a friend from an acquaintance. As Eustace Budgell wrote in *The Spectator* almost two hundred years ago, "Friendship is a strong and habitual inclination in two person to promote the good and happiness of one another."

True friends can be a great comfort when things aren't going your way. A good friend elevates us with their concern for our well-being and gives us the feeling of not going it alone. It's not that difficult for many of us to make friends, but to become close friends is work, just like any other relationship. A true friend is one who will be on your side no matter what, even if you're wrong. Anyone would be on your side if you're "right," but if there were a job description placed on friendship, it would certainly include supporting a friend whether they're right or wrong. It's easy to support a winner but much more difficult to stand up for a friend in a losing cause.

Our lives are partly what we make them and partly what is made by the friends we choose. You need to choose friends wisely. They are the few people who will come to know you best, and despite that, will still like you. If you're experiencing trouble in your life, the first person you'll likely call will be a good friend, not a relative. As Euripides said in *Orestes*, "One loyal friend is worth ten thousand relatives." I don't think I'd go that far, especially with the respect I have for the members of my family, but you're more likely to confide in a friend and tell that person your innermost thoughts, than you would anyone else.

You're also likely to have much more in common with your friends, as compared to relatives or acquaintances. If you become very close to someone, you each might take on characteristics of the other; personality traits and mannerisms and things like that. Sometimes that's obvious in the similar way friends dress. We all realize the importance of close friendships. Life wouldn't be nearly as rich without them.

Having a close friend also gives us the opportunity to be generous. It's so much fun when you come across something you know your friend would love to have. If you have the resources, I highly recommend that you act on your generous impulses. Don't analyze it to death and go back and forth in your mind about it—just do it. One rule I follow is to never stifle a generous impulse, although I'm very much in favor of not being impulsive in most things. But, this is the one exception I allow myself. Recently I came across a beautiful Celtic cross that was framed under glass on a plush green background. I knew a friend who would just love it because she's devout and it would match her décor perfectly, and I knew she liked things like that. So I bought it and shipped it to her. One thing about giving is if you take the time to make sure it's something you think the person would really like, and not only something you think that possibly they may like or you'd like, it's so much more appreciated. Friends appreciate thoughtful actions, especially if they come out of the blue.

Although our lives are enriched by friendships, ultimately, as conscious people, we realize that our happiness depends on ourselves. No matter how good a friend, how caring and helpful, friends can't manufacture your happiness for you. They might be happy for you when something good happens in your life, but they can't provide that happiness no matter how much they'd like to. Friends to us are more the icing on the cake of happiness, than creators of it. In no way should we expect our friends to provide it, but it's more in the line of sharing it with them.

I've been quite fortunate to have some very good and close friends. True friends will always do things for you that others wouldn't, and sometimes you wish they hadn't, but that's all part of friendship. Years ago, I was on a training exercise just outside Death Valley. We arrived at the fort at 3:00 a.m. after riding all night in a convoy. We were bone tired and knew that reveille was in two hours. Unfortunately, we also knew that all the trucks, Howitzers, and equipment had to be secured. All the men undressed the second we got to the barracks and jumped into their bunks, hoping to get two hours sleep and also hoping that if we were in our bunks we'd be spared. It was like we were a bunch of kids, if we closed our eyes and looked asleep no one would bother us. It didn't work as a kid and unfortunately it didn't work in this case either. We were all hoping someone else, anybody but us, would have to drive the trucks and howitzers to the secured yard. Our chief of section was a close friend.

We'd gone to the same college, and I was his number-two man, the gunner.. He was responsible for getting that done. So, it wasn't at all surprising that my attempt to fade into the background and not have to go out in the freezing cold didn't work. The desert can get brutally cold at night in the winter. I got the tap on the shoulder as I knew I would. My friend needed help and he didn't want any hassles from the rest of the other men. There was no chance that others would go quietly. So, another buddy, who did it as a favor to me, got dressed and spent the next hour or so securing all the equipment. My friend knew that we'd do it with a minimal amount of complaining because we were close. He knew he could count on us to do what nobody else wanted to because of our friendship. I didn't consider it as him taking advantage of our friendship, but more as a duty to him as a friend. I was a sergeant so I could have picked someone else to do the job for me, but since my friend had asked me specifically, I went ahead and did it myself.

No matter how long or well you know someone, sometimes their generosity catches you by surprise. When I was going through a period of health and money problems some years ago a major and unexpected bill arrived. Actually, it was more of a court order. Years before I'd gone in with another person on a condo. I paid the mortgage off and was in the process of clearing up some bills on it when the court order arrived. It actually was sent to my sister Nikki for me. I distinctly remember that day. I just arrived home from Maui, and she called. She asked me how the vacation was and what kind of mood I was in. I told her I'd had a great time and was in a very good mood. She said she'd change that when she told me what had occurred. The court order basically told me I owed in the neighborhood of thirty-five thousand dollars on the condo. I was shocked since I had paid the condo off completely, and didn't have a clue to what this was all about.

The person I went in on the condo with had declared bankruptcy and he never put the deed in my name as he said he would, and I mistakenly believed he had. That was supposed to have been done five years before. There was a judgment against him including interest and penalties totaling one hundred and seventy thousand dollars. He had defaulted on a loan. I didn't even realize that he had done that, until I got this paperwork. I had to get an attorney to see what I could do because I was having trouble paying my own bills. I found out there wasn't much. Since he'd declared bankruptcy his creditors were going after anyone they could to get back as much as they could. I should have known better. (One time I had to bail him out of Burbank jail right before Christmas. It was on some old traffic tickets. The bail was $156 cash. He wrote me a check to cover it, and the next week I was bouncing checks all over town. He'd given me a bad check.) They determined what they considered his share of the condo was worth, and since he hadn't taken his name off the deed as we had agreed to, they came after me.

I learned a lot about bankruptcy law, more than I ever wanted to. So, now I was stuck with this huge bill. It goes to show that life isn't always fair, and if one lives it consciously and learns to accept such things, fair or not, the ride is a lot smoother. I was living somewhat of a conscious life at the time, at least I was trying to, so I handled the bad news pretty well. I didn't once fall prey to resentment. I was going through chemotherapy then so I had to make a point not to get too stressed. (I'd allowed myself to get stressed during chemo before and it made the situation much more unpleasant.) Trying to figure how to pay my portion of the medical bills now got a lot more complicated. If I didn't come up with the thirty-five thousand, my condo would have been foreclosed on and auctioned off. And I'm sure it wouldn't have done my credit rating much good. While all this was going on I got a letter from the California Board of Equalization (sales tax) telling me that my business was being audited. That's when I was so glad I was honest. One problem with the audit was now I would have to prepare for it and I was feeling absolutely awful. Another was the fact that our first accountant set up the books wrong when it came to our collection of sales taxes. We were collecting on the wrong things and only later found out that prescription eyewear was taxed differently than anything else.

Our new accountant told me to expect the worst. If we couldn't convince the auditor it was an honest mistake, I could have been liable for three years' worth of sales tax. Sometimes things work out okay, that's one reason why it is imperative you don't project your thoughts into the future. Let things play out and if you've done your best, whatever will be will be, and you can more readily accept the results. If you can do that at least you didn't worry yourself sick about it. Since worrying about what's going to happen tomorrow or next week is totally counterproductive, if you can train yourself to stay in the moment, at least you won't make the matter worse. In this case I lucked out and the auditor understood. Even though we were doing it all wrong he took into consideration the fact that we paid all the tax we collected and it actually came out the state made more money than if we'd done it correctly. My accountant told me it was the first time any of her clients didn't have to pay anything at all. That was a huge relief, but the clock was ticking and the time for me to pay the thirty-five thousand was fast approaching. I couldn't afford to close out much more in my retirement accounts but I bit the bullet and took fifteen thousand dollars out. That left me twenty thousand dollars short. I didn't want my condo foreclosed on. I didn't know what to do, so finally when I was out of options, I knew I needed to borrow it. That was a big chunk of change to hit someone up for, so I decided to ask four friends to loan me five thousand each. My friends readily agreed and I paid that huge bill, so there was one less thing I had to contend with. But now, I owed twenty thousand to my friends, which I decided had to be repaid as quickly as possible. That's even though they told me to take my time. Neither my friends nor family ever charge interest to each other on any loans, so I knew each day I had their money was interest lost to them. It took me a while but within a year and a half I had paid three of my friends off.

On my fiftieth birthday I went to my sister Nikki's. We had arranged for her to take me out to dinner, which is a family tradition. I had just completed a week's worth of chemo and felt awful. When I opened the door to my sister's house, the place erupted. She had put together a surprise party for me. To say I was surprised would be an understatement. My sister's only fear was that with all the excitement, I'd have a heart attack. (I have an irregular heartbeat now due to the medication.) There were forty or fifty people there. I had friends from Northern California, San Diego, and relatives, including my brother Joe, from New Jersey. Others came from New York and Connecticut, just for the party. I was so heavily medicated and exhausted, I don't remember too much about what went on. The people who couldn't make it all called during the party. My good friend John, who lives in Northern California and was one of the four friends who loaned me money, called. He was the only one I hadn't paid back yet, because he's the one that needed it the least. After wishing me a happy birthday, he said he had a present for me. The present was, the five thousand dollar loan was forgiven. As a gift he told me to forget having to pay him back. I'd never even considered something like that, and after a few half-hearted protestations on my part, gladly accepted his offer. His generosity was the result of twenty-five years of friendship.

When he moved I was the only one who helped him. I took three days off work, but because we were so close for so long, I was glad to do it for him. Now, he was in a position to do something nice for me and he knew that in doing what he did, a big load was lifted off my shoulders. Sometimes friends' generosity can be a wonderful thing and true friends are the ones who do the greatest things. Because his gift was totally unexpected, it had an even greater impact. As I've said, true friends are the icing on the cake of a conscious person's happiness.

When I was younger I always felt that asking for help was a sure sign of weakness. I felt that a person should sink or swim on their own, and if they needed help in any way that they were in something over their head, it was their own doing. That's even if the help was offered. It was, I later realized, just another case where ego got in the way of sensibility. Friends genuinely want to help a friend in need, if given the opportunity. It took me most of my life to come to that conclusion. I couldn't have made it through the hardest times, and in the beginning, only grudgingly accepted help when I had no other option. But because I needed so much help and support these past few years, I came to accept the fact that sometimes it's a necessity. I never realized how much it meant to others when they were able to lend a hand. But, that's what makes friendships so special. You know you can count on them when no one else is there for you. They don't have an ulterior motive. They only want to lend a helping hand and they know if the situation were reversed, you'd do the same for them.

If my story rings true, try not to make the mistake of taking friends for granted. Consciously and thoughtfully make it a point to remember all their kindnesses, and consciously make it a point to push to the back of your mind their weaknesses. Accept them on their own terms as they are. Each friend is a unique individual, and it goes a long way in cementing your relationship when you take the time to treat them that way. It's important that you always make the effort to understand their likes and dislikes and try to accommodate them in any way you can; just as you'd expect them to do the same for you.

CHAPTER FIVE
AGING AND DEATH

It's interesting how people's perceptions of themselves evolve over time. If there were no mirrors to bring us back to reality we'd think of ourselves differently. As we get older, at least on the inside, most of us still feel young, and our self-image doesn't change as fast as the actual years that go by. When you're fifty you easily might feel the same about yourself as when you were thirty. It's as if we are living a real life Dorian Gray situation. We age, but until something major happens to affect the image we have of ourselves, we still feel ourselves the same. Instead of the picture of Dorian Gray getting older as he stays young, we have the mirror, which doesn't lie. If you asked the typical middle-aged person how young they feel, and not how old they are, it wouldn't be at all surprising that the person feels half their true age. It's hard for us to see ourselves getting older. That's for other people. How many times have you heard someone say, "I don't feel old enough to be a grandparent"? When we think of grandparents we think old, because when we were young our grandparents were old to us.

If I want to feel real old I just have to remind myself that when I was born in 1947 there were still a few survivors of the Civil War alive (that's a fairly sobering thought), and there was no such thing as a calculator. Television was in its infancy (our first TV had a nine-inch screen with a big magnifying glass bolted on the front), so forget color and transistors. Everything was heavy, from the telephone to appliances (in rural areas crank phones were still common).

The computer didn't exist, almost all cars were black, airliners used props instead of jets, there were no cell phones (see, there were some advantages), and just about everything we take for granted today and "need" to survive was years away from invention. It was a much simpler time and I actually preferred it that way.

I dislike the Internet because it is so cold and impersonal. Outside of work, how people can sit in front of a computer for hours is way beyond me. I guess some people need to feel somehow connected to the outside world without having to actually go out into it. It has many wonderful uses, but like everything else, it should be used in moderation and always in context of your life and balanced activities.

I feel about the same with cell phones. I know people who couldn't even walk down the street without the phone to their ear. There is a woman who owns a store near mine who, if she has to work eight hours, will literally be on the phone for the entire time. It's as if these people can't stand to be in their own company and are tethered to their cell phones as if it were their life support.

The older we get, the more weird little things start happening to our bodies. You begin to notice things that for all your preceding life were not there. At first you get a little freaked out because you have something either growing on you, coming out from you or sprouting in the weirdest places, and it wasn't there yesterday and you realize it's not going away tomorrow. Whatever it is we're now stuck with it. And, it's never an improvement over your former self. Even with all that, we still don't feel as old as our years.

After the initial shock of noticing, for the first time, you're starting to look like your mother or father, you just have to accept the fact that that's life, and not worry about it. It's a new experience and if it helps we can think of all the people before us who have gone through the same thing— at least everyone fortunate enough to live that long. Even though we've been aging our whole lives we don't notice it too much and it doesn't become an issue until we really start to feel it. All of a sudden we can't read small print anymore. There are aches and pains and a lot of other nasty surprises that seemingly pop up on a weekly basis.

I think the youthful approach, that is keeping the youthful outlook, is a very healthy and beneficial way to approach life. When we're younger, life is usually a lot easier. There are less responsibilities, and fewer health problems, so even though you are aware of how old you are in years, to feel yourself younger is to live younger. The real beauty of it is as you get older you get wiser, at least through experience you should. That's how we get the attitude about childhood being wasted on the young. If we knew then what we know now we'd have made a lot of different choices, and appreciation of that kind of freedom would be one.

I always loved that line: "If I knew I was going to live this long, I'd have taken better care of myself." Unfortunately, we come to realize that mistakes of our past sometimes do in fact come to haunt us later in life, sometimes when it's too late to do anything about them.

For example, if you've eaten a lot of fried food your whole life, there's a good chance it will eventually catch up with you and manifest itself in heart disease when you get older. Try to think about things like that, and make it a conscious choice, to always remember there are consequences for even seemingly minor things we do. In a case such as this it's really not that difficult to eat better. You don't have to become a vegan. Instead of a hamburger eat a turkey burger, instead of fries, eat a side of fruit. If you do begin to have health problems as you age, make sure you're not the one responsible for creating them. Doing beneficial things for yourself instead of harmful ones is a conscious and deliberate everyday choice. So, get in the habit of consciously making the right choices and there's a much better chance your habits won't come back to haunt you.

I think you should always make a conscious effort to keep your image of yourself youthful in the sense that you don't impose limits on yourself. Don't ever be the one to say: "I'm too old for this." It's never too late to do many of the things you either didn't have time or money for when you were younger. Just as it's never too late to try new things, take up a new hobby, change jobs for the better, etc. But, that's as long as you're not deluding yourself into thinking you're younger than you really are. Age can be an attitude just as surely as happiness is. What you don't want to be is the old guy who dresses like he's a kid and who thinks the only women worthy of a second look are half his age. Even though others' attitudes aren't really that important you really don't want to be perceived as the old fool who's trying to recapture his youth by dressing and acting like his grandchildren.

Start doing things that make you happy, even if you think you were too old for them. If you've always wanted to learn something more about a particular subject, take a class. No matter your age, each moment spent in a happy frame of mind is one less spent in not as good a place. It doesn't matter your age or what others think, but even if you're at the end of your stay here, it's best to wring out as much happiness as you can, and end your life on a high note. Since the past is no longer and your life is being lived in this very moment, every day you get up is a fresh new beginning. Explore, have fun, live life, do whatever it takes to make each day special and you'll find that no matter your age, life can a be wonderful thing. I'm at the point where every day feels like a vacation day.

PART V

APPLYING THE BASICS TO REAL LIFE

CHAPTER ONE
ACCENTUATE THE POSITIVE

There was recently a Latino photo exhibit at one of the local galleries. It depicted everyday life as seen through a Latino perspective and featured Latinos of all economic and social strata. It was an uplifting and well-documented display of every day life. One local Latina took exception to that. She wrote a long article in the *Los Angeles Times* decrying the lack of suffering being depicted. It's as if every depiction of Latinos should include their struggles or somehow it isn't valid. She must be afraid that if for one minute we're allowed to put to the backs of our minds the hard times many Mexicans and Central Americans have suffered here and still do, then everything is lost. We should never see them happy in their work or enjoying life.

I don't get it. As much as some of these people have suffered, they are certainly no worse off than African Americans who were forced to come here, or Native Americans who were royally screwed at every turn and endured centuries of systematic persecution. I very much doubt Black or Native Americans want only their suffering depicted. What would the point be, to make people feel sorry for them? I would think that would be the last thing they'd want. We're all aware of what happened to them and we have hundreds of laws on the books specifically written to make sure nothing like it ever happens again, at least not government sanctioned. We also are aware there is discrimination, not nearly as much as there was thirty years ago, but still persistent, no matter the law. And, we're quite aware that we all have some prejudices, whether we want to admit them or not. I'm not discounting the tremendous disadvantages poor Latinos encounter in their everyday lives, nor am I discounting the problems my grandparents endured when they came to this country from Italy. But, as a conscious person my tendency is to accentuate the positives and to focus on all the advances made instead of constantly harping on the negatives. Good things happen to Latinos as well as other minorities who are temporarily relegate to the lower rung of society's ladder. That's a fact just as discrimination by some is also a fact. We might not like it, but that's the reality of the situation. Just as Jews make every effort, and rightly so, to make sure the Holocaust is not forgotten, I think we all need to be reminded that some in our society are not reaping the benefits of our prosperity. And, I think, as conscious individuals, we should do everything in our power not to be part of the problem, but through our examples, by our accepting and nonjudgmental ways, to be part of the solution. We need to make the effort to understand the plight of others and show compassion. If we lead exemplary lives, our actions will influence the behavior and thinking of others. We don't need to hit someone over the head with a stick twenty-four hours a day to get their attention, but by our example of understanding and compassion, influence the thinking of others to be more open minded.

I feel to constantly harp on the negatives is counterproductive because people get to the point of compassion overload and in always complaining, risk a backlash. People, no matter how sympathetic, want to see some of the fruits of their efforts displayed at least occasionally. As conscious people we learn to accept the good with the bad, but it's not all bad. Compassion is a cornerstone of conscious living—trying to understand the struggles of others through their eyes. If we can understand the problem better, we can be more effective in trying to help solve it.

There are so many people in our midst who through no fault of their own, and despite hard work, live in poverty. Discrimination has a lot to do with it, as do lack of education and basic English skills, but I think that Latina writer must understand that things are changing for the better. People are becoming more aware and are trying to help, but we do need to see the good sometimes. In this instant gratification world people have no patience for gradual change. But, it takes time for many people to change the way they've always thought, and, unfortunately in the case of discrimination and ethnic hatred, it takes longer than most other things. Being conscious is being patient. It also means being realistic.

CHAPTER TWO
REMOVE YOURSELF FROM UNHEALTHY SITUATIONS

When I had an employer, he would get incensed if we ever received a bill from a vendor before we got the product. Even if it was just one day. He thought that to be the ultimate nerve on their part. I remember him calling one company threatening to drop their line of eyewear if they had the gall to do it again. As with everything else with this man, he expected, actually demanded others to toe the line when they refused to do what he expected them to do.

This guy was no Albert Schweitzer. He was in it for the money and for no other reason. I distinctly remember talking to him about a client who was having a lot of trouble with a product we dispensed. I was concerned that he was doing damage to his eyes and the first thing my boss asked me was if the client paid his bill, and not how the client was doing or what we could do to remedy the problem. I told him I thought his attitude was wrong, and that we always collected his money, but, I would have thought he would be more concerned about his client and the trouble he was having. As you can well imagine, that didn't go over too well.

This man actually charged his father cost for his glasses until his wife finally made him stop. I always felt funny when I had to ask his father for his credit card. That's although he thought nothing of having our lab make numerous free pairs for himself until the lab took the unprecedented step of denying him any freebies. That's the only time I've ever heard of a lab doing that. Normally clients couldn't leave without paying but as I've said some entertainers requested that we bill them through their managers. That was always "fun" as he hovered nervously over us making sure we had the correct billing information. He thought nothing of doing that even if he had a client waiting for him. He hated it when people didn't pay on the spot. The person's chair would still be warm and he would be harassing us to send the bill. Never mind the person's glasses wouldn't be ready for a week and their manager would receive the bill well before the glasses were to be delivered (his own pet peeve). Until we actually had the bill in the envelope with the stamp on it, he would badger us every ten minutes or so to make sure we wouldn't forget. There was fat chance of that. The guy was so anal he'd actually walk out on a client to get on our case, six times on one occasion. It didn't matter that he'd already asked us to do it, and that in the past we'd always taken care of it. Every day was like our first day.

We were extremely busy and usually had clients in the office and on the phone all day, every day, so anything else would get priority over sending one bill out. So, we'd every once in a while get a little revenge. That's something I would never do now, nor should you. We exacted our revenge by doing everything else under the sun but send the bill. We figured if he was going to drive us crazy we'd take him with us. The way we saw it, he had a much shorter trip. He was like this about almost everything. We'd be swamped and he wanted us to book appointments every fifteen minutes or so, so if we got lunch on most days by 4:00 we'd be lucky. To give you some idea, the specialists we send all our clients to today take well over an hour with each person we send. With my former employer, you were lucky to get twenty minutes. One day he had a personal Fed-Ex package he wanted shipped, so we decided to see how many times he'd walk out on a client or some other client-related activity, to tell us to make sure the package went out that day. We very purposely reassured him early in the day that we'd take care of it. It didn't have to be ready until 4:00; if we called Fed-Ex at noon it wouldn't have gotten to its destination any faster than if we called later. We held off making the call for about three hours and in that time he managed to "remind" us nine times that the package was to go out that day. That was pretty typical of how he approached everything. I remember he and I having one of our little talks one day because he was upset about something. He was usually upset about something. After I finally had enough, I told him he was the problem in the office and that he had a really good thing going, but he was going to screw it up with constant harping about every little thing. He actually apologized and said he'd try not to be such a pest when we were swamped, but that never happened.

I would bring up the fact to him that he couldn't stand anyone billing him first but thought nothing of doing it himself. I asked him if he saw the irony in his actions. I'm sure you're all familiar with the reply: "It's not the same thing." Of course it was, but he'd never admit it or he'd have to look at himself in an honest fashion, something he'd never done in all the years I worked for him.

He had a television on his desk so he could play the stock market during the day. I wouldn't have given it a second thought but he started spending more and more time doing it. It got to be an addiction. Since we were a busy office, people with appointments would start to pile up in the front as he was stock trading in the back. He was the only one who could perform his task there, so you can imagine the problems that it caused. People would rightfully get upset and the staff would have to deal with them. We couldn't tell them what he was doing. This was minor stuff compared to everything else that went on, but I'm mentioning it to make a point.

Every year I worked with this person, I would lose more respect for him. I won't go into details but suffice it to say he did so many things I considered bizarre and morally disturbing, so frequently, that after a time we all looked at him as being a weak and dishonest individual. Together we had built the business into one of the most successful in California. After I arrived, business doubled in less than three years. When I left we were doing quadruple what he'd done before I got there. When I spoke to others in the field, they were astounded by the amount of money the office generated. We were doing two to three times what other successful practices were, and with no more staff. With all his shortcomings he was a very intelligent man and oddly, outside of work, was a very nice guy. He knew the best way to keep quality help was to pay very well. Because he realized he upset us so much with his odd behavior it wasn't at all unusual for him to apologize to the staff at the end of the day. It reminded me of the old television show "The Honeymooners" where Ralph Kramden would screw up royally on every show but at the end would apologize to his wife Alice, and they'd kiss and he'd be forgiven, until the next show, where the whole thing would start over again. That was us, except after a while we were less and less forgiving.

At the time I wasn't leading a conscious life so it became a dilemma for me. I was fast becoming a stress case of major proportions. But, I was making more than just about any one else in my profession. I truly believe that a lot of my physical problems I'm dealing with now are directly attributable to that stress as both my terrible allergies and leukemia struck two years after I started working for him. They were the two most stressful years of my life.

Until that time I was the picture of health and hadn't missed a day of work. To give you some idea, in the six years of junior high school and high school I'd missed a total of three days, and that was all at one time caused by the flu.

This has nothing to do with anything, but it's funny. Speaking of flood length pants. When I went to my Senior Prom I rented a tuxedo as we all did. The thought never occurred to me to try it on before Prom Night. When I did put it on the night of the prom the pants were about six inches too short and they looked more like clam diggers than formal attire. For some reason, my Prom picture was blown up to a large size and was prominently displayed at the photography studio above their cash register. I'm not exactly sure why they did it, but I think I've got a clue. I still have the picture and always get a good laugh when I look at it.

Back to my work situation, I was becoming so distressed by my boss' behavior that my personality was changing and I started dreading having to go to work. My dilemma was that I loved my job, the actual work itself, the people I came into contact with and grew to know over the years, my fellow employees, the fact that I was helping people, and I was extremely good at what I was doing, and I was making quite a bit more than I ever had. The downside was him. Instead of just allowing his behavior to roll off my back as I would do now, I was allowing it to get to me more and more. Where I'd been pretty carefree, I no longer was. For the first time in my life I was becoming impatient and nervous. Looking back on it now I can easily see what I didn't then. Today there would have been no dilemma at all because my priorities are no longer askew. Money is not the driving force anymore, and if this were to happen today I would quit in a minute and get on with my life. I didn't and I believe I'm suffering the consequences of prolonged stress. That's exactly the point. If you haven't learned this lesson as yet through personal experience, take a lesson from my life. Never allow yourself to stay in an unhealthy situation if it is at all within your power to get out. Don't walk away, run away. If this situation reminds you of something you're going through now, I urge you to get out of it if you can't change your attitude regarding it, and decrease your stress level. When one door closes, other doors will open. Always look at the big picture. Are you willing to jeopardize your health or something as important as your day-to-day happiness just for a job when there's a whole world out there to discover? As I've said, you only get one shot at this so all the time you spend getting stressed can't be made up.

If you love what you're doing or don't but can't take the chance of finding a suitable replacement job, you need to consciously determine to accept whatever is causing you the stress, and make a concerted effort not to let it get to you. Maybe if others at your work are having similar problems you might get your heads together to try to figure a way to lessen the stress. If the situation is out of your control than acceptance is what you need. But, if you get to that point I urge you to look for an out. That's even if you've been with the same company for a while. You're not running away from your job, just eliminating an intolerable situation. You can explore other possibilities while you're still working at the stressful job.

If you do that, and find another job, while you're still working at your old job, it's your responsibility to yourself and the company to keep performing at the top level till the minute you walk out the door for the last time. You're still being paid and you still have the same responsibility.

But don't allow stress to become a way of life. There is no rule that says if you have a job it must cause you stress. No matter how bad the situation, many people are loath to change because of several factors: people are resistant to change even if it's for their own benefit out of fear of the unknown; laziness (it's easier to just keep doing what you're doing than trying to find something more suitable); they can't afford to take the chance financially; their co-workers have become like family. You know, no matter how much you promise each other to stay in touch, after you leave, that rarely happens. You know what? Your peace of mind is more important than all those factors combined. Any time we decide to make a big change, fear and apprehension seem to take over our thinking. Change causes stress, that's normal. Realize there will be some discomfort with your new co-workers, new surroundings, new job, new boss, etc., but you have to realize all those discomforts are only temporary and if your new position is more relaxing and less stressful than the one you left, then you did the right thing in the long run.

I should have left that office five years before I did. It was an unhealthy situation for me and I knew it, but because it was easier for me to get up every day and go to that job, instead of taking the initiative and finding a less stressful job, I didn't until my hand was forced. That's not at all the way you want to do it. You don't want to wait till you're at the point of desperation because then you're not entirely in control of the situation, and you might have to settle for a lesser job than if you took the time to find the best situation. I talked about leaving for years and was even offered other work, but it was nothing more than complacency and sheer laziness that kept me there. And, I suffered the consequences of my inaction. If you don't know what you really would be happiest doing then it behooves you to find out.

If you've seen others' work and thought it might be for you, ask about it. Don't expect good things just to happen, unless you make them so.

If you're satisfied and happy doing what you're doing, then by all means, don't change. Change just for the sake of change doesn't make sense. Consider yourself very fortunate. But if you're not—if you take the chance, only then will you know if things could be better. If you don't, you'll never know. It's never too soon or too late to act. You have time, so consider what you want to do very carefully and then your chances of making the right decision will be greatly enhanced.

In an address to the Massachusetts Supreme Court in 1942 Leonard Hand said it this way: "We accept the verdict of the past until the need for change cries out loudly enough to force upon us a choice—the comforts of further inertia or the irksomeness of action." This also goes for anything else you're involved in, including personal relationships. People's tendency is to stick with what they find comfortable and continuity is comforting. I'm not at all advocating jumping ship at the first sign of trouble, or even the tenth one, in your job or in a relationship. But, you have to weigh the benefits of keeping going, especially if the situation continues to deteriorate, against what you're willing to pay in terms of both physical and mental price to your well being. It's much like me and the medicines I need to take. Sometimes the medication does the job but the side effects are so bad I just have to discontinue using them. There are other medicines for me to try and without such uncomfortable side effects.

Since relationships can get complicated, especially those with children involved, you might have to do what's best for others before you can do what's best for yourself. Sometimes you can't leave even if it's the healthiest thing for you. In that case you're going to have to make the best of the situation. If talking to your partner hasn't produced the desired results, if you can't make some accommodation, the only thing you can do to make the situation livable is to consciously approach all aspects of the relationship to re-set your thinking.

To do that you'll have to forget and forgive what happened in the past, whatever it is that brought you to such a point. You won't get very far if you harbor resentment and you'll only be hurting yourself. You'll have to emotionally accept your partner and accept everything that's caused you so much trouble in the past. It's over, so rehashing it over and over is counterproductive. That's not easy, especially if you don't want to be there. But, since you can't leave at the moment, what other choice do you have? If your attitude changes you might even see a difference in the way you're treated by your partner. Remember, your attitude and the way you approach others has a big impact as to how they'll react to you. That is a very important point to remember at all times. What you put out, you'll get back. So, being more accepting and not harboring resentment will go a long way in helping you deal positively with the situation. If there are children involved they'll also notice the shift in attitude in terms of how you deal with things that previously caused friction. That will be a positive step in relieving some of their stress caused by the circumstances. You never want to put your partner down in front of them or anyone else for that matter, no matter what is said about you to the children, friends, or family. If you take the high road and don't ever resort to past practices that might have contributed to the problem, you'll be rewarded in subtle ways that show in the appreciation of the children and others who are directly involved. Another major benefit is that you'll feel even better about yourself for doing the right thing in the right way.

CHAPTER THREE
FIND A ROLE MODEL

If I were to pick a role model I would choose someone who I thought lived an exemplary life, not someone who spends his life in self-promotion. The two people I most admire are my father and Abraham Lincoln. My father worked very hard as a factory foreman to provide as comfortable a life as he could for his family. He never made much money, but we were always well provided for and never felt anything but love from him. Although, if he said more than ten words a day that was a lot. He was very family oriented and was very protective of his children. When I was around five he had half his stomach removed because of ulcers. The day he returned from the hospital was the only time in my life I ever saw him short tempered. I always considered that quite amazing especially since he was under pressure in having a wife and four children that he needed to feed and clothe.

Abraham Lincoln was a great man and possibly the greatest American of all time. He had a wonderful sense of humor and was expert in the art of understatement. He could be quite sarcastic when provoked. Civil War Union General George McClellan was a great organizer but to put it mildly, a reluctant battlefield commander. Lincoln once wrote him asking if he could borrow the army for a while, since it was clear the general wasn't using it. Lincoln had his faults just as the rest of us, but I admire just about everything that I feel important about him.

What I always thought was interesting was the way George

Washington, another man whom I greatly admire for a number of reasons, went about his life. When he was a teenager he decided he wanted to be the best person he could so he wrote up something he called "Rules of Civility and Decent Behavior," which he borrowed from a French book of maxims. In it were one hundred and ten rules by which he lived his life. He wanted to make sure he lived up to the eighteenth century ideal of the gentleman in everything he did. When you read Washington's rules of conduct you get a much better picture of the life he led. It was important to him to be accomplished in the art of "perfect self control." He was living a form of conscious life without realizing it. He had an ideal and was making a concerted effort to live up to it. Although many of the rules are outdated and are pretty funny when you read them, this is what he was all about, and I think his work at conscious self-improvement was quite admirable. If you've never read them I thought you might enjoy a couple of samples. My favorite is Rule #13: "Kill no vermin as fleas, lice, ticks, etc., in the sight of others; if you see any filth or thick spittle, put your foot dexterously upon it; if it be on the clothes of your companions, put it off privately; and if it be upon your own clothes; return thanks to him who put it off."

Rule #32, which is an interesting glimpse into the workings of an eighteenth century gentleman's mind: "To one that is your equal, or not much inferior, you are to give the chief place in your lodging; and he to whom it is offered ought at first to refuse it, but at the second to accept, though not without acknowledging his own unworthiness."

Washington also believed in "modeling" himself after people he most admired. He would studiously adapt the traits of others he felt would make him a better person. "Modeling" is an interesting way to go about life in that you get to pick and choose approaches to all facets of life, and adapt them and follow them. In your own life I advise you to follow Washington's example. If you admire something about someone, imitate that quality and make it part of how you act. Since others will have traits you consider better than your own in any number of things, why not learn from them? "Modeling" is not phony or a sign of weakness. I think it's a very smart way to become a better person consciously.

When you try to improve in any area of your life or modify your views to more fit the current conditions of it, you are evolving. That is never a sign of weakness, but a sign of confidence and strength.

Some people think that if you change your opinion on a particular matter, you're being weak and wishy-washy. That couldn't be further from the truth. If you are willing to admit to yourself that your views might not have been all they should have been, you're consciously and deliberately making an honest effort to come more into line with your current, evolving thinking, and I think that is correct and admirable.

People can be role models for you in any number of ways. For instance, if you've always admired a particular person's ability to stay calm no matter what the circumstances, watch that person, study them and their responses to stressful situations, and then incorporate their style into your own life. Think of it as if it were a blueprint on how to proceed. When you have a model to go by, the guesswork is eliminated and once you incorporate that style it becomes yours as assuredly as it is theirs. Two thousand years ago Seneca, in *Letters to Lucilius*, put it this way: "We need someone, I say, on whom our character may mold itself: You never make the crooked line straight without a ruler."

As you can see, modeling is not a new concept and has been successfully used by great people for thousands of years. There are good models everywhere. It could be a famous person from history or it could be your next-door neighbor. You shouldn't have to look far. It can also be several people, all of whom have some characteristic you'd like to incorporate. Just choose an area or areas in which you're not happy or that you find confusing in how best to act. I wouldn't choose more than a couple to get started, and go from there. Once you've decided on who and how, adapt that model and customize it for your own use. Personalize it and make sure you incorporate that model in the next situation you're confronted with, and from then on. Life is so much smoother when you follow a path already blazed for you.

CHAPTER FOUR
THINK BEFORE YOU ACT

One of my favorite silly sayings goes: "If you can keep your head when all those about your are losing theirs, perhaps you've misunderstood the situation." I always thought it was very clever—though wrong. To my thinking it's just the opposite. If you can keep your wits about you under even the most challenging situations, you're the one that will see things for what they really are, making you more effective in coping with them. Being conscious means that since you always think first, your perceptions under all circumstances are clearer than if you didn't. Conscious people have the ability to stay calm no matter what is occurring at the moment and that's due to our acceptance of things not in our control. And, that goes for all things, under all circumstances, no matter when they occur.

One of the great benefits of living in the moment and thinking things through, is that your life will flow in a straight line, without fear of how you'll handle things in the future. Two thousand years ago Seneca wrote: "We are more frightened than hurt. Our troubles spring more often from fancy than reality." Reality is the key here. The more realistic your perceptions, the less you try to justify aberrant behavior, the fewer problems you'll encounter. And when you do encounter bumps along the road, the easier it will be for you to handle them. That's only as long as you perceive them for exactly what they are, and no more, and have confidence in your ability to handle them when the time comes. A situation that might occur in the future should have absolutely no bearing on your present thoughts. Whatever will happen in the future is no more than con-jecture on your part. It's like events of your past. They no longer exist except in your mind. If something troubling from your past keeps replaying in your mind like an endless loop you need to tell yourself that there's where it truly is. It no longer has any life except what you give it. When you think of things that went on before, especially those that you found troubling, and that involved others, remember they've moved on and there is a good chance they've left it there, and so should you.

Our perception of time is pretty fascinating. How time seems to fly by sometimes and drag by others. It's a situational thing. You know how a two-week vacation feels like only two days, and it's over before we know it, but a long day at work can feel like two weeks. Clock-watchers are especially prone to this phenomenon at work. So, time is like most things, perceptions come into play that affect its movement. If you can keep yourself living each moment as it comes, and not projecting into the future, time will become more regulated in your mind. Most of the time I don't even know what day of the week it is and don't really care. Wouldn't it be nice if that two-week vacation could actually feel like two weeks and a long day at work not feel like it will never end? The one way to assure that is moment-to-moment living. If you can keep your concentration fo-cused on the present, the factor of time either flying by, or not seem-ing to move at all, doesn't come into play. The second you realize your mind is taking flight, consciously bring it back to the present. In the beginning it will seem like that's almost all you do, because our minds tend to wander all over the place no matter how hard we try to control them. But, stick with it and after a while the new habit will start to take hold and it's amazing how long you'll be able to focus, as long as you don't let yourself slide.

One more point on work. When we get rushed or have a deadline to meet, we tend to accelerate the pace of everything we do (more on this later). We speed up our walk and even talk a little faster on the phone. There's a sense of urgency. Unfortunately, that urgency is also transmitted to the brain, and it takes on more of a crisis mode than necessary. You get ahead of yourself thinking of all the work you need to do and you might start to get a bit overwhelmed. And you can even get a little depressed thinking about the load. My advice: Slow Down. Regroup. In the first place, when you consciously slow everything down you feel less tense. And in the second place, you'll wind up being more efficient and the quality of your work will improve. As G. K. Chesterton wrote, "One of the great disadvantages of hurry is that it takes such a long time." It's very important to cut yourself some slack in this regard.

You can only do as much as you can in a certain period of time. No matter what others' expectations are, you can't produce any more than your best effort. That's an important point to consider when the stresses of the job and outside obligations get to be too much. Americans are the most efficient workers in the world, even ahead of the Japanese, so a lot is expected from most of us. Keep your perspective on work and don't allow the stresses of it to take over your life and keep you awake at night. If it does, tomorrow is another day and that gives you ample opportunity to re-group and start the next day at a consciously measured but productive pace. We all want to do a good job, it's important for our self-image, but doing a good job can be accomplished much more easily if you do it on an even keel and don't get too caught up in it. Relax. Take your time but don't waste time. If you push yourself too hard, it will affect all aspects of your life in a way that's not beneficial to you. It is totally within your power, although with your boss looking over your shoulder, it often doesn't seem that way. If you can go home every night knowing you gave your best effort that day, that's all you or anyone else can realistically expect. Remember realistic goals and expectations go hand in hand.

Unfortunately, there is a world out there full of people who are not looking out for your best interests, on the contrary, they're out there trying to use you to further their own interests. Having good friends can give you the comfort to know that on dark and stormy nights you'll always have a warm shelter where you can turn, and there you'll find a willing ear to listen. You can't buy true friendship.

Even if you only have one true friend you have an awful lot, and an awful lot to be thankful for. So, if the urge strikes you anytime soon to do something unexpected and nice for a friend, by all means, do it. Since conscious people already try to treat all individuals equally and accept them the way they are, we tend to make good friends. And, since loyalty is such a prized virtue, we tend to keep the friends we have. In my own life I can count six very good friends. We've been friends for twenty, twenty-one, twenty-five, twenty-six, twenty-eight, and forty-eight years, respectively.

As I've said there are a lot of people out there who purportedly are out to help you, but in actuality that's not their real purpose at all. Some of these people are completely legitimate and are well respected in their fields. And, it's not what they do that is the problem. It's how they go about doing it. Some of the less legitimate ones, even without breaking any laws, aren't really providing any service at all. For the legitimate ones who actually are professionals at what they do, the intent is usually not to defraud. For example, if you ever watch CNBC during the day, you'll see a lot of talking heads who are stock analysts for various stock market related companies. These people give their opinions on how individual stocks will do according to their research, talking with representatives of the companies themselves, experience, etc. In the year two thousand, the Nasdaq fell more than thirty-nine percent. Stocks are rated by analysts as "strong buy," "hold," "accumulate," or "sell," with different companies using different terminology on some of their ratings. To lose close to forty percent value in one year is pretty astounding, especially since the fall was so swift from the nineties' dynamic market. Many highflying stocks came crashing down and it wasn't at all unusual that a stock lost half its market value or even much more. So, in 2000 there were a lot of dogs out there. But when the analysts rated stocks, which they did thousands of times, no more than two or three dozen were ever rated "sell" during the whole year. Obviously, something is wrong when that happens. How can analysts justify giving the recommendations that they do in the face of plain fact; and the fact is the market stunk. If the market stunk that obviously means that so did many stocks. Keeping a "buy" recommendation on a stock that's sinking faster than the Titanic, especially when it keeps falling, doesn't make much sense. People are supposed to use analysts as only one tool when they're trying to uncover the next big one, or just trying to make an educated trade. Unfortunately, people act like people and even with their hard-earned money at stake, they either get lazy or don't understand the other available tools or how to use them. Understanding an analyst rating takes no special knowledge other than the ability to read, and they're available seemingly everywhere. It comes right out and tells you if you should buy or not or just hold onto the stock. People buy only on the basis of analysts' recommendations all the time. I wouldn't be surprised if a large portion of individual investors' money was played that way. The analysts provide a service, but, for whatever reason choose not to rate stocks as critically as they should or they rate them too optimistically.

I knew nothing about the stock market before I began investing. I literally didn't know the difference between a bull and bear market. So, when I decided to start investing, I bought books and watched anything that had to do with the market. I also had help from a friend who's a financial advisor. Not until I was ready did I make my first investment. That's the conscious approach. That goes for anything else you're involved in. Always go into anything you pursue with your eyes wide open and your chances of success will improve greatly. Unfortunately, even if you do your homework you aren't guaranteed success by any means. That's what happened to me. I started investing from a small inheritance from my mother just as the market took the huge nosedive. I listened to analysts and for the most part they were still bullish on the market's prospects, and most of what I read said the same thing, so I stuck with my investments. Right now I'm down about forty percent. I knew when I went into it that, no matter how well the market performed in the past five years, there was no guarantee of future success. It just came a little sooner than I had hoped. But, since I knew the risk involved, I accepted it when things got bad. I didn't blame anyone else, because it was 100% my own doing. Sometimes we learn expensive lessons in life that we'd rather not. I guess I learned to be a lot more careful, now that I have considerably less than I did. Lately I've been reading that the tech sector where many of my investments lie might be down for a few years, not months, more. Such is life.

For some strange reason some people will take the advice of other people, almost always strangers, on chat rooms sponsored by the company who's stock is being discussed. Why someone would invest their money on the basis of a stranger's opinion is way beyond me. In the first place you don't know what the stranger's motives might be. They might just be trying to talk up the price so they can sell and make a nice profit, or talk down the price to short sell. You don't know the person's level of expertise. Maybe they're honestly just trying to be helpful, but you never know. I made the mistake of buying a few shares of Commerce One, which, like many of my stock buys last year, quickly sank. I researched it so I felt rather confident I had made a wise choice. It had a nice run up before I bought it, but there wasn't anything to indicate it wouldn't last a while longer. I was checking the stock's chat room, something I almost never did, and there was a plea from a woman for someone to give her advice. She had bought Commerce One at around sixty dollars and she wanted to know if she should sell it, so she'd at least break even. It had just gotten back to that level the previous day. She got a reply from another investor in the chat room telling her to hang onto it because in a few months it would around a hundred and twenty dollars. This occurred a few months ago. From the terminology he used he sounded like he knew what he was talking about. But, how he felt confident telling this woman what he did, I'll never know. She replied to his reply, and thanked him for the advice and said she was going to heed it. I hope she didn't. The last time I checked the stock was sitting in the low teens. That was about a fifth of the price she bought it at. She took advice from a complete stranger, even if she didn't know anything about him. She obviously didn't think things through, or she wouldn't have been asking a stranger, any stranger, advice on the matter. The stock market is like anything else in our lives. If you're going to invest you must go about it in a conscious manner and that entails research, and understanding the fundamentals of the stock you're thinking of buying.

And, as I've said, that goes for anything you do. Just as you need to try to understand other people, you have an obligation to yourself to do the best job you can in understanding what you're getting yourself into. You would never blindly give money to strangers if they promised you a huge return on a gold mine. That wouldn't make sense. The old saying is true, if something sounds to good to be true, it probably is. But, it's human nature to look at only the part of the picture and many of us have the tendency to gloss over a company's shortcomings, in our hopes of striking it rich. We sometimes allow ourselves to be blinded to reality in our zeal to make a killing. If you work hard for your money it behooves you to take special care not to waste all the hours you worked to accumulate it. Strangers don't have the same commitment to you as friends, so if you're going to take their advice always take it with a grain of salt. Always try to discern truth form wishful thinking and if you do come out on the short end, it won't be for lack of honest effort, and you can feel good about what you did, even if it didn't go as planned.

Another thing I find troubling is the fact that some people will allow others to dictate how the lead their lives. I have trouble understanding why certain things are still legal, or, at least don't come with a warning label. The most obvious example is the "Psychic Help Lines". The only thing they're helping is themselves to your money.

(It's as phony as those infomercials where the man excitedly extols the virtues of a product he's trying to hawk, and the woman, his partner in the little charade, feigns amazement at how well the product performs. But at least when you spend your money there, you get a product in return.)

Even if there is a disclaimer telling us that the psychic predictions are for entertainment purposes only, which limits their liability, people who actually believe this stuff take it as being real. You see the commercials for them all the time. We get to hear "callers" being astounded by the supposed knowledge these "psychics" have of their lives. I'm not saying some people don't have some extra sensory perception, I'm just saying it's not necessarily these people. Again, many people put great stock in stranger's words. I find it baffling. Do the callers have so little confidence in themselves that they think some stranger knows what's best for them? Especially someone who's charging them by the minute? I'd think the only requirements to getting some of these jobs as a "psychic" is the ability to talk slowly and stretch the conversation for as long as humanly possible.

As a conscious person, since you take your time and think things through, and learn to accept the conditions of your life that you can't change, a psychic hotline would be about the last place you'd look for guidance. I find it hard to believe that someone who could actually predict the future would have nothing better to do with their time than sit by the phone waiting for you to call.

I think astrology, although somewhat more accepted and mainstream, is just as bad. You'll never convince me that over five hundred million people are going to have the same experiences as others born around the same time on a particular day. Divide the world's population by the twelve astrological signs and that's what you get. Astrological forecasts are even listed in the daily paper. Here's an example from one given for Cancer (July 21-July 22) in the *Los Angeles Times*: "Look behind the scenes for answers, take initiative, don't follow others. Avoid heavy lifting, if possible. Take a chance on romance. Protect self in emotional clinches." The one thing you should take from that "forecast" is the admonishment not to follow others, especially the person writing this. The astrologer would have us believe that over five hundred million of us specifically will have problems today if we pick up something heavy. And, if you don't like your chances with what one astrologer says for a particular day, read another's, because it will be different. How accurate could it be if it's open for interpretation, among other things. Another forecast tells us we'll be the "talk of the town". I rather doubt it. Many people put a lot of stock in this. I find it hard to believe that some poor soul in Bangladesh who is struggling on a daily basis just to survive is going to be the talk of the town. Since so many otherwise rational people believe in this, I wasn't at all surprised that Nancy Reagan used an astrologer to dictate her husband's schedule on some occasions. That's pretty scary, having someone with such great influence determining things that affect the entire world based on some astrologer's forecast.

As conscious individuals we tend to develop a confidence in our own abilities brought about by our constant work at self- improvement. If you're going to listen to psychics and astrologers you might as well buy some fortune cookies instead. You'll get the same level of experience as some of these people have and save some money.

Whenever I read *USA Today*, I turn to the sports section for a good laugh. There you'll find advertisements for sports handicappers. Again, we have "experts" trying to convince readers that they're providing legitimate service, when in fact they're providing nothing except a way to separate you from your money. According to a study I read a few years back you'd be as well off having your dog pick the games for you as you would one of the handicappers. Just looking at the pictures of these guys would frighten away most readers. And, it's always the same thing. Every week it's the game of the year for a guaranteed 5 and 0 record for the weekend's betting. It's either that or it's the "blowout of the month". These guys aren't public servants and if they actually had a clue on how the action is going to play out, they'd be in Vegas betting for themselves. Why go through the expense and hassles of advertising and setting up a phone bank if you really know what's going to happen in future games? You could kick back and collect your winnings on a daily basis. And we all know these guys aren't doing this to give back to the community. They really don't know more than you do because unless the game is fixed there's no real way to know who'll win or beat the point spread. And, it's "only" twenty-five dollars a call for many of these predictions. They use the word "only" a lot, especially when it comes to your money. And, when you use their service, you can be confident because the results are "guaranteed". That's a real big of them to guarantee winning results. You've already paid the twenty-five dollars, so if you lose you'll get some more of their "exclusive" picks for free.

In these cases, to add insult to injury, you not only lost the twenty-five dollars, you've also lost the money you bet using their picks. How generous. It costs them nothing to guarantee results, so they could feel safe in guaranteeing you the moon. Say you placed a bet using one of their "guaranteed" winners and you lose. Why would you go back to them for your "freebie" when they've already given you a bum steer? So, the whole thing, if scrutinized, doesn't make a whole lot of sense. They must make good money at this or they wouldn't be able to advertise so often in a national newspaper. Handicappers are totally unproductive members of our society. Even if they had a real clue as to what would transpire in the future, what exactly have they accomplished? What benefit do they provide to society? To me they're as useless as cyber squatters.

If you consciously deliberate before acting and make it a point to have faith in yourself and your abilities, while maintaining a realistic approach to everything, there's much less chance of you being played for a chump.

Another way some are taken for their hard-earned money is through the constant pleading for money for donations from TV evangelists. Some of these evangelists are truly sincere and actually believe in what they tell you and really do help some people. But, others found a way to strike it rich by playing to the vulnerabilities of gullible and easily influenced people. I've had a few "evangelists" as clients over the years and there hasn't been one occasion when they didn't spend large sums of money on themselves. Every time one showed up I knew I was going to have a big day. A friend who owns a dress shop has one evangelist for a customer and the last time she showed up she spent fifteen hundred dollars on herself. Two days later, she came back and spent another fifteen hundred. And, this woman, who ostensibly is in the business of saving souls, does this numerous times each year. This is only one dress shop. I can't even imagine what she spends on other things for herself. This money is from contributions from her flock. It leaves the impression that her flock is being fleeced instead of being "saved". I find it sad that people with limited means who are experiencing trouble in their lives, turn to these people, and through their donations, support those who are richer than they'll ever hope to be. It winds up being a case of those with limited means supporting a lavish lifestyle of people they trust with their spiritual well-being. Why wouldn't someone go to their local church or synagogue and have a heart to heart talk with their pastor or priest or rabbi? That will cost them nothing and they'll be seeking advice from a person who really does have their best interests at heart.

People do things that defy logic and, much of the time, work against their own best interests. I guess it's easier to just flip on the TV and get their spiritual guidance that way. Many, who are confined to home, don't have much choice, and this can be their only source of spiritual guidance. Given the fact that many of these people derive comfort from TV preachers, they're more willing to donate because it means so much to them. I just hope they're getting their money's worth.

As you are well aware in your own life you need to take special care when relying on the "expertise" of others. Sometimes it's obvious that you're being scammed and sometimes they're slick enough to hide it. I get that kind in my store all the time. Sometimes I think more people come into my store trying to sell me than the other way around. Some of these guys have their shtick down pat. Recently I had a very well dressed man come in just before 7:00P.M. and he asked me to show him some eyewear. He came in just before closing, when most salesmen are long gone home. This guy was smooth. He wore an expensive suit and was a very glib individual. The whole purpose of his visit was to sell me something, not to buy eyeglasses. He timed it perfectly so I wouldn't realize what he was doing until he was already into it. But, I've pretty much seen them all, and although I never treat these people with disrespect, I also make it a point not to buy anything from them. I didn't care for his sneaky approach, much less the fact that he took a half hour of my time trying to set me up. There are smooth talkers everywhere who, if they never make an honest nickel, would be quite happy with the fact. It's a shame though that so many people, honest and hardworking are such easy targets. You might put in a forty or fifty hour week to support yourself and family but if some of these people can figure a way to separate you from the money you worked so hard to make, they'd be more than happy to do it.

As with anything else there are degrees of slick operators. Sometimes, they are not so much dishonest as they are sneaky. If you're in business you've more than likely gotten a call from one of these boiler room phone salesmen who tell you they're your company's copy machine supply company. They're supposedly calling to check up if you need any supplies. I've probably gotten this call twenty times over the years. It doesn't matter if you have a copier or not, it's a cold call, and the salesman hopes to get a gullible person who'll believe him, and who can be convinced he's actually their supplier. Again, it must work often enough to make it worthwhile for them to keep doing it. In your initial contact with this person the first thing out of their mouth is a lie. They don't care because they see you as more of a mark than a customer. That's just the way they do business and if they have to lie to you to make the sale, they're more than happy to do it. Most people would be embarrassed if caught in a lie, but not these guys. They just hang up and call the next business on their list. In their minds it's just business. These guys aren't too bad. The worse that could happen is you'll overpay for copier supplies.

The truly bad ones are the boiler room operators who are the vultures that prey on the elderly. These people are the bottom feeders of the pond we all inhabit. They're the lowest of the low, the pond scum. There should be a special place in hell reserved for them. They make their living by picking at the bones of our society's most vulnerable citizens. To specifically target such a group is unconscionable. I think what they do is ten times worse than almost any other non-violent crime. They remind me of the Hyena's who choose the old and infirm out of the herd for easy pickings. Obviously, if I call these cretin's vultures, pond scum, and hyenas it leaves no ambiguity as to how I really feel. Even for a conscious person it's hard to accept that these people exist and do what they do.

Being conscious isn't always easy but, as I've said, you just can't pick and choose when you want to act in a conscious fashion. I bring these people up for exactly that reason. No matter my opinion, I make it a point not to get my negative emotions going when I read about them or see them getting away with it.

It can break your heart when you see the devastation they cause people who placed their trust in them, if you allow it to. But, I've trained myself, although this was a tough one, to accept the fact that these people do cause untold misery all for the all mighty dollar. There's not much a single person can do except to warn any elderly person you know to be careful. What you can't do is allow yourself to go, even a little, down the road of revenge or hatred. And, that's an easy thing to do in a case like this. But, any time you head down that path you're getting further away from where you want to be. If you do, you're going in the wrong direction. Situations involving this type of person do definitely cause negative emotions to well up in you, it's only natural. But, if that type of feeling starts to build a head of steam, it's hard to get it under control. If you consciously and deliberately tell yourself that, your getting upset is totally counterproductive and in no way helps the victim, it makes it much easier to accept. If somehow it did help the poor victim, that would be a different story entirely. But, it doesn't, it only hurts you. And, if there were anything you could do, I hope that you would.

CHAPTER FIVE
TREAT EVERYONE WITH RESPECT

You should never dismiss others or their accomplishments in any way. That's just as we've all known people in our lives that for some reason, we don't think of being as valuable as others we know. We might tend to not dress well when we know we'll be spending time with them or not return a call to them as fast as with others, or maybe not at all. I'm not sure why, but we don't see them as being up to par generally. We have a tendency to take this type of person for granted, and not appreciate their uniqueness. There could be a number of people in your life that you might dismiss as more a part of the furniture than a friend. That's even if that person is the one who's always there for you and comes through when the chips are down. But, I don't think that's at all unusual. And, this person could be quite successful and really not a bad person at all. If one realizes that they do have this perception of less value in another, it's not that difficult to change thinking, and I think it's the right thing to do if you do realize that's what you're doing.

It's an important concept that we treat everyone, no matter who, the same. Just make a conscious effort to remember that person is a valuable member of the human race, as we all are, and should be treated with the same consideration as others. Wouldn't it be a revelation if you found out you were the one others viewed as not being quite good enough? That would hurt. You wouldn't want to be thought of as being less valuable than your peers and neither does anyone else. Even if your circle of friends all felt the same way about one individual, break from the pack. If you're seen treating the person as an equal, with respect and dignity, others will surely follow. Their perception of that individual might change if for no other reason than it's just the right thing to do. That person will appreciate you going the extra mile on their behalf, because even if they never mention a word about having been relegated to second class, they're more than likely quite aware of it.

I went to a small high school, where there were only a hundred and eighteen students in my graduating class. Everybody knew everybody, and most of us went through grade school and high school together. So, it was a tight knit group. As with any high school there were cliques. The "cool" people hung out together and everyone had their own circle of friends. We all got along and I was, for some reason, considered "cool" enough to be included in all the "A" activities if I so chose. But, for the most part I chose not to. For some reason I've always gone with the underdog. People who were unique and sometimes even a little unusual. So when it came to choosing who I spent the bulk of my time with, I'd choose people who didn't have the same "standing" as me. If I decided to participate in any activity the "in crowd" was involved in; it was understood by my friends, who weren't considered "A" material, that they would be allowed to join in too. And, much to their credit, the "cool" people really were, and always welcomed my friends, who they knew but didn't hang out with. I think we were pretty much ahead of our time when it came to accepting others who were cut from a different cloth. There were two obviously gay members of my class, but not once did I ever see them treated any differently than anyone else. They were elected to class leadership positions and were widely popular.

When it comes to you, if you see what you feel is an injustice being done, it's your responsibility as a conscious person to make it a point to show leadership and accept the person on their own terms and try to include them in as much as possible. If you really don't like the person, that's another matter entirely. Remember, if the shoe were on the other foot, you'd appreciate the same consideration.

When I was a sophomore I was voted the Citizen of the Year

Award by my teachers. In reality the award was considered by us students to be more like the Dork of the Year Award, so I was not thrilled that I won. The winner was decided by a vote of the faculty, and I can't even imagine why I won. But, much to my chagrin, I did. To add insult to injury, the award was presented in front of an assembly of the whole school. Moments before my name was called, my buddies and I were cracking jokes about who this year's loser would be. I was dazed when my name was called and don't remember walking up on stage to receive it. My brother Joe had a great time at my expense. That's all I heard for a month. So, during the graduation ceremony I got sweet revenge (pre-conscious living) when my brother's name was called for the same award for the senior class. I think that model of how everyone was treated in my class as more or less equals would be a good one to follow by all society.

We don't have a defined class structure as they do in England, but our society does definitely have class distinctions. As I've said, ours is more defined by money and fame as opposed to title and heritage. The perfect society would never be along the lines of Communism, where there were supposedly no class distinctions, and everyone worked for the good of the whole. At least that was the theory behind it. In reality, it didn't work that way at all and the ruling class was corrupt and were the only ones to enjoy all the perks. It was an ill-thought-out and unworkable system for a number of reasons and one was there were no incentives to do a good job and your only chance to share in the wealth was through nepotism. The idea of social equality was on the right track but, unfortunately for them, since most humans take care of themselves first, everything else in their master plan was off track. I think the idea of a classless society, where everyone is given the exact same opportunities, educational and social, if modified to account for individualism, is not such a bad idea. And I think the United Stated comes closest to the ideal in practice. That's one of the many advantages of being a citizen here. Hard work can be rewarded regardless of a person's background.

Everyone, especially here in America, sees individualism as a basic right and one of the very reasons for our success. We more than most have the individuals who look at things from all different points of view, thus creating advancements and new opportunities for all. That's why it is up to us as conscious people, to do our part in leveling the playing field whenever the opportunity arises. If we make it a point to treat everyone the same and with equal respect, then we've done a good job. You can't force others to act like you do, but you can influence their perception of others by your attitude.

In order to counterbalance those social misfits who do prey on the vulnerable, it behooves you to make it a part of your everyday lives to be kind to everyone with whom you have contact. There is no such thing as being too nice. The old adage of nice guys finish last is a lot of nonsense. With your attitude of treating everyone the same, in a respectful and in an obliging manner when at all possible, you elevate others to do the same. As you know just about every situation has a myriad of potential responses from which you can choose. It's up to you to make the right choice. Some people mistake kindness for weakness, but the two aren't really the same at all. You can accomplish more by your attitude of equal worth for all than if you butted heads with these same people. If you're the only one who, for instance, let's someone pull in front of you on the freeway instead of speeding up so they can't, that's something positive. I could never understand why people don't. What's the big deal? It's not as if the person was trying to do them harm, all they're trying to do is to merge into traffic. But, to some people it's taken as a personal affront, when all it is is part of driving and not a personal situation at all. But, if you do allow someone to pull in front of you, you've done the right thing, the unselfish thing. It's small potatoes, but even so, the person you accommodate will appreciate your kindness. And, if you don't receive the traditional "thank you" wave it doesn't matter. You didn't do it for the thank you. You did it because it's the right thing to do in the situation. And, it doesn't slow you down or cost you a thing.

When you multiply little kindnesses like that over the course of the day it makes other people's lives a little more pleasant having had contact with you. The thing I most enjoy about my job is that, with little effort or time expended, I can help make a stranger's day better. I think it's nice that I have the opportunity to do that. Over the course of the last seventeen years I've fixed literally thousands of non-clients glasses. When I tell them there is no charge for the service, they have trouble believing it. Most of us aren't used to getting something for nothing. But, it only takes me a few minutes. It's also good for me for two reasons: first, I enjoy helping people and second, I've just made someone happy so there's a good chance when they need eyewear they'll remember what I did for them, and come to me. It's good customer relations and good human relations. When someone's glasses are unwearable, depending on the severity of the prescription it can have a negative effect on whatever they do. They might experience headaches or can't read a menu or drive or it may be causing them eyestrain. With a little expertise on my part the problem is easily solved, and I'm more than happy to do it.

Whenever the opportunity arises, make it a point to do little kindnesses for friends or even strangers, and you'll find when you need a little T.L.C., there's a much greater likelihood it will be there for you. If you make others' lives more pleasant, they'll be more inclined to treat you and others in kind.

There was a front-page article a few years ago in the *Los Angeles Times* that depicted a particular aspect of everyday life in Israel. I'd never heard of this before but the entire article focused on people's attitudes toward others in that society. What the article detailed was how if a person did a small kindness for a stranger, in society's eyes, that person is considered a real sucker. They even have a word for it: "freier," which means sucker. It provided specific examples of situations where in Israel kindness is truly equated with weakness. One example was the driving situation where if a person needed to merge into traffic, others would literally think of you as a real patsy and pushover, and actually think less of you if you allowed them in. According to the article it wasn't only a few people who had that attitude, but society in general. That was the entire point of the article. It reminded me of an old Three Stooges bit, where the saying went: "All for one, one for all, and every man for himself."

I assume the article was correct in it's assertions as they documented their findings with numerous quotes from interviews with Israeli citizens saying as much. What a perverse way to go about life. I find that attitude odd because over the years I've had numerous Israelis as clients and gave no indication that's how they would behave. If society in general accepts selfish behavior as the norm, what does that say about that society? American Jews certainly don't act that way in our society, on the contrary, many Jewish people are some of the most generous and down to earth people I've ever had contact with. As a matter of fact, if I had no Jewish customers I'd last in business about a week. In the town I grew up in you were either Catholic or Jewish, the two predominant religions there. That's why I found it so odd when I learned about that attitude in Israel.

Obviously it's not any kind of inherited trait, I doubt if that attitude could be passed down in your genes, but more a societal thing. It's really pretty sad when nastiness is not only condoned but almost encouraged and accepted as an every day fact of life. I can't imagine living in a society where surliness is considered acceptable behavior. For that reason alone I have absolutely no desire to go there. If I wanted to be treated rudely I'd go to France. As least I'd get some excellent food and top-notch museums for my troubles. Life can be difficult enough for many without others thoughtlessly adding their woes. We have enough nastiness here in our own country without having to go looking for it. The difference is that here it's not condoned or considered acceptable behavior, although that doesn't seem to have much effect on the frequency of it occurring.

When people are treated unkindly enough they might start to think it's their own fault when it necessarily isn't. They might even start to get a little gun shy when dealing with others. You've probably experienced that sensation in your own life at one time or another. You have words or disagree strongly with a friend, business associate or a stranger, or one of any number of other unpleasantries that is out of character for you, and before you've fully recovered from that something else happens and you're at odds with someone else. And, that's the last thing you wanted at the moment. That's when you might even start to think "is it me? Is there something wrong with my attitude?" That's also when you start doubting yourself and think that maybe you're not quite as good a person as you thought you were. At that time more than most, you need to hear encouraging words from a friend or at least some pleasant interaction with another to assure you that you really are a good person, and your positive self image is correct.

When your self image takes a battering and you need reassurance, you'll more than likely get that from someone who really cares for you and wants you to feel good about yourself: a friend. Although, after a couple of rough goes when you are beginning to doubt yourself, you'll take whatever you can from whomever you can get in a sense of positive reinforcement. Even a kindness of a stranger or acquaintance, maybe no more than a pleasant hello and a smile, or even a little pat on the back, goes a long way in making you feel better about yourself. You don't feel as emotionally alone after a few kind words. Most of us go long stretches between arguments or other unpleasantries and are very happy that is the case. Most of us don't feel good after arguing and that's one reason we try to keep such things at a minimum.

If a person gets in the habit of being belligerent and argumentative they will obviously be involved in more altercations than the average person. If that's the case, many times the aftereffects of that argument aren't as severe for them because they're used to it. But, the other person involved in the altercation isn't. That's something frequent arguers don't take into account. If they're in the habit of being belligerent they might move on soon after the altercation. The other person doesn't, and there will be a lingering resentment for having been dragged into a situation they didn't want to be part of in the first place. Remember this; if you have the habit of being argumentative, people don't forget, even if you do.

But, if a person doesn't live consciously there is always that fear of the next occasion when, no matter how much they want to avoid it, they're going to have a similar problem, and the real fear is of reacting poorly and the after-effects on their self esteem. It's possible that something unpleasant can affect your whole day and you'll more than likely take an emotional pounding home with you to ruin your night also. If those feelings do persist into the night, a lot of times we resent the person with whom we had a falling out even more, because now it's affecting the time you need to relax and get emotionally ready for the new day tomorrow. It's taking away precious R&R that we all come to depend on to get ourselves rejuvenated and refreshed. You might have a hard time bringing yourself around and can't get the situation out of your mind no matter how hard you try or what techniques you use. When you go out in public, to counteract that feeling, you might go out of your way to treat others even better than you normally do, at least for a while, while you're still harboring lingering aftereffect of the unpleasantry that caused the negative feeling in the first place. When you do that, you're making an effort to reassure yourself that you are really a good person and the problem was more or less the other person's fault. "See it's not me, I'm here with others and we're getting along just fine."

Even if you live a deliberately conscious life, every once and a while, and far less than most, relations involving you and another aren't on the friendliest terms. A short while ago I had a slightly contentious difference of opinion with a client. That almost never happens with me. If something like it happens every few years, that's a lot, and I deal with thousands of people. I try to be as accommodating as possible when it comes to my clients but when I think someone is trying to take advantage I will probably balk at their demands. When I say "contentious" there was no argument, I don't do that. But, to a conscious person, since problems of that nature are so rare, even a few slight words or the wrong attitude on another's part, is so out of character of our every day lives, I use that terminology to distinguish it. That's what happened in this case. The client had purchased an expensive pair of glasses from my shop over nine months ago. She came in and demanded I make her new lenses because there were a few minor scratches on a lens. Her lenses cost me over a hundred and eighty dollars. Her reasoning was that she never had a scratch on a lens before on any previous pair so obviously this pair was defective and warranted free replacement. Having done this type of work for so long I get that story a lot. Their old glasses never had any problems and they had them for years. They can't admit to the fact that lenses do indeed scratch or that they could be the one responsible for causing it. Living consciously precludes you from purposely zinging another and as I've said, in the heat of the battle I never had the problem of later wishing I had said something.

But I've learned to keep my mouth shut. I thought her request was very presumptuous. If she bought a car and a year later there was a scratch on the paint, would she think she was entitled to a new car because her previous car didn't have a scratch? But, and this is one of the benefits of living life in a conscious fashion, I held my tongue to give my brain a chance to catch up. I decided there was no need for me to exacerbate the situation. It wasn't only what she said, but how she said it. Not only did she demand new lenses, when I asked he if she could give up her glasses for me to have the new lenses made, she said no, that I was use my pair from stock to be used as a "sizer" and when the lenses were ready, she'd come in for me to insert them at her convenience. Having consciously slowed down in order to handle the situation in the best way possible I didn't come back at her with my first thought but actually agreed to do it. As I've said, I really try to be as accommodating as I can, inside business and outside business.

But I also made clear that I thought her demands were unreasonable and that the only reason I was going to do it is because she's been a long time client and I would like to keep her business in the future. I didn't allow my ego to intervene. I know for a fact that in most optical stores if she tried that she'd have been shown the door, even if she didn't realize that. I didn't get upset with her attitude or the prospect of losing the money because I just accepted that these situations occasionally occur in business. It's the price I pay for independence and it's a very small price indeed.

We didn't have words but there was a chill in the air. She came in with an attitude but I took the wind out of her sails when I didn't take the bait. Nothing seems to upset people who have little control over their emotions more than dealing with a person who does. Or, as Oscar Wilde once wrote: "Nothing is as aggravating as calmness." It's true. If you keep your head when others are freaking out and are out of control, they'll resent you that much more for it. That's not at all the intent, but that is the result. Remaining calm when you ordinarily wouldn't is a very liberating feeling, and it gives a tremendous boost in how you feel about yourself. In this case, I'd never been anything but friendly with her in the past and although I answered all her and her husband's questions in a professional manner, I wanted her to know that the only reason I was accommodating her was despite her attitude, and not because of it. There is no doubt that in this case she got more upset the less I did. So, I stayed on an even keel not to aggravate her but to keep myself in a consciously accepting state of mind.

The next morning there was a message on my store's answering machine telling me not to go ahead with the new lenses, she would buy a new pair instead. I didn't expect that but I think she might have thought better of her demands when she went home and had some time to reflect on what happened. She walked in feeling like the aggrieved party but after what transpired, felt a little foolish when she left. She could have gotten what she wanted but a little more than she bargained for in the process. By stopping and thinking first and not just going ahead with my first impulse, I kept the potential for a more serious disagreement from developing, and at least I know I handled the situation in a way that I had no regrets. In business you have to take care to have your client's leave with a feeling that they were treated fairly and have a positive image of their experience and your service. The statistic is if a client is happy with the overall experience they'll tell, on the average, three people, if not, they'll tell ten people. And, those ten people will probably tell others, so one occasion of unhappiness can snowball into a bad image for your business in the eyes of many more people than the one who's experience was negative.

It's important that people feel comfortable around you. One very easy way to make people more comfortable is to use their name.

It's a little thing but means a lot to many. Try to make it a habit when conversing with others to do that. Not only in business but in social settings. When you use a person's name when talking to them it makes them feel that you think enough of them to personalize your speech. When I worked for someone else, I remembered almost all the clients' names and there were five thousand of them. I made it a point to do that. My boss couldn't remember any so it wasn't unusual for him to slip into the back room where I was working and ask me to peer around the corner so he could address them properly. I remember people complimenting him all the time for remembering their name and many said they appreciated it. He knew I would remember, so in speaking to them he made them feel more comfortable.

You make a much better impression and make others more comfortable when you take the time to remember others' names and use them. It makes a person feel special that you took the time to care. I had a client who said one of the main reasons she liked to shop at my store is that she was always greeted with personal, and not the generic "can I help you?" greeting. I'm sure you like people a little bit more when they show you the same courtesy. It's not some trick to get people to like you, that shouldn't ever be a problem when you lead a conscious life, but more of a conversational tool to make others more comfortable in your presence. That also goes for remembering things about their personal lives. If you ask about their kids and go so far as remembering their names that goes a long way in cementing your relationship.

Another thing you can do to make people more at ease with you is to never argue while in the company of others. There's not a more uncomfortable feeling than being at a social event and having two people going at each other, especially if you know the combatants. I could never understand when a couple comes into my store in mid-argument. Not only is it disrespectful, but it can also make me feel ill at ease in my own business, at least it used to before I started living life consciously. No one wants to hear it. I guess in the heat of battle they don't realize they're airing their dirty laundry in public, or maybe they just don't care. Either way you shouldn't be arguing in the first place. That's only for people who can't understand their own emotions, and who can't handle a situation in a more conscious and less contentious way.

I always found it odd when people say that in all true relationships they'll always be arguments. Some how I think these people confuse the concept of being committed with being combative. Of course, couples won't always agree on everything, but there is the concept of disagreeing without being disagreeable. There is no law or rule that states if you have a disagreement it has to be contentious. If you really love someone, why would you ever say things to them that you wouldn't dare say to a stranger? Just because they're close, it doesn't give you free reign to treat them any worse or with less respect than you do others. It baffles me that people who supposedly love each other can treat their partner in an offhand and dismissive manner. We have a tendency to get used to each other over a prolonged period of time, but that doesn't mean just because you're familiar with them, and everything about them, you should ever show them contempt. It's odd that some people treat the people who supposedly they care deeply for the worst. In many cases their partner is taken for granted even if they are the ones turned to when no one else is there. If you're married or in a serious relationship you should always remember, and make it a point, to treat your loved one at least as well as you treat others, and hopefully even better.

When people argue many times it's because they can't control their tempers. They may be able to control many other aspects of their lives but when a person allows their temper to dictate their actions, they're really not in control at all. Many people who argue often or have bad tempers don't even realize there is a better way to resolve conflicts. They've probably been doing just that for all their lives and it's like anything else, it can easily get to be a habit. I find it strange when I see an elderly person throwing the adult version of a temper tantrum. You'd think in their seventy or seventy-five years they'd have mellowed a bit. It's even scarier to think this might be the already mellow version, when you see their antics. Most people do mellow as they get older, it's just a natural progression. It takes that long for many to come to the realization that all the little things that tick them off aren't worth the time they spend hassling them. As you age, you learn to pick and choose your battles in a much wiser fashion, and realize that ninety percent of the stuff that used to upset you enough to get into an argument about, couldn't matter less.

But, until people finally come to that realization and reach that stage, their lives aren't nearly as happy as they could be.

Temper equates to stress. When we can't resolve our differences through more peaceful means we add even more stress to our already stressful lives. How can we fully enjoy life when we fear how we'll react in certain situations? If you can't trust yourself to stay on an even keel no matter what the circumstance, you worry that since a certain situation caused you to get upset and lose your temper before, that will be the case when a like situation develops in the future. It's a very uncomfortable and totally unnecessary feeling. You need to be able to be completely comfortable with yourself in all areas of your life. I think the reason most smokers can't possibly be a hundred percent comfortable with themselves is that they know that they're doing themselves great harm and even knowing that, persist. Since smoking is more addictive than heroin, it's a major problem for many to quit although they might want more than anything else in their lives. There has to be a gnawing feeling in the back of their minds that never fully goes away, until they quit.

While having a bad temper won't give you emphysema, throat cancer, or lung cancer, it's the equivalent in a mental deficiency of a serious nature. No one wants to be around a person who can't learn to control their temper, just as no one wants to be around a drunk. And, what really mystifies me is that many of these people don't seem to realize that. As a conscious person there is really no chance of that happening, after you reach a certain point. That's due to the fact that being conscious is being in control of your emotions, not sublimating them, letting them run wild, or denying their existence. As I've said, you always need your intellect to dictate to your emotions and not the other way around. Since conscious individuals don't put pressure on themselves, making situations unnecessarily do or die, the chances of overreacting and making problems out of situations, is much less great. It's a very liberating feeling when you know that no matter what happens and no matter what day or time of day, any situation that confronts you won't cause you angst; and, it gets even better. That's because now any situation that you previously dreaded due to the way that you feared how you'd respond, doesn't cause that fear any longer. When you have the confidence to feel completely comfortable with your actions and responses, then you've come far on your path indeed.

I use the term liberating because when you know you're in control and always will be, it's like shackles being removed from your thinking patterns. You're now free to move about the cabin of your life without a worry about your future and how you'll respond to it. Worry is just a form of fear. When you eliminate the reason that you fear something by conquering it, the cause of the worry is gone, the less stressful your life will become. If you do have a temper you have trouble controlling, that is the perfect thing for you to work on. When you do teach yourself to slow down and consciously keep a level head you'll kill two birds with one stone. That's much better than initially eliminating only one area you find troubling in your life. It will allow you to see early progress on your quest to reach the ultimate goal of happiness, tranquility, and serenity. If you attain one of those goals you've attained them all. That will encourage you to do more. It allows you to conquer more things in your conscious life and your business and social lives as well. When you don't have to any longer fear how you'll react, number one, you'll eliminate worry about it, and number two, you reduce your stress level as well.

So you see why it's so important to get a firm handle on the situation at the earliest possible time. This is what you should do should you start to lose your temper. Slow yourself down until your body and brain can work their way out of the crisis mode. Do this consciously and deliberately. Relax to get the adrenalin to stop pumping so you can retake the reigns to get yourself back in the right direction. Take some deep breaths. Tell yourself that this situation is not life or death and therefore your response is in your power to control. Accept the fact that whatever is happening, is, and you'll approach it in a conscious manner, i.e., willing to listen to and try to understand the other person's point if someone else is prompting this negative feeling in you. Even if you start to get just a bit irritated use that as a practice situation for bigger things. Allergies and temper have one thing in common. They're both cumulative, in that the longer they're allowed to continue without intervention the harder they are to control. If you can nip it in the bud when you first feel the signs of irritation, you won't allow the negative feeling to develop and grow until it's out of control or very difficult to get a handle on. The important thing is to consciously take charge of the situation. If done correctly, it's as if you're giving yourself instructions as you proceed. And, the reason for that is, that's exactly what you're do- ing. It's like when you started to drive and the instructor gave you step-by-step instructions, so you wouldn't get confused or learn to do things improperly. Relax, accept, and think before acting or speak- ing and you'll be amazed at how well you can do at this.

It's important that you don't take people's words personally, even if that's their intent. Eleanor Roosevelt once said: "No one can make you feel inferior without your consent." The same holds true for anger. No one can make you angry or lose your temper without your consent. When you allow that to happen, you're playing their game and only hurting yourself.

Many people who can't control their temper have a habit of living much of their lives in a foul mood. That's logical in that these people really don't exhibit much control in one aspect of their lives so there's really no reason to think they'd exhibit much control with another along the same lines. So it follows that people that tend to habitually have bad moods also habitually have bad tempers. They exhibit that tendency maybe not every day but enough where you can detect a pattern. I'm sure you've all known people like that, we all do. It's pretty much a vicious cycle for them of surliness followed by regret. It's as if the person were a puppet being controlled by outside sources that they seem powerless to control. Unfortunately, for all of us who have contact with these people, they tend to take their bad moods out on others. Sometimes you can understand it if they're not, for instance, feeling well or are going through a rough patch, but no matter the cause, that certainly doesn't excuse it. Nobody likes being in a lousy mood and nobody likes to be around those with that tendency. Again, I find it truly amazing that often times these people don't realize that.

People who exhibit the patterns of temper and bad moods really can't like themselves all that much or have a high opinion of themselves or they wouldn't be so careless with their emotions. If you love yourself, and not in a narcissistic fashion, you'd never want to exhibit that face in public. If you really cared about others and their feelings there is no way you'd behave that way because when you do you negatively affect the mood of all those around you.

You'd never go out in a public place if you were infected with the measles; that would almost certainly result in others catching the virus. So, why would you go out and infect all those around you with your negativity? It's really not fair to others. As a conscious person you want to elevate those you come in contact with, not drive them away. Unfortunately, as with people with communicable diseases, we can't quarantine them or treat them like children and make them go to their room until they learn to behave in public. If they would just "stew in their own juices," they wouldn't affect (or infect) the rest of us, so it wouldn't be so bad. It's extremely uncomfortable when you have to tiptoe around on eggshells for fear of upsetting them even further. Once headed down that path it doesn't take much to make matters worse, as it starts snowballing, and you need to watch out not to get crushed. You could be in a truly wonderful mood but if you're not living consciously, you could easily be sucked in. When they do have an effect on the mood of all those around them, that's just basically bringing others' down to their level. You can't always avoid them so you just have to learn to live with them. But, surliness is one tough neighbor.

If you see any of this in yourself, you realize there is something you can do about it. Patterns that have developed over the years can be changed. You might have gotten into the habit of spreading bad moods in the past, but that's just what it is, the past. It's to be forgotten.

Each day starts off with a clean slate. What you did before has nothing to do with how you act now or will act in the future. Forget the past, it's over and it's not coming back. In my own life I've come far enough where bad moods, for the most part, are a thing of the past. I still have a lot of days where I don't feel well, the vast majority actually, but I make it a point on those days not to let it significantly affect my mood or how I treat others.

I also feel that I'm no longer somehow missing out on things as I once did for that very reason. I know that no matter how good I feel, if I didn't feel crummy physically, I'd feel that much better. But, I've accepted the reality of the situation and feel very fortunate to be as good as I am. Every once in a while I get a window when physically I feel as good as I used to, and in those moments I try to take advantage of that feeling, and try to make it last as long as possible. Sometimes it's only a few minutes, but I feel fortunate to have them, because I didn't have them for many years.

When you start living consciously the occasions when you're feeling a bit surly and are not in the mood to deal with most things or most people, become less and less. Since you now have a guide that basically tells you how to handle such times, if that type of feeling starts to well up in you, you can now change it to a more positive approach before it gets too far along. Your moods are totally in your control, although sometimes keeping positive and remembering what you're trying to accomplish is more difficult. Nothing less than you ongoing happiness is at stake. As La Rochefoucauld wrote in *Maxim* over three hundred years ago: "the happiness and unhappiness of men depends as much on their turn of mind as on fortune." It's your responsibility to yourself to take care to consciously steer your thinking in the right direction, no matter what else in going on in your life, or even at the moment.

Each moment you stay in a positive frame of mind is less that

you're in a neutral or negative frame of mind. You should start enjoying as opposed to just existing day to day. Once you develop faith
in yourself to do the right thing in any circumstance and not to allow
outside forces to affect or determine your moods, you'll come to
realize how much easier and less complicated your life will become.
Things that always caused you dread in your past life, no longer will.
That's due to the fact that you can now see through all the clutter and
know what's important and what's not. You'll realize that things you
took for granted or felt relatively unimportant, really are some of the
most important.

It all starts with attitude. Since you can now see the importance of things such as mood, even for a short period of time, you can
now place greater emphasis on developing skills in coping with them.
We all know that what kind of mood we're in affects how we feel
about things, so just accepting the fact you're in a crummy mood and
just riding it out until you start to feel better, is no longer acceptable.
Even putting up with a foul mood for a short time takes you away
from a flowing life for too long a time. Instead of just passively
accepting negative emotions and hoping they'll soon go away, you
realize that you can change them for the better through conscious
effort. You don't have to be on vacation to be happy, just in the
proper frame of mind. Once you get that feeling, you'll start to get a
little greedy, you'll want to experience it more and more. That's a
great sign because once you get a taste of true sustained happiness
and you develop techniques that move you in that direction, it becomes easier and encompasses more aspects of your life. When
you've practiced living in the exact moment you're in and not two
minutes ago or tomorrow and learn to accept your moods as control-
lable entities, working on them becomes part of your life.

Determine to stay in a positive frame of mind and the hard
edge that was once your life starts to soften. That nervous feeling in
the pit of your stomach that almost never seems to go away completely, will be replaced by a placidity and calmness that you might
not have felt since you were a child. Everyone is in the same boat,
and no one is immune from the trials and tribulations that life seems

to bring on in a constant barrage. I'd say that ninety-nine percent of us don't know what you do now, which puts you at a major advantage to others you have contact with.

Some people have a habit of being overly critical of other and their accomplishments or lifestyles. Even if it's none of our business we're quick to criticize others, be it fact or assumption. I could never understand, for example, some people resenting mixed couples. What business is it of theirs? It's not their life and has no effect on them in any way. People should learn to mind their own business and concern themselves only with things that actually have something to do with them. That's the same thing with gay or lesbian couples. What right do you have to try to dictate how others lead their lives? This is not Saudi Arabia where they have "morality police" that dictate standards. Let others live their own lives and only concern yourself with yourself.

As a matter of fact, facts sometimes get in the way and are often ignored. It's much easier to be critical than correct. Famous people are criticized all the time and much of their lives are lived under a microscope. Their every move is scrutinized, their every action, eagerly watched. That's the price people pay for notoriety. I'm always amused when famous people complain that, because they are under the microscope, they can't lead normal lives. These are the same people who live in homes so sumptuous we can't even imagine them, receive preferential treatment in every facet of their lives, take vacations in places we didn't even know existed, have access to powerful people that the rest of us don't, get the best tables in restaurants, drive the finest cars money can buy, get paid unheard of amounts of money for minimal work, travel only first class, stay only in the finest hotels, have personal chef's cook their meals, send their children to the most exclusive private schools, get free perks the rest of us have to pay for, hire people to do the mundane that the rest of us spent untold hours doing, socialize with the crème de la crème who determine everything from fashion to what we read, are more able, through their notoriety to influence the thinking of others, wear the finest clothes money can buy, and just in general lead lives on a scale not available to others.

So, if these people are criticized more than the rest of us, it's just part of the territory. It's hard to feel sorry for them, unless a personal tragedy strikes one of the elite, and causes them to look more like regular folk in the public's eyes. As I said, it's hard to feel sorry for them, but, with all that, treating these people more critically than others isn't right. Many of those who are overly critical do so for two reasons: jealously and resentment. They can see glimpses of that lifestyle but it will never be theirs, and when they go home at night, it's to the same tired old house, on the same old tired street. Instead of being thankful for everything they do have, they spend much of their time worrying about what they don't have or what other people do.

I'll admit that it can be easier for the famous to be happy than for the rest of the population, just for the fact that their lives are more comfortable, and problems are handled by others for them. Most of us would eagerly trade our hassles for their hassles in a minute. How many times have you read, after a celebrity is arrested for breaking a law, and one of the favorites seems to be associating with prostitutes, that their lawyers showed up in court and the celebrity was somewhere half way around the world vacationing or working on a movie. They can leave the responsibilities of every day life to others, and don't seem to suffer the consequences of their actions unless it gets to the point of ridiculousness. Some celebrities don't seem to handle their fame too well and become arrogant and egotistical. When that happens they can come to believe they're above the law and their money and notoriety will take care of any problem they cause. In all the times I've had contact with celebrities, though, there has been only one occasion where when asked for an autograph, they blew the person off. This person is a very famous singer who has a reputation in this town of being arrogant. That's pretty amazing in itself. But, for the most part celebrities are smart enough to know who butters their bread.

Celebrities are in an elite group that constitutes less than one percent of the population. Our lives will never be like theirs, but that really doesn't mean a thing. Even if we have to do the laundry, take out the garbage, do our own food shopping, or whatever, that really doesn't matter. Who cares? Doing those things on a regular basis is just part of the scheme of our lives, and aren't really that distasteful if you go about them with the proper attitude.

It's never what you have to do, it's always how you do it. Just as there are no "only" jobs, as in he's only a waiter. If that's what you are, determine to be the best waiter you can possibly be. You have the same opportunity to achieve happiness if you're "only" a gardener than if you're the president of a large corporation. It's all how you go about it. The only thing that you should ever concern yourself about when it come to making you livelihood, is being the best you can at what you do.

I'm much more impressed with a poor man who puts in the time to provide for his family, no matter what he does, than I have respect for that singer who blew off the autograph seeker. So, if you have to personally go to the supermarket, is that such a distasteful chore? Can't shopping with the proper attitude be pleasurable? Of course it can. No matter what you do or have to do isn't really an issue. The only thing that is an issue is your attitude about it. So, when you start to envy others' lifestyles, always remember all the good things you do have in your life. Don't ever go comparing your life with others' lives because that is meaningless. As long as you're doing the best you can, then you're doing just fine. Remember, that it's not so much what you have as what you do with what you have, and how much you take the time to truly appreciate it. As I've said, the only thing you might want to compare yourself with is your former less conscious, self, and that's just an exercise in wasting time. Some people feel better about themselves when they make comparisons of their life with someone they know that isn't doing so well. That type of superficiality has no place in a conscious life.

No one likes to be criticized. If someone asks your opinion regarding something they've done or said, most of the time what they're really asking for is validation. As W. Somerset Maugham, wrote in *Of Human Bondage*: "People ask you for criticism, but they only want praise." You have to decide if being one hundred percent truthful when asked to be critical will cause more harm than good. When someone requests your opinion on a matter, the first thing you should ask yourself is if you tell the whole truth, will you be hurting the person doing the asking? If it will, you need to determine the importance of the matter. For instance, if someone wants your opinion on a matter such as if you think they're qualified to start their own business, that's a pretty serious matter. If the person asking holds you in high regard, then your opinion will carry some weight. If you don't think they're qualified, you need to tell them as much. But, as with everything, there are different ways of going about it that can be constructive. The best way in this case would be for you to state your reasons why you think what you do, but at the same time offer insights into how you think they can go about rectifying their deficiencies so that in the future they'll more likely be qualified. It's so easy to be critical, anyone can do that, but to offer solutions with your critique is a very positive approach. If the subject is of little importance or even no importance at all, say you're asked your opinion about a recipe a friend tried for the first time, there's no reason not to tell the truth. Although again, there are ways of going about it while keeping the others' feelings in mind. If you can't stand the taste of it I wouldn't use those words. Even then how you say it is as important as what you say. Why hurt their feelings and make them feel unnecessarily self-conscious?

There are ways of getting your message across without being harsh. Sparing someone's feelings who you care about isn't being dishonest, it's just being kind, and there's almost never an occasion in our everyday lives that kindness is not the right thing. Think how much better and more pleasant our lives would be if everyone made it a point to make a point to be kind to others. Again, it costs you nothing and if the right words or way of saying something help to elevate another's day and is in your power to do, there's absolutely no reason not to. That also goes for something someone does that is praiseworthy. People most certainly do appreciate hearing praise if they do something that warrants it. If someone puts out the effort to do a good job, then you should make it a point to show that you appreciate the effort. That is especially true if someone tries hard but fails at the task. Honest effort should always count. Since it is just as important the way you say things as what you say, always stop and think, and make it a point to get your point across without offending. Something as easy as that for you to do also has an effect on how you feel about yourself. If you use kind words instead of blunt or ill-thought-out words, you've taken the high road and because of that your self-image has one more positive aspect to add to the growing list of good.

Since attitude is more important than other factors when it comes to your happiness, that is one area you always need to pay particular attention to. No matter what the situation or when it happens, how you view it counts for everything. I keep harping on this one point because of its importance.

CHAPTER SIX
BE HONEST

A lot of us take on too much. We get overwhelmed. We should be taking small bites and not try to consume the whole enchilada in one gulp. If you find yourself not finishing things you've started, you may be either doing the wrong thing, taking on too much at once, or complicating the matter. Either way, something can easily become out of hand if you don't think it through before tackling it. In that case, you've created a problem where one shouldn't exist.

One thing that keeps people from solving their problems is that they're expert at making excuses. More time is spent trying to lay blame on someone else than trying to solve the problem. Cardinal DeRetz in his memoirs (1718) said it very well when he wrote: "One of man's greatest failings is that he looks almost always for an excuse, in the misfortune that befalls him through his own fault, before looking for a remedy, which means he often finds the remedy too late."

As a conscious individual you realize more than most the futility of trying to wriggle out of things that, through actions or words, you've caused to happen. What needs to be done is to honestly look for the root cause of any particular problem, and attack that, especially if the culprit is you. Making lame excuses to oneself is pretty pathetic. When you can't accept responsibility then you don't really have a grasp of what being conscious is all about.

The good thing is that when you've reached a certain point you realize that blaming yourself or others is counterproductive. There should never be blame assigned. It's amazing how easily problems, that before would cause you much consternation, are easily fixable, when you just accept the fact they exist and immediately start working toward solving them. As long as you take them head-on they don't get a chance to cause even more problems. Some say problems are just opportunities in disguise, I say problems are just that, problems, and should be identified as such. I guess the opportunity is to fix them.

Honesty is the best approach. For example, if I make a mistake at work, say I'm writing up a prescription for eyeglasses and transpose numbers, that delays the client getting their glasses. Since people are usually anxious to pick up their new eyewear, the delay doesn't go over too well. If I honestly explain that I've made a mistake people appreciate the fact that I'm not making excuses and are more willing to be patient. There are a number of reasons not to make excuses besides the ones I've already mentioned. Practically speaking if you lie (which many excuses are) or just make an excuse, you have to remember what you said. If you're at work you have to make sure your co-workers know what you said and are willing to go along with it. You might be asking them to do something they find morally wrong. You can see how this can lead to even more problems. If you're esteemed in your colleague's eyes, they might lose some respect for you if they think you're a liar or one to make excuses for your behavior. You only have to be caught once in a lie to lose all credibility.

Let's say I have a good client who's spent thousands of dollars in my store over the years. If I mistreat him once or get caught lying about something, all the past good will I've built up is destroyed. It's difficult to build people's trust but so easy to lose it, at work or not. I want to make something clear. I don't feel lying is always wrong. It has to do with the importance of the subject matter and other variables. What I consider okay are the little white lies and only then to spare someone's feelings. Just about everyone does it to some degree. If your friends just had a baby and the poor kid is not very cute, as a matter of fact he's downright ugly, you would never say that. If a relative gives you a polka dot bow tie for Christmas, if you told the truth about what you really think of it you would unnecessarily hurt their feelings. Because the matter is of such little importance it's wiser to spare their feelings and make them happy than to be honest and possibly hurt their feelings. You don't always have to be a straight arrow or always right, sometimes the heart should be given the chance to do the talking for you. But, again, only limited situations and only to spare someone's feelings. I'm sure moral purists disagree with that, but I think the positiveness of being kind outweighs the negativism of not being truthful in some cases.

Lying, can become delicious and hypnotic, especially when you get good at it with practice. But, what a phony way to go about life. In the years I worked with that man, I don't think a day went by when he didn't lie about something. He was about as transparent as they come, and even though he didn't realize it, we all knew when he lied. His fellow employees got to the point that everything he said was suspect. It's hard to respect someone when you're not sure if what they tell you is the truth or just another fabrication. Part of being a conscious person is being an honest person. That holds true even if telling the truth isn't convenient under the circumstances. People have to be able to believe what you say if you want to be taken seriously or thought of as a reliable friend or co-worker. Even if the truth of a particular matter doesn't fit into the image we portray to the world, that shouldn't matter. I'd much rather be truthful and have self respect than try to garner others' respect through telling people what I think they want to hear. In almost all occasions, with minor exceptions, telling the truth is morally right, lying is morally wrong. You don't need me or the church or any other institution to tell you that. Although institutions that give moral guidelines certainly have their place, we all should have a moral code by which we live. Morality is a subject that doesn't seem to get much play nowadays outside of church. It's a shame too, because now, as at most times, we could use a little moral leadership. Maybe this will change after September 11, 2001.

To always do what's right and fair just feels good even if it's the more difficult path to follow sometimes. Being moral, distinguishing right from wrong, and by that how you conduct yourself, is a matter of ethics. Many people feel that as long as something is legal then it's right. That's like saying if you're capable of doing something, you should do it. Since we're all responsible for our own ethics, it's something we should always keep in mind no matter what we're doing. That's even though it sounds old fashioned. The greatest people in history had this much in common—a strong moral foundation. Think Gandhi and Lincoln. The famous people that didn't have a strong moral foundation are remembered also, but not for positive reasons. Think Hitler and Stalin.

Just because we live by rules doesn't mean you should expect others to adhere to them. In a perfect world we'd all have the same high morals, but obviously that will never happen, especially as it seems many people have little or no moral foundation at all. One thing we need to be careful with is not feeling superior to those that seem to be morally adrift. Either they'll see the light or they won't, but that's their personal choice and their life.

Even if people you know and love think you are on your high horse when it come to this, especially in today's every-man-for-himself world, we all should take it very seriously as our obligation to ourselves and those who come into contact with us. It absolutely makes life that much easier because you always follow the same guidelines, in any situation, whether it be in your personal or professional life. Once you've decided the proper and prudent way to act, you never have to think about it. That's only as long as you have only one standard of conduct, and not a different standard that's open for interpretation and manipulation. It's as simple as making the rules and following them. It's true that telling small lies sometimes keeps us from getting grief from somebody and many times it keeps us from having to go into detailed explanations regarding something we really don't care about (lies of convenience), but it's not a good thing to get into the habit of doing. There are degrees of lying just as there are degrees of anything else.

I once worked with a man who had a very unusual last name. From the sound of it you really couldn't tell the derivation. Since the name was so unusual many people would ask him where his family was from. He always told them that he wasn't sure and they were from somewhere in Europe. Now, this man wasn't adopted so he obviously knew his ethnicity. Have you ever met a person who didn't? I was curious so I asked his father because the son had given me the same line. His father said the family was from Poland. (This is a different man than the one who changed his name.) He never knew his son tried to hide his roots, and I didn't tell him. The son obviously was embarrassed to tell anyone as if there were a stigma attached to being Polish.

As a conscious person it's hard for me to even fathom that attitude. You are what you are, as sure as what is, is. The man lived a lie because he felt if he told the truth people would perceive him differently. It didn't matter that no one else cared one bit. He was born and raised in the United States as was his father and mother. I guess being an American of Polish descent wasn't good enough. The image he had of himself precluded him from telling the truth. He was dishonest in that way and was dishonest in many other areas as well.

That's something I've noticed over the years. You can be pretty sure if someone's lying about one thing, that's just the tip of the iceberg. It's easy to slide down that path once you start. If he's going to spend his life lying about something as insignificant as his heritage, especially in a country as diverse as ours, you can be pretty certain that his moral compass is broken. And, in his case, it truly was just the tip of the iceberg.

People sometimes become very creative in excusing themselves from the liability of the lie. That's nothing new. My favorite new euphemism that seems to be getting a lot of play south of the border is a classic. Once the charade was found out and it was discovered that he really didn't have the degree in management from Harvard that he'd always claimed, Mexican President Vicente Fox called the decades-old lie an "imprecision," Not to be outdone, his spokesperson, who claimed to have a Master's from Cambridge and who is now his wife, got caught in a lie about her education. The spokesman's exact words were, "It's another imprecision." Hers was a bit easier to uncover because she claimed she attended Cambridge in Dublin, Ireland. If you're going to lie you might as well take the time to get the facts straight.

These lies were uttered for one reason only—to present to the public a false persona. The mission was to leave a certain impression to mold people's perceptions of them to fit the public image they've been portraying over the years. Obviously, both these lies were blatant and were told to fool people into thinking they are more qualified than they really were. But now who looks like the fool? And it was totally unnecessary.

He would have been elected either way. But for many that's not nearly good enough. They need to impress.

Since many lies cause no real damage, people see no harm in telling them. I agree that most of the time they're not told to be malicious, but, still taking the easiest way out isn't necessarily the right way. I think if we spend less time in fabricating stories to others and just stick with the truth, we'll know others will find that our words are as good as gold. Others will become certain they can take whatever you say to the bank. And, since that isn't always the case with others, it's a comforting feeling for them when they know they can trust you. When you get into the habit of lying eventually you'll get caught and then your credibility is shot. An Ashanti proverb says it this way: "One falsehood spoils a thousand truths." Once you're caught in a lie people will have trouble believing things you say even if you tell the truth. It's a matter of trust. Things you say from then on will be "taken with a grain of salt." As Aesop said in *The Shepherd Boy*: "A liar will not be believed even if he tells the truth." There's even a good chance that when you do get caught, you won't even know it. A very good chance. The other person might not say a word. So, why take the risk?

There is another type of lying that has nothing to do with others. Many of us lie to ourselves, and just about every day. Basically what we're doing is letting ourselves slide when it comes to certain matters that we find troubling. We allow ourselves to make excuses to ourselves. Even if we realize we're doing it, it's such an ingrained habit it's hard to break. It's just easier to look the other way, even if we're the only one there. The problem with that is if you can't even tell the truth to yourself, how do you expect to be truthful with others?

In my years as an optician I've heard it all. The lies normally come when a client brings in a pair of broken frames that were purchased from me. The usual line is: "I don't know what happened. I took my glasses out of the case and they were broken." That's possible but frames don't have a habit of breaking themselves. Especially nowadays with the high quality of material used. Or, a strong number two: "I was just cleaning them and they fell apart in my hands." They don't seem to take into account my knowledge of eyewear. After all that's what I do for a living. I can usually tell by just looking at the frame if they were abused or if they wore out from normal wear and tear. In every case, whether I thought they were fibbing or not, I never challenged their assertions. What good would that do? Since everything I sell comes with a guarantee, I just replace the article and go about dealing with them as I always had. I've gotten to a point where I expect to be lied to in certain situations. I don't condone what some clients do but I understand it. They've probably been given grief in another store at one time when they tried to return or exchange something. So, they think, in order to get what they want, the easiest way to go about it is to lie. Although, that makes it harder for me to believe what they say in the future. They're under the false impression that their fibbing actually worked and they got away with a little something. These are good people but in this instance they risked future credibility for the sake of convenience. Not everyone is as understanding as me so if they tried the same thing with a different person the results could have easily been otherwise.

I know people, and you might, too, who've lied to us as long as we've known them and still do. They're the ones who can't own up to mistakes or failures and are in the habit of covering up their shortcomings, as if no one notices. So, instead of just admitting a mistake, which no one really cares about, they compound the situation by lying about it. I've come to expect it. They're pretty transparent and aren't fooling anyone, except themselves.

Since morality is such a personal thing, and since you might hold it in higher esteem than some others, you never want to go around feeling superior or lording it over others. Living with a strong moral foundation also manifests itself in a high confidence level. When, in a situation some might have a hard time deciding what to do, you'll just naturally "do the right thing." Being a more conscious person, one thing you'll notice right away is that everyday life becomes easier. Since life doesn't have to be inherently complicated, always doing what we feel to be the right and moral thing takes away a lot of stress and also the guesswork.

If you think "this is not only the conscious thing but also the moral thing" you'll discover they are one and the same. Since a conscious person usually thinks before acting or speaking, there is time to reflect before you act.

CHAPTER SEVEN
JUDGE NOT

Sometimes people think they're better than they really are. They have a habit of thinking they are more skilled at a particular job than others and many of these same people have a habit of discounting others' abilities. I'm sure you know a person that fits the bill. Probably someone you work with. When we were kids we called that type of person a "know-it-all." Most of the time that person isn't nearly as good as they think but you'd never convince them of that. Again, this is the person who doesn't seem to have any trouble finding fault with others but doesn't recognize the same in themselves. I like the way that sentiment was addressed in an old proverb: "He can see a louse as far away as China but is unconscious of an elephant on his nose." Most of us love for this type person to fail. There's even a term for that, "schandenfreude," which means taking pleasure in the misfortunes of others. Unfortunately, it's not at all uncommon for people to have that same attitude about friends. In that case, it's more jealousy than anything else. But, when it comes to "know-it-alls," we don't at all mind seeing them get knocked off their high horse. The confidence they project is nothing more than a smokescreen they use to mask their feelings of inferiority. They think by projecting the image of being all knowing others will perceive them as being superior, and knowledgeable. But, most of the time they are pretty clueless as to how others really see them. Elbert Hubbard in *The Notebook* says it: "Let a man once see himself as others see him, and all enthusiasm vanishes from his heart."

Although it's human nature to wish someone would knock

the wind out of their sails, conscious people shouldn't. No matter how much we feel these people are in need of a reality check, conscious people never get satisfaction seeing someone get what's coming to them. Who are we to decide if someone is due for a comeuppance? In the first place we never feel the need to gloat at others' misfortunes, self-inflicted or not. We understand people are going to act how they will and since we really don't have and don't even want control over that, we must accept the fact that that's how they are. If the "know-it-alls" do fail, many tend to feel a bit superior. We think: "I could have done it a lot better but they wouldn't listen." You have to allow others to do for themselves and for you not to feel superior, even if you are on a certain matter. They're probably better at other things than you are, so things tend to balance out.

You should always, regardless of the circumstances, try to approach life in a positive, nonjudgmental fashion.

An elderly gentleman came into my shop recently and before I knew it, he had taken out a bunch of small figurines and placed them on my desk. I started to say that I wasn't interested, but he didn't want to hear that and just kept talking and selling, all the while taking out more and more. As I've said, sometimes I have more people trying to "sell" me in my store than I have customers in a day. So, initially I just dismissed him as another salesman, although I still treated him as I treat all others in the same situation. That is, with respect. I really wasn't interested in the figurines. That didn't faze him and he just plowed ahead and didn't stop his sales pitch, no matter how much I protested. At the time, I didn't realize he was homeless because he carried himself so well. Then he said something that really caught my attention and reminded me how difficult some people's lives are and how truly blessed mine is. As he put the last figurine on my desk he said: "I'm sorry to be a pest, but if you don't buy some I won't eat tonight. My very survival is at stake." I was shocked by his plight and his candor. He immediately changed from being "just another guy trying to sell me" to being a human being in need of a kind gesture and words of encouragement and a meal. What I did in that situation meant little to me, in the overall scheme of my life, but everything to him. I realized the importance of handling the situation in the correct manner, and I wanted to make sure when the man left, he left with dignity. To me, that was even more important than the money and I came to find out it also meant a lot to him. Because we see so many homeless people nowadays we sometimes build an immunity to their suffering.

I have a tendency to give more to women, young and old, and the elderly because living on the street can be much tougher for them, and I see them as being defenseless and easy prey for other, younger, homeless people. On the streets it's back to basics and definitely survival of the fittest. So, if I can help, I'm happy to. Most of the older homeless were at one time productive members of our society and in many cases, it's not their fault for their predicament. When I see people on the streets struggling for even the basic necessities of food, clothing, and shelter I always think, and so should you: "There but for the grace of God go I." The safety met we all have and take for granted is just not there for them. When you see someone so down think how you would feel if you were in their position and always try to keep that thought, and make it a point not to judge. Try to see things from their perspective so you can understand better what they're going through.

Sometimes we get "compassion overload" because there are just so many people in need. When we were growing up we didn't have the homeless problems that is now endemic in our society. We thought of those people at the time as shiftless drunks. And, for the most part, at the time they were. Remember when homeless were referred to as "bums"? In New York they were called "Bowery Bums" because they tended to congregate there and in the downtowns of other big cities. You would never see a homeless person in the suburbs. They just didn't exist. In the '80s when we legislated people out on the street, the Reagan administration spoke often of the safety net that was supposedly provided for the least fortunate but in reality for the most part it was removed faster than private social service agencies could take up the load. Instead of balancing on the high wire with a net below to break their fall, these people had only the hard concrete to crash down on and unfortunately for many of them to sleep on.

Although this gentleman that came into my shop was indeed homeless, he had a nobility about him. From speaking to him it was obvious he was very intelligent and I could easily tell he was embarrassed to find himself in the plight he was in. The last thing I wanted to do was to add to that. Usually I carry some cash for the specific purpose of giving it to some of the more needy homeless people that abound in the beach area. I had twenty dollars on me so that's what I gave him. I wish I had more but I didn't. His reaction was worth the twenty dollars a thousand times over. He was very thankful and tears welled up in his eyes, as he thanked me for my "kindness". I told him to keep the figurines and sell them to someone else. He wouldn't hear of that and insisted I take at least one, which I did to make him happy. I did that because he could now consider this a business transaction and not a handout. And, in turn, would not lose any more dignity than he already had.

If I were homeless I know it would be terribly embarrassing and even demeaning to have to stand in line for a handout. If things got bad enough I'd probably do it, but only as a last resort. On the other hand, if I could help this gentleman, I would feel great in the knowledge that I was helping him in a basic way that would remove a lot of stress from his life and provide him with one thing that he needed.

As a conscious person I feel it is my responsibility, if the chance arises, to help a fellow human being in need. I can separate the emotional side from the practical side. As you know as conscious individuals we make it a priority to elevate those with whom we have contact, without letting negative emotions such as pity get in the way.

Let me propose a concept for you. It's up to you to take it or leave it. If you see a truly needy person, one who is in a predicament not of their own making and not of their choice, if they are incapable of providing for themselves, make it your mission to lend them a hand on an ongoing basis. If you have the means, make sure that you take the opportunity that is presented to you, to take a few dollars out of your own pocket, or more if you can afford it, to insure that person has at least enough money to eat a good meal every day. It only has to be one person, if ten thousand of us did just that it would make a huge difference in others lives. If you are willing to do that, you'll find it is about the best karma that you can manufacture and the good you provide by doing that small act will come back to you a hundred fold. Just think how you would feel if you found yourself in that predicament and someone showed you that kindness. If you can add just one small shred of dignity to another's life, you've done one of the greatest goods a person can do, and it took none of your time and a small amount of money and effort. If it means that you can't eat out one time a week, that small sacrifice will add so much to your life, and the image you hold of yourself, that you'll find it more than worth it.

Unfortunately for some, life isn't the fantasy world as portrayed in movies. In life, if someone is crying, that's real, if someone is hungry, that's real, if someone is being abused, that's real. Real life is fraught with real consequences, whether they're good or bad.

In the fantasy world of the movies we can decide when we want to go along and suspend belief and when we want to remember where we really are. For instance, if we see a very heartwarming, tender scene that almost brings us to tears, we can go with the fantasy and just enjoy the moment. If, on the other hand, there is a scene depicting cruelty to children or animals, we tend to remind ourselves that it's just a movie and the people involved are merely actors. If we couldn't do that there would be a lot fewer people going to the movies. We can consciously choose which way we want to view it. In real life, we can't really do that if we wish to have a realistic view of the world, and not walk around in some kind of fantasy of our own making. Unfortunately for many, fantasy is a much preferable place to reside then having to live the misery their real lives have turned out to be. Because there are real consequences for life's actions, whether intended or not, life can be unpredictable and even the best-laid plans, or the most meticulous attention doesn't guarantee the desired results. We just don't know and unless we're clairvoyant, there is no way of predicting how our lives will play out.

For example, since I was the picture of health for most of my life, I could never foresee or even imagine all the health problems I've been going through for the last fourteen years. If I didn't have the family and friends I have that made sure I was provided for, I could have easily found myself in a predicament that I couldn't overcome. Without the support, financial and emotional, I could have easily found myself in the precarious position of being homeless, literally. Just because a person always had a home doesn't mean they always will. I'm extremely fortunate. I've always been a hard worker, but hard work, although it is a virtue to be admired, isn't a guarantee of success. That's why when I see some of the older homeless, who could have done "all the right things" for their entire lives is such a sad state, I don't subscribe to the notion that they alone are responsible. It's possible they are, but we don't know, and their plight just as easily could have been the result of a series of misfortunes out of their control. They probably didn't have the type of support that I had or they wouldn't be where they are.

That's why it's so important that we treat everyone, no matter if they're dressed in rags or two thousand dollar Armani suit, the same, and with respect. If we're in a position where we find ourselves living life comfortably, and not worrying about where our next meal might come from, then we're extremely fortunate. If we have a place to go home to every night, and people who care for us and our welfare, we have everything.

Before you judge another and you know you shouldn't, you need to take into account all the variables, and try to see life through their eyes. I can't even imagine the loneliness these people are living every minute of every day. It must be terribly difficult to see happy families with well-dressed children all around them and to realize that lifestyle will never be theirs. They are so close to it that they can touch it, but they might as well be on Mars, for all the chance they have to experience it ever again. So, when you have all the problems that we all go through always remember how very fortunate you really are, and never forget "there but for the grace of God" go you. Appreciation of everything you do have will help you keep things in perspective.

As I've said, many people resent the success of others instead of admiring that person for their good work ethic or a particular skill they've developed. I recently read a letter in *USA Today* that perfectly illustrates that very point. This letter appeared a few days after Julia Roberts won the Oscar for Best Actress, written by a woman from the entertainment industry. In it she derides Roberts' acceptance speech. She complained that Roberts looked "selfish and foolish" and her speech was "all about her." Well, it was all about her for those few minutes! How often does an actress win an Oscar? I think the word "petty" is an apt description for the type of response that only small minds are capable of.

Let others resent them or feel superior to them or gloat when they fail, you're secure in knowing what you know. That is, conscious people tend to view things realistically, so we, more than others who tend to work more on the emotional level, understand our strong points and our weak points. On the other hand, one thing we never want to do is underestimate our abilities. That's one sure way of not reaching our potential. If you can view things realistically and not how you think they should be or you want them to be, your chances of underestimating your abilities are much lower. And since you really don't know if you're capable of doing a particular thing or not if you've never tried, why not try? What's the worst thing that can happen? Even if you fail miserably, at least you made the honest effort and found out.

You never want to make the mistake of assuming things. Either you know something for a fact or you don't. You might think you're somewhat knowledgeable about a matter but unless you know for sure, then you really don't know. That's why things need to be investigated. We all make assumptions based on personal criteria, to judge a situation or a person. Let others assume things, conscious individuals go by, as Joe Friday would say: "Just the facts." Much of the time when we assume things we're wrong. We base many of our assumptions on past experiences. If a person looks remarkably like someone from our past, we might assume they'll act like them our sound like them. If a situation is developing like one we've experienced we tend to feel it'll play out the same way. That's not necessarily true, as we've all found out. Since each person or situation is unique, a resemblance to something past might mean nothing at all. Each person or event stands alone and can only be taken on their own merit.

If we see an obese person we normally assume they overeat. We don't know that for a fact. But, that's what we automatically think, given our cultural biases and experiences. But, in doing so, we're discounting what might be the truth. We don't know if the person has a slow metabolism or a glandular problem or any number of things. It never serves us well to jump to conclusions about anything. I always prefer to give the benefit of the doubt about people until I'm proven wrong. I still try not to judge them either way. What's the rush? Make it a point never to make up your mind until you know all the facts. You'd appreciate it if others would offer you the same courtesy.

When I was in high school I was on the wrestling team. I also played football, but that's only so I wouldn't have to play in the marching band any longer. Some people have a proclivity for certain things and are just naturally good at them. That was me and wrestling. After four years I became pretty good at it; never great, but good enough to be offered a couple of college scholarships. In my senior year I was participating in a wrestling tournament at the end of the season. I had a good enough record during the season that I got a "bye." I automatically advanced to the second round without having to wrestle the first night.

That first night I watched my future opponent literally destroy the kid he wrestled. His opponent is what we called in wrestling terminology a "fish," meaning he flopped around and wasn't very good. In boxing the equivalent term would be "tomato can," as in, "he boxed a real tomato can tonight." It was wrestling etiquette in a situation like that to just take care of business and pin the fish at the earliest opportunity. That's just as in team sports where you don't run up the score on an inferior opponent. The object was to get the match over with and not embarrass your opponent any more than necessary. But, that's not how this guy went about it. He even tried to hurt the poor fish and was obviously enjoying himself immensely. He was playing up to the crowd, which in reality wasn't amused. He didn't try for the pin and instead showed off by racking up as many points as he could. That's even though it is a team sport and a pin was worth more to the team than winning on points, no matter how many you scored.

He was out to make an impression. I found out later he was trying to impress me, his next opponent. I watched with obvious interest as he demolished the "fish." The final score was eleven to nothing. That was extremely unsportsmanlike and I felt sorry for the guy who just got beat up. The winner thought it was a big joke when his opponent needed assistance to get off the mat when it was over. He wasn't like any wrestler I'd ever seen—his punk attitude and his attempt to injure an opponent were not at all normal. I'd never seen a wrestler get that beat up before. He was bleeding heavily and was obviously in a lot of pain. I was in the first row sitting with my friend Mike, who also had gotten a bye that first night. The wrestler who won thought he was a real tough guy. You didn't have to assume anything on that. He was from a tough section of a pretty gritty town. He was from a large school so we didn't wrestle his team during the season, and we'd never seen each other before. I know for a fact that he proudly wore the image of a thug because I was sitting in front of his buddies, and heard everything they said.

I thought what he did was cruel and any respect I might have had for him as a wrestler was gone. As he passed by me he made a comment. I didn't quite catch it but from his tone I knew he wasn't wishing me happy birthday. I didn't realize he knew who I was but he obviously did. He walked a few more paces and then came back. He literally snarled at me and said: "Are you the 147 from Ridgefield?" He was referring to our weight class. I told him I was. He looked me up and down and got a stupid smirk on his face and just laughed at me, and without saying anything, walked away. He was basically letting me know that I was in for the same treatment he had just administered to the "fish". His friends thought this was funny and they all had a good laugh at my expense. Being the bully that he was, and seeing things through his eyes, I could see how he'd gotten am impression of me. I was wearing horn-rimmed glasses and looked as if I couldn't fight my way out of a paper bag. He made an assumption and judged me solely by my looks. I was wearing a jacket at the time so he really had no idea about how I really looked. I was a little over six foot one and a hundred and forty seven pounds. I wasn't skinny, I just looked that way in my jacket.

The next day was our turn to wrestle. He was sure I'd been cowed by last night's performance. He hadn't heard what I said to Mike after he laughed at me the previous night. After he'd passed I turned to Mike and said: "He's going to pay for that." Mike appreciated that. This guy obviously wasn't very bright. For at least a few reasons. He had never seen me wrestle, but I'd seen him wrestle the previous night. So, right there I had an advantage. I had gotten a bye, which you only get if you are seeded highly—higher than he was. That should have meant something to him, but obviously it didn't. I had the reputation as a pretty good wrestler. He also didn't take that into consideration. His perception of me as some kind of skinny nerd was so strong it overrode warning signs that any other wrestler would have taken into consideration. I don't think he was capable of changing his opinion of me even after others told him it might be a good idea. Because of the way I looked, his image of me was firmly entrenched. Even if his own brain told him that I just might be a tougher opponent than his last one he obviously just dismissed that. His perception of me, it turns out, wasn't correct.

He'd done two things wrong in my mind: One, he unnecessarily embarrassed and tried to injure his first opponent, and two, he laughed at me. Now, at the time I was far from living a conscious life. I didn't even know the concept existed. I wasn't at all afraid of him as he obviously believed. His tactics and assumptions were about to backfire on him. He had a choice as to how he could have acted.

He could have done what he did, or do the right thing, and get the match over with as quickly as possible. He also had a choice as to how he perceived me and approached our match. He chose to ignore the facts and went with his biases and prejudices instead.

We make choices every day and almost all the time. What you choose each time has a lot to do with how successfully you live your life. In this case, if he'd done the right thing on the mat and kept his big mouth shut off of it, things would have gone a lot easier on him. Things never just happen. There is always a cause. That's just as there is no such thing as an accident. No matter what the result and how improbable the circumstances, there's always something that causes it to happen. This guy was the sole cause of what happened to him. I also knew what he didn't in another area. I had my father's genes and I was extremely strong and well muscled for my height. To give you some idea, my friends and I didn't lift weights but decided to see how much we could lift. It was more for bragging rights than anything else. At that time I weighed a hundred and forty-five pounds and on my first try easily bench-pressed two hundred and sixty pounds. I might have done more, but that's all the weights we could find. Anyway, I knew but he didn't. When it came time for all of us to warm up I took off my wrestling jacket for the first time.

He was on the same mat doing the same thing. He'd been trying to intimidate me that morning also, but, when he saw me without a jacket for the first time the intimidator became the intimidated. I could see the split-second transformation plainly on his face. He wasn't laughing anymore and neither were his friends. The upshot is I won the match thirteen to nothing. I did that on purpose. I wanted to score more points on him than he had the night before on his first opponent. I could have pinned him anytime I wanted to but I was in no mood for that. In my mind it was payback time. The match had to be stopped three times because he was bleeding profusely. I broke his nose.

In a bit of irony, at the end of the match he had to be helped off the mat. I hadn't realized the people in the stands had taken such a keen interest in our match. When the referee, who realized what I was doing halfway through and warned me to cut it out, raised my hand in victory, the place went wild. I was surprised by the response. Evidently everyone was happy to see the bully get his comeuppance. At the time I didn't think much of it but all day people came up to me to thank me and to congratulate me. After all that I was feeling pretty good about myself. I had taken it personally because he had mocked me in front of everyone, and I was still upset with the way he treated his first opponent. I had never taken a match personally before.

Thinking back on that I now know what mistakes I made that day. In the first place in my zeal to knock the wise guy off his perch I changed my personality and lowered myself to his level. When it was all over I was really no better than he was. Just because he was a bully was no excuse for me to turn into one. What I should have done was go out there and do what I had trained to do and pin him, and score more points for my team. That personal vendetta I carried onto the mat cost my team points even if it went over well with the crowd. My responsibility was to my team first, and any personal feelings should never have entered it. But now, being a conscious person who would have considered that the right thing to do, I got carried away with the moment and let my team down. In spite of the fact that none of them complained and they too enjoyed watching the bad guy get it. There were some college scouts out there who, ironically because of that match, wanted me to wrestle for them.

I went into that match seeking revenge. Revenge is never something a conscious person should ever be involved in. Revenge and bacon make a good analogy. Just about everyone loves bacon, but at the same time, we know it's not good for us. We love the taste of it, just as the taste of revenge is sweet, but there's a potential price to be paid for that pleasure. It might be sweet at the moment but the price we pay for revenge is a major setback in our conscious path.

Revenge can't normally be achieved as quickly as mine. Instead, the negative feeling is inside you and just grows and festers. You're the only one being hurt. Every second you think about what you'd like to do to get even is time taken away from enjoying your here and now. You're spending precious time that can't be made up, thinking and planning and stewing while the object of your planned vengeance is merrily going along with his or her life. There's a good chance the person has already moved on so you're the one left holding the bag. I realize it's not an easy thing to do, especially since revenge can be so satisfying, but what you need to do is to just let it go. Forget about it. Wipe it completely from your mind. Every time the thought of revenge enters your mind you need to quickly change the subject in your head. No matter how often the vengeful thoughts pop up, immediately bring yourself back to whatever is happening in the moment you are living. Don't give it a chance to develop. Planning revenge is fun. Dreaming about what you'd like to do to that so-and-so can make you feel better. Realize that whatever caused you to get to the point of having those thoughts is something that happened in the past, and therefore is no longer a part of your life. File it in the dead file. Get on with your life and the more you do that, the faster the need for revenge will dissipate.

That doesn't mean you need to let people get away with things. Many people are like children. If they get away with something that emboldens them to push to see how far they can go, and how much more you're willing to take. But, if you want to rectify the problem you'll have to go about it another way and without malice in your heart. Remember, the other person is probably not churning inside, you are. No matter what the other person has done to you, and no matter how tempting the prospect of seeing them pay, as a conscious individual you can't pick and choose when you feel like being conscious. It's not something you live only when it's convenient and easy, but especially when it's difficult and your instincts tell you otherwise. As Francis Bacon wrote in *Of Revenge*, "In taking revenge man is but even with his enemy, but in passing over, he is superior."

The worst extreme of being judgmental may be hypocrisy. I'm sure you know hyprocritical people: they can find all sorts of faults with something others do but when they do the exact same thing they don't seem to notice. They have a double standard. They hold other people accountable for mistakes or the way they do something or any number of things, but if you told them that's exactly what they do—somehow that's news to them. They might even get angry if you bring it up. Their perception of themselves is so fragile that any criticism or comment, even if it is plainly evident to everyone else, just can't be tolerated. That's not a good thing because having that attitude hinders their growth. They can never improve in that aspect of their life for the fact they can't accept the reality that that's how they indeed do act. With that being the case there's no way for them to consciously try to change it. It's obvious if they find some thing to be an unattractive quality in others they don't think it's a good quality at all. You really should never set the standard you consider acceptable behavior higher for others than you do for yourself. As a matter of fact, since you shouldn't be judging people or setting any kind of standard for them to live up to at all that should be a moot point.

Since so many of these people who try to slide by believing the rules apply only to others, a common trait to be found in this group is hypocrisy. What make hypocrites so despicable is the fact that they have the nerve to make moral judgments, and are usually more than willing to tell others how to lead their lives, when their own lives are in disarray.

An example we're all familiar with is the case of Jimmy Swaggart. Talk of being self-righteous, this guy takes the cake, although he's far from being alone in that. If he had spent less time with hookers and more time leading the life he demanded of his followers, he wouldn't look like such a pitiful soul in the public's eyes. If you saw his "apology" with the tears flowing, he carefully didn't mention what he actually did, all he said was: "I have sinned." Euripides in *Electra* almost 2500 years ago hit the nail on the head when he said: "Often a noble face hides filthy ways."

And, the worst thing about Swaggart is that instead of having a live and let live approach to life, he extols his gullible flock to lead a straight and moral life, while he's doing just the opposite, all the while pleading for more money. I guess that proves two things: Prostitutes can get expensive, and some people just have no shame.

All of us, and not just the conscious ones, can see this "moral" person is nothing of the kind. If you're a hypocrite, by definition, you're a liar. When confronted about their behavior they'll say something like: "Why would I ever do such a thing?" and will probably act insulted that you had the nerve to bring it up. They use their supposed morality as a smokescreen to hide their true lives. If someone gives me that line or a similar one that sounds logical, the first thing I think of is "watch out. You have to be careful when talk that way: "Why would I ever do such a thing?" "How could you think I would ever say that?" "I can't believe you'd think I'd be a party to something like that."

We've all heard those lines. It's possible they're speaking the truth, but just as likely it's the "moral indignation while talking out of both sides of the mouth double speak." They might be 100% guilty of whatever it is, but they try to deflect blame by acting indignant and questioning the motive of others for having the nerve to even bring the matter up.

It's as if the matter were beneath them and not even fit for them to bother answering; although it in reality might be exactly what they're doing and how they're living their life. They have trouble admitting their shortcomings to themselves, much less others. Logic seems to be in short supply when they come to assessing themselves, but apply it without a second thought, to the behavior of others.

For example, it's only logical if you expect other people to live their lives in a certain way, you'd follow the same rules you apply to everyone else.

When we see people who are in a leadership position and who, through their good work over the years, have improved the lives of countless others, but are found out to be hypocritical, we find it very disappointing more than anything else. That would be the case with the Rev. Jesse Jackson. When people with ostensibly impeccable moral fiber get caught, they hurt many more than their family and close associates. Whatever causes they espouse also become the victims and the hypocrisy becomes fodder for anyone plotting to discredit their work.

Hypocrites become expert at the art of talking out of both

sides of their mouth, a skill developed by constant application. They conceal and lie, even to themselves. If a person lies enough they can start to believe the lines they gave others, themselves. If a person says something enough no matter how outlandish or untrue, since they're in the habit of "letting themselves slide" when it comes to the hard choices we all need to make, it's not a long throw from telling others untruths to believing it.

I truly believe, for instance, that O.J. Simpson has convinced himself that he really didn't kill his wife Nicole. That sentiment was put well by Andre Gide in *The Counterfeiters* (1921): "The true hypocrite is the one who ceases to perceive his deception, the one who lies with sincerity." O. J. wasn't around at the time, but Gide might as well have been speaking about him. I've met O.J. and one time my friends got paired with him on a local golf course. They weren't too thrilled about that, but if you know golfers they'll play with Satan if it means getting a tee time. I've probably seen him half a dozen times on different courses. The local joke is that he's check-ing out all the area golf courses to find Nicole's real killer. I don't know if you remember, but at the time of his murder trial he made it a point to tell everyone he was going to track down the real murderer. But, why not have a little fun while you're at it? There's no way he'd ever admit to the facts for number of obvious reasons, but the one reason that isn't so obvious is he can't even admit it to himself. Ev-ery time I've seen him he was joking around and laughing. I'd be a happy guy too if I got away with what he did, but then again, would you or I?

Sometimes our best efforts to not judge don't seem to be enough. I'm sure we've all noticed recently that it's not that hard to offend a person or a group. It's almost as if people are looking for something to get upset about. Amercia is noticing that political cor-rectness is starting to get out of hand. You might innocently make a mistake and use the wrong terminology in describing someone or something. It's hard to keep up with the designated correct terminol-ogy du jour for any of the seemingly million or so advocacy or inter-est groups. You can't be sure if you're putting your foot in your mouth when you open it. For instance, you now can't call a little person a midget without offending. But unless the preferred designation is posted for everyone to see and you haven't recently had contact with someone of short stature, how are you supposed to know? Osmosis? Innocent mistakes are no longer taken that way. That attitude of perceived slights is now everywhere. From groups taking offense in the naming of sports teams to obscure advocacy programs you've never heard of and who seem to spring up out of nowhere, or could even imagine existed.

There was an article in the paper recently where in Nepal three people were killed in rioting. Why were they rioting? Someone had started a rumor that an Indian film star said he didn't like people from Nepal. The fact that no one ever heard him utter the slur didn't seem to matter. Both the television station that gave the interview and the film star himself even stated that nothing of the kind was said. It boggles the mind the lengths people will go to right a perceived wrong that didn't exist in the first place. If it weren't for the fact that a young girl was killed by a stray bullet while she was at home reading, it would almost be laughable.

You have to be sensitive to other people's concerns and if possible accommodate their wishes when it comes to ethnicity or religion or any subject that can touch a nerve. Even if you can't fathom why the sensitivity is there it the first place, or see how it could possibly be. Things that are irrational to some are completely rational to others. For the life of me I can't understand why some Native Americans think it's a terrible thing to have Atlanta's baseball team called the Braves. I can see why Washington's football team, the Redskins, could cause a negative reaction among Native Americans, but the Braves? I'm sure they have their reasons but I'm not sure even if they were explained to me that I'd completely understand them. I don't see the negative connotation or understand how that denigrates Native Americans. I can't see through others' eyes or have their perceptions of things or their history and experiences to go by. But, just because I might not understand it, doesn't mean I shouldn't be sensitive to others' feelings on the matter. That also doesn't mean you'll always "do the right thing." Just as most of us don't understand the workings of a jet engine, we still know it works.

We don't have to understand everything and we shouldn't be expected to when it comes to many matters. As conscious individuals we know not to take offense at slights, real or imagined. Whereas others will display righteous indignation when they feel someone is putting them or their group down, we don't. We understand that we can't control how others think or talk, and if they choose to go through life ignorant or without trying to understand others' feelings, so be it. If someone called me a "dumb wop," what concern would that be to me? It's not my life's work defending Italians against stupid people. If someone has hatred in their heart, they're the ones who have to live with themselves, not me. If they think that way I almost feel sorry for them. Can you imagine having to inhabit such a narrow and unforgiving mind?

Since our true life is lived in our brains, and the outside world is just incidental, being narrow minded and hateful must be a terribly unpleasant way to go through life. Serenity will never be achieved by people who are not willing to see others' points of view or accept people the way they are, but spend life resenting and distorting the world they see. Serenity will always be out of their reach, but is always close to ours.

CHAPTER EIGHT
BE COMMITTED AND FOCUSED

Again, using the stock market as an analogy, you don't want to go through life being a day trader. Flitting in and out, and not staying long enough to really master anything. If you're now planning on starting to spread your wings and attempting new things you need to stay with them to find out what they're all about, and if you'd like to proceed further. Day traders contribute nothing and have a very narrow sphere of reference. Most of them lose money and even if they eventually do make money, what exactly have they accomplished? To my eyes—nothing. That hit and run, in and out lifestyle really can't be all that rewarding. People who have the fortitude to stick with something, even if they're initially not very good at it, are amply rewarded by their gradual improvement.

You might not be the best Yoga student in the world, or never really get very good at it, but who cares? If you enjoy it and keep at it, you'll become the best Yoga practitioner you can be, and that in itself is a worthy goal. I never imagined myself writing a book. It never entered my mind. But here I am writing and enjoying every minute of it. Right now I can't think of anything I'd rather be doing. Part of the fun is knowing that people will be helped by reading this. I'll change some people's outlook on life for the better. That's a great motivator for me. It's something that takes a lot of my time and even takes me away from other things I enjoy. I haven't taken a long walk on the beach in months, something I'd always done, although the beach is just four blocks from my house. I couldn't care less. It's important that you don't ever let the fact that you feel inferior about a particular subject to influence you in any way. Everyone is good at something, and nobody is good at everything, and **absolutely no one is better than you**. Remember that. If you can master living your life in a conscious fashion, you've done one of the hardest things anyone can do. When you reach a level in your thinking where you feel you've taken control of your life and not the other way around, you'll firmly believe that with concerted effort you can do anything you set your mind to. If you enjoy what you're doing, no matter who's better or worse at it, then in my mind you've mastered it. You've mastered the most important thing—getting enjoyment and fulfillment out of something. And that is as worthy a goal as any I can imagine.

For most of my life I had a bad habit of working on impulse instead of consciously deciding whether doing something would be prudent. My mother had always told me that I was intelligent but lacked common sense.

When I went to college I never gave much consideration about what I wanted to do with my life. I've come to realize that I'm a late bloomer. A very late bloomer. Things that most people spend time considering at a fairly early age, didn't occur to me until years after most people have already moved on. I'm slow, but if my life lasts a couple of hundred years, that should give me just about the right amount of time to catch up. Even after two years of college, when most people put enough thought into it that they can decide their major with some confidence, I was still totally clueless. I always had an interest in history, so without any reflection at all, I chose it that as my major. I was never a great student but because I looked like a nerd and wore horn-rimmed glasses people assumed I knew what I was doing. Their perception of me was not at all accurate and I pretty much wasted my four years in college. Having not initially thought it through, I basically just went through the motions and was more concerned about where the next party was. I graduated with a B.A. in history and absolutely no job skills. There's not much call for people with training in something like that unless I wanted to teach, but I didn't, and even if I decided to, I didn't take the right courses that would allow me to get my credential. So, when I graduated I wound up in retail management.

Retail management and real estate sales are the refuge for people like me, with a college degree and no real relevant job skills. In retail I was pretty successful but was still clueless as to what I really wanted to do. After five years with the same company I quit my retail management job, and again with not a bit of thought, I packed up and left Southern California and moved to a small town in Northern California, where I went into the restaurant business with a good friend. I had no idea if I'd like it or not, and since I didn't think it through at all I didn't know what to expect. Owning a restaurant is extremely tough. We worked eighty hours a week with only one day off every third week. We had a small stage in the restaurant and on the weekends would have bands playing after the restaurant closed for the night. They were usually rock and roll and sometimes bluegrass (for the locals). Since neither of us could stand country and western music, that was the only music we didn't have. On Tuesday nights we'd have Jazz and on Wednesday nights Contra Dancing, which is a type of Square Dancing, also for the locals.

We held benefits for the neighboring Hoopa Indian tribe and even staged plays and comedy nights. It wasn't at all unusual for us to start our day at 9:00 a.m. and finish up the following morning at 4:00 a.m. We'd get some sleep and start all over again. You can only do that for so long and after about a year I quit. My friend stayed on a while longer and he eventually sold the business. I moved back to L.A. and had no job and no prospects. So, I drifted back into retail but with a less prestigious job than I had in my first retail stint, and worse, making a lot less money. I still wasn't consciously planning my future. But, by now, I finally had enough of the drifting, of the "Even a blind pig finds an acorn in the pigsty every once in a while" theory of success and life. For the first time I thought it might be a good idea to start planning before it was time for me to retire.

So, I went to one of the local colleges and had them give me a job skills test to see what I was best suited for. I was now thirty and still drifting. As I've said, I was a late bloomer. The results of the test showed I'd have made a good pharmacist. Having neither the desire nor the money to prepare for that profession, I felt I was no better off than before. But, at least now I was making an effort to try and find my niche. When I was at a four-day managers meeting in Chicago for the company I was then working for, I decided I couldn't keep blundering my way through life without any plan or foresight. I wasn't paying much attention to the meeting anyway, so it gave me time to think. I needed an occupation, and I knew if I thought about it hard enough and took my time I would make a much better choice. I didn't want to make the same mistakes and later realize I wasn't suited for this new line of work.

At the time I was studying Ken Keyes' *The Handbook to Higher Consciousness*, so I was for the first time actually starting to get a clue. Reading that book six times started me on the road to conscious living. Almost overnight my murky thinking began to crystallize and I began the real search for some way to make a living that I enjoyed. That's basically what I was looking for. That was more important to me than anything.

I read an article written about the optical industry and it sounded interesting. I studied up on what occupations were available in that field. My sister Nikki had wanted me to become an optometrist. For some reason she just thought that line of work would be appealing to me. I am very fortunate to have a person such as her and I consider her one of the most quality human beings I know. Again, I didn't have the money to go back to college to get a degree in optometry so I thought since optician was the equivalent of a pharmacist, that would be a good choice. Since I'd already gotten a four-year degree all I needed was three hundred and sixty four hours of instruction in Optician School. I was working full time so I went to class at night. For six months I'd go to school four nights a week for four hours a night. When I graduated I had no problem finding a job. I was making more than twice my retail management salary and was for the first time in quite a while, doing something I enjoyed. No offense to retailers, but I wanted a profession where I'd be doing something that entailed different skills. Being a good retail manager was easy for me so, now I wanted something I found more challenging and more interesting.

It took me an eternity to finally come to the realization that life works best when you put some thought and effort into it. That's the point of this whole thing. If you want to enjoy all the wonderful things life has to offer, you need to consciously and deliberately work at it. You can't just sit back and let things happen and hope that it will work out fine in the end. It doesn't work that way for most of us. And, you should never just settle for things.

Recently, I spoke with a friend who'd been working at Fox Studios here in L.A. as a secretary, and she and her husband had just lost their jobs. She was a bit depressed with the prospect of having to look for work again. She'd always wanted to be an actress (and is attractive and has acted). She asked for my advice. I know it might sound odd after reading this book but I'm not one to give advice, and if I do it's only when asked. I asked her if she was still interested in acting and she said she was. I basically just told her that she's still young and if acting is what she really wanted, then that's where she needed to direct her energies. I pointed out that if she gave her best effort and failed she'd at least have chased her dream. But, in order to not shortchange herself, she had to make an honest effort at it and not just a half-hearted attempt.

This conversation took place about six months ago and when I spoke to her this week she was very excited because she just landed a part in a commercial, and she was flying up to San Francisco to shoot it. Her diligence and determination was starting to pay off. In the meantime she's working at a retail store to help make ends meet, at the same time going on auditions whenever her agent sets one up. If she succeeds then she'd be one of the few people fortunate enough to do what truly makes them happy. In situations such as that, you are presented with a chance to actively take hold of your life and change its direction.

In this case, by losing her job, the decision to change was already made for her. The opportunity was there for her to seize and not to passively let the circumstances dictate her actions. She could always find another job, but the chance to find your life's work, something that would make her happy, is not something that comes along every day. If opportunity doesn't knock on your door, as it did with the young actress, it would be a good idea for you to look for it. Life is much more meaningful and fulfilling if you can wake up each morning looking forward to the day, every day. Even if doing what really makes you happy isn't possible, there are always other things, maybe not exactly your dream, but still rewarding. Sometimes you just can't make a living or the opportunity isn't there. Since no one else can or will kick start you, it's your responsibility to yourself to give yourself the best chance to find daily happiness. Don't be complacent. We all have a tendency to do just that. Make it a point not to sit back and wait for something to happen. Because, unfortunately, the things that seem to happen when we're complacent aren't usually good.

In order to keep a positive self-image, it's important that whenever we do anything we always do it to the best or our ability. Once you have the self-image you're comfortable with you have to maintain it. That's accomplished by doing our best in everything from our jobs, to exercising, to writing a letter, to attending a class, to relaxing. We don't want to be the type of person who always takes the easy way out. When you went to school I'm sure you knew people, or maybe you even did this yourself in a pinch, who used Cliff's Notes as a crutch. The old line that usually follows discovery of its use is, "you're only cheating yourself." It may be a cliché, but we all know it's true. In that case, since the person really didn't learn anything of substance, just an outline of the book they were supposed to read, it was pretty much a waste of time. When the person had the opportunity to enrich themselves, they instead made the choice not to. The time spent diddling away, doing other things, when they should have been reading was misspent. The problem with quite a number of people is that they cut corners on just about everything they do. They're constantly looking for some kind of angle, some weak spot—anything that can be exploited. The thought of taking something head-on never occurs to them because that's not the way they think. Unfortunately, there are a lot of Rosie Ruiz clones out there. One of the drawbacks of that approach to life is that the image you hold of yourself, which sometimes may be a fragile thing at best, is not allowed a chance to grow positively. When you take shortcuts and try to constantly slide by, even if you fool everyone else, as you know, the most important person, you, is being short-changed. That's even if it doesn't feel so at the time. You know how you always feel a little better about yourself when you accomplish something, especially when it took great effort; you and others value the hard work and honest effort you've put in and rightfully so. It does mean something to try hard and counts for much in our feeling of self-worth and give us confidence in our abilities. You might wind up with the same results, but since the process is at least as important as the results, effort, and not time trying to find an angle, counts for much. We tend to appreciate things more if we worked hard to attain them than if they were given to us or we cheated to get them.

Along those lines, the first army expression I learned in basic training was "It's close enough for government work." That's an attitude that was prevalent in the way many of the men went about their duties. If you had to paint something, they'd slop some on, after all "it's close enough for government work." If they had to dig into a position, they'd do the minimal so they wouldn't get hassled, and besides, "it's close enough for government work." When you have that kind of attitude, there is absolutely no pride in a job well done. Instead of enriching your own life (after all no one else can do that for you) you add nothing positive to it. As a matter of fact, you're doing just the opposite, and detracting from the positive image you should be developing of yourself and your abilities.

The Los Angeles Marathon was recently run and for the second year in a row the same man was caught cheating. What I'd like to know is what's the point? Even if he got away with it, he's achieved nothing. I guess some people just have a very high humiliation level to go with a low work ethic. How bright can this guy be? Most people are smart enough to learn from their mistakes. Not only did he act foolish, he looked foolish. In any situation if you don't want to put out the effort then it's best not to do it at all. At least that way you won't be doing more harm than good to yourself.

If an opportunity to do something will help make you a more well rounded person, make sure you take advantage of it to the best or your ability. There is nothing too big or too small when it comes to that. If you're not doing it now, make a rule for everything you do to always try your very best.

Along those lines, you only get one chance to make a first impression. Most things aren't all-or-nothing, but first impressions are. Since someone you meet for the first time doesn't know you or anything about you, they can only make a judgment of your character by how they see you act. If you act confident and caring, that's how your character is etched in the new acquaintance's mind, because they have nothing else to go by. This should be done with an eye more towards how you view yourself than it is in trying to impress the new acquaintance.

CHAPTER NINE
TRUTHFUL EXPRESSION

One of the great benefits of living life consciously is to always **say what you mean and mean what you say.** Be open and honest with yourself and others. Never be a party to anything that doesn't fit your own moral parameters. Stand up for only those things that you've taken the time to filter through your screen of what you feel is moral and right. And be at peace with yourself in the knowledge that you've made the right choices.

So, in speaking, you should allow your true self to come out. If you say something out of character, and if you're beginning to live consciously, you'll immediately notice it and regret it. (Although you'll find the more conscious you are, the less you'll regret.) One, you'll think before you act or speak so you'll be much less prone to doing or saying something regrettable. And, two, you get to a point where you'll always take lessons from your mistakes, and instead of regretting, you learn from them so you won't repeat the regrettable act, and then you move on.

Conscious people don't try to build themselves up by knocking others down. It's more important to respect yourself than almost anything and regrettable speech takes you further from that. Publilius Syrus over two thousand years ago touched on just that when he wrote: "Speech is the mirror of the soul; as a man speaks so is he." And so he is perceived by others. So, it's at least as much for ourselves that we keep to the moral high ground, not only in actions, but also in our everyday speech, as it is for others.

Don't say anything about someone you wouldn't feel comfortable with them hearing. Being conscious means not putting ourselves in the position of having to apologize for ill-thought out speech, or to feel regret afterwards. You don't want to be worrying that something you've said about another that you really shouldn't have said, will get back to them.

Another reason that you need to always think first and monitor your speech is that what you say can have a profound affect on people, not only how they view you, but how they view themselves. Unkind words hurt. Words might not be able to hurt us, because as conscious people we learn how to view them, but not everyone knows how. And, you know how easy it is for people to be hurt. It's not a stretch to say that you can actually ruin another's day with an ill-thought-out or off-hand remark. If you try to hurt someone, it's not hard at all to do, and even if you do it by mistake, it hurts just as much. That's why it's so important to think first, speak second.

As I've said, I used to have a very bad temper. I could be quite intimidating if I wanted to. My first roommate many years ago was another Italian with a worse temper than mine. Some combination. He could and would intimidate people twice his size, and rather enjoyed doing it. At times he could be downright nasty. We both were managers for the same company and didn't know each other too well when we decided to split the rent on an apartment. We were both in our mid-twenties at the time. On our first day in the new place he unpacked all his kitchenware first and used every drawer leaving no room for mine. He also took the biggest bedroom with the private bath, without the courtesy of even asking if it was okay with me. The guy didn't even consider me when he did it. That wasn't such a good idea at the time. I started unpacking and soon discovered what he'd done. I thought that rather selfish and told him so. Immediately he started in with the heavy guns, no preliminaries at all—he just started ranting and screaming in an effort to hurt me and make me back down. He'd always gotten his way doing just that and expected to this time also. Unfortunately for him he picked the wrong guy at the wrong time. He was about five foot nine and I'm over six foot one. I got right in his face, or in this case the top of his head, and told him that if he had a desire not to spend his first night in the hospital instead of his new big bedroom, he'd better rethink how he was going to go about this roommate arrangement.

At the time I really didn't take any crap from anybody. That's because I had more ego than brains. I could see the shock on his face when he saw the veins on my neck getting bigger and bigger, and my face getting redder and redder. He wasn't used to people standing up to him. By that time I wasn't talking, I was yelling. We must have made a real good impression on our new neighbors. I told him we were going to settle this right on the spot, and if he didn't like it, to do something about it. I said if he wanted to use all the drawers he could pay the majority of the rent, although I had no intention of actually letting him get away with it. He was bald and he looked a lot like Larry from the Three Stooges. I wasn't above using anything at the time so I started calling him Clarabelle, the clown character from the old Howdy Doody Show. I knew he absolutely hated being called that so that's why I chose it. I Clarabelle'd him this way and that, until he had enough and gave in. Although he was still muttering under his breath, he cleared out half the drawers. I didn't care about the bedroom. In the couple of years we were roommates he never even came close to raising his voice to me, although to everyone else he was still a tyrant. People would always ask me about that because everyone noticed how well he treated me. I just told them we had reached an understanding and left it at that.

The point is, if we disregard the feelings of others, we can, much of the time, get our way. But, just because you are capable of doing something, it doesn't make it right if you do it. Even if it's expedient for you to act in that fashion, and it makes it easier to get what you want, it's certainly not the right way to go about it. The ends don't always justify the means. And, just because someone else does it to you, you're not justified in reacting in kind. I could have gotten the same results by staying calm, answering him in a firm, measured way, and standing my ground, but, at the time that wasn't in my repertoire.

People can't have their way with you without your permission. If you are right and stand up for yourself, no matter what the other person is doing or saying, you can't be forced into something that you think is wrong. You are in control of what you do and no amount of haranguing or intimidation should ever have any bearing on what you decide. Have faith in yourself and when you say no, mean it.

Conversely, if you have a desire to do something, and you've thought it out and decided it's the right thing to do, go ahead with it even if others don't approve. Don't ever allow someone else to do the deciding for you. If you do things consciously, you'll develop the confidence in yourself to make the right decisions.

In the case with my roommate I blew up. That's something I would never do now. In the past ten years I've lost my temper only twice, both with the same person, and that's after some major provocation, and in the last five years I haven't lost my temper once. One reason I never allow myself to get to that point anymore is the fact that whenever I really lost my temper I'd always feel bad about it afterwards. That's even if I got my way. I call it the "regret test." It goes for anything. No matter if it's in speech or action, if you regret doing it after your emotions die down, you can be sure it wasn't the right way to approach the situation.

One of the problems I had was I was insecure and my ego could be easily bruised. It seems like the louder the mouth the larger the ego problem. Since most of us have some insecurities we have a tendency to over-react to what we perceive as provocation. But, if you want to feel good about yourself at all times your ego really shouldn't come into play.

Another obligation you have to yourself in regards to speaking, and this has a lot to do with how people perceive you, is to speak only when you really have something to say. Many people talk when they really don't have anything of importance to say. It's as if they like to hear the sound of their voice, even if nothing of value comes out. The problem with that is when they do have a valid point people tend not to pay as much attention because it gets lost in the avalanche of words. It's like sitting down to a delicious meal. If you overeat it loses its appeal, but if you eat just the right amount, the experience is satisfying. I listen to people's conversations all the time, not that I eavesdrop, but in the normal course of the day, you overhear things. Ninety percent of what I hear is what I call "filler." Most conversation is "filler." A conscious person may not be the most talkative person but at least when he or she speaks the listeners know there will be some value to what they have to say. Phillipe de Commynes in his memoirs put it: "One never repents having spoken too little, but often of having spoken too much."

The more you say the more prone you are to saying not only too much, but the wrong thing. People don't normally think about that. We've all on occasion said things that as soon as they left our mouth we wish we could retract. We've all done it and had the same reaction. "Why did I say that?" Sometimes we don't even know why we say what we do, and that has a lot to do with not thinking before speaking. This is a subject that I've heard only a little about, and it's often overlooked when discussing speech. But, to live a conscious life it's an everyday part of how we go about things. Don't just say anything that pops into your head.

Remember that you do have influence on others and how they view things, so be careful how you influence others. A particularly insidious form of manipulation is gossip. As a conscious person that's something you need to take care to avoid. If you're involved in a conversation and the person starts gossiping, speaking disparagingly about another outside their presence, and you feel yourself getting sucked in, the best thing to do is to stop and not get involved. Many times people will relay gossip with the express intent of influencing how you feel about another person, and it usually doesn't put them in the best light. Either tell them you're not interested or if you're afraid of hurting their feelings, don't give them any feedback when they start. Change the subject if possible.

Many times gossipers want you to join in because if they respect you, and you join in, they feel you're validating their position. If you don't, they're pretty much left hanging and will probably start to feel a little uncomfortable. That's because since we were children we were told gossiping is not the right thing to do. They know that – but relaying some juicy gossip is a hard thing for most of us not to do. In the first place it's always fun when you know something your friends don't, especially if it's at all unusual and everyone knows the parties involved. Although you may just be relaying what you heard, you get to weave a story, interpret it the way you want, and feel almost a part of it in the retelling.

A friend recently called me from his home in Maryland. He'd just done something really stupid and for some reason felt the need to tell me. It turns out he was being hauled before his company's attorney to answer to charges of sexual harassment. If you knew this guy you'd never think he'd be the one to have someone charge him with that. He's an accountant and looks and acts pretty conservatively, usually.

The poor guy couldn't get more than a few words in without me interrupting him asking why and what. I knew I shouldn't have interrupted him but it was so out of character for him I had trouble believing he was telling me the truth. I'll put it this way, he brought some pictures to work that didn't show his best side, and foolishly showed them around. A lot of my friends are his friends, and as he filled me in on the details of his stupidity, the first thing I thought was, "I can't wait to get off the phone, because as soon as I do, I'm calling Lew," a mutual friend. I left out all the details in relating this, but, suffice it say, something like this doesn't come around very often, not at least in my life. And, it wasn't over, there was more to come. He now has to drive to Baltimore for sensitivity classes. It was a gossip work in progress, the best kind.

We'd been friends for at least twenty-five years and at one time worked for the same company and were even roommates for a while. One thing about leading a conscious life is that since you hold yourself to a higher standard, you can't let yourself get away with things. *I wanted to relay what I'd just heard, but I knew he had told me, not our mutual friends, so it would have been a breach of trust to blab.* Of course, if I asked him if it was okay, and he said yes,

I was free and clear to start dialing. So, I did. And, since he didn't mind I was now free to tell a few other mutual friends. If he said no, that would have been the end of it, and I would have kept my mouth shut. Our friends were as blown away as I was, and we all had a good laugh about it. It was actually a very minor transgression and a very funny story. My female friends enjoyed the story as much as my male friends.

I lost no respect for him but now thought of him in a different light. You don't often hear people relate tales about themselves that make them look foolish, but in this case, he was almost gossiping about himself. I think if the matter were more serious, he would have kept quiet. One thing you always want to remember is that when you gossip you tell more about yourself than you do about the object of the gossip.

Another way people try to change our perception of someone is through innuendo. They don't actually come right out and say what they really mean, but give enough not-so-subtle hints to make sure you get the idea. I think they feel if they don't come out and just say something, then it's not really gossiping, and it's okay. It's not. That's just someone trying to justify aberrant behavior to themselves. You're left with enough information to draw your own conclusions, which can be a problem since they deliberately left things out. You could easily jump to the wrong conclusions. Then you're playing a semantics game, and games are for children. Since people may feel if they don't come out and paint the full picture then somehow they're not responsible for spreading the gossip, it makes it that much easier for them to justify their actions. If you ever do something, gossip or not, and have to justify your actions, there's a good chance it wasn't the right thing to do. You should never put yourself in the position of having to justify anything that you do or say. As with gossip, it's best to leave the innuendo to others, and let them justify their words, whether others believe them or not.

A close cousin of gossip and innuendo is rumor. For many of the same reasons as the other two, spreading rumors or being a party to hearsay is unhealthy. People's lives have been ruined because someone started a rumor about them. I think rumor is probably as old as man's first language. They're easy to start. Just make something up, or embellish something you've heard, preferably negative and titillating, and pass it along as fact. Rumor can also contain a kernel of truth, but is presented in a way that sheds negative light on the person being rumored about. Rumors can be used as a strategy to gain the upper hand, especially in politics or during war, or to hurt someone who's on the "outs." Besides besmirching an individual, if the rumor you help spread is found to be groundless, you're left with egg on your face. It's another one of those instances where you'd be much happier if no one ever started a rumor about you, so obviously others would appreciate the same courtesy. An old Spanish proverb puts it: "Whoever gossips to you will gossip about you." That also goes for innuendo and rumor. If you dish it out, you're more likely to have to take it. Another reason you never want to get involved with any of the above is trust. If you want to be respected, not talking negatively about someone outside of their presence is all part of that.

As you can see, it's really not that hard for perceptions to change, or be influenced to change. So, as a conscious person, you realize your responsibility to monitor what you say about others. You can be counted on by friends and family to say only what you know to be true, and not pass on what you don't know for a fact, and if you are entrusted with a personal matter they can be sure you'll keep it personal.

Even when we aren't trying to gossip, we can easily color others' perceptions. If someone talks something down, that person is devaluing whatever it is in others' eyes. It's like putting "only" in front of another word. "He studied really hard for the test and only got a B." By using the word "only," someone is now giving an opinion instead of just relaying what transpired. They might not have meant it, but that's what they did, and we go by what people say, not what they mean to say. That's why you always need to think before speaking so you'll say exactly what you mean and not be ambiguous. If you describe something to someone else don't make it an opinion unless that's exactly what you mean to do. Since you only need one word to change an entire meaning, you need to choose your words carefully and thoughtfully.

People who walk by my shop will often say something like this when they read our sign: "Oh, it's another sunglass store, just what we need." That little piece of sarcasm reduces years of hard work that we've put in to no more than an afterthought, all with one flippant comment. If the person that they're walking with is new to the area anytime they hear of Blue Moon Optical, they'll think, "oh just another sunglass store." In reality, we're trained and experienced optical professionals, but because of that type of comment, we're reduced to nothing more than sunglass peddlers in some eyes. People who do business with us know the truth. We're good at what we do and keep up with all the latest advancements in lens and frame design. We're expert at choosing the correct frame and type of lens best suited for our clients' needs. I truly believe that our clients are fortunate in doing business with us because you never know when you walk into any situation for the first time if you'll be treated fairly or not. There is a lot of misinformation given out by some opticians either through lack of education or sloppiness. People come to find that when they come into the shop that they'll not only be treated fairly, they can also be assured we won't be trying to sell them expensive add-ons they don't really need.

It's always a crapshoot when you go someplace for the first time. You don't know what type of experience it will be, short and smooth or long and unproductive. The reason people who deal with us are so fortunate is that the experience is surprisingly painless and even fun for them. That's something we consciously try to always supply. A positive experience. And, it's not like people don't notice. I've been told countless times by clients that they are so glad they found us and their experience in our store was nothing but positive, and they always walked away with a good impression and would do business with us in the future and will recommend us to their friends. If a client recommends us to a friend, we do everything in our power to live up to that trust. They also give us the war stories of their experiences they've had in other optical shops. It's amazing how many people who deal with the public don't know the most important quality any business can have is good customer relations. That's just like me when I was young. It's really very simple, just treat everyone like you'd like to be treated. That's how all your dealings should be framed, with anyone, anywhere, and at any time. It makes life that much more pleasant when you follow that rule everyday and in any situation. The Golden Rule is as relevant now as it was when it was first postulated. So, we're far from being "just another sunglass store."

Even the tone of voice can give new meaning to the same words. That's why it is so important that you clearly enunciate what you're trying to say. Say exactly what you mean to say so there is never any ambiguity. You don't want people to have to try to figure out what you really mean. I call that politician-speak, when someone has to read between the lines in an effort to get at the message you're really trying to convey. There is no need for that.

I think we all know someone who speaks just like that. I knew a man who would never answer my questions directly. Even if it were something of little or no importance he would dance around the answer and never answer directly what was asked. It was very frustrating for people to try to get a straight answer out of him. There is no reason to ever do that. Either you answer or you don't, it's pretty clear-cut. But, there is no excuse for purposely being vague or evasive with your answers.

With too many people, their language is vague because they really don't want to commit to anything. They feel if they say "the wrong thing" it will cause friction with others, so when they speak they really don't say anything of substance at all. As conscious people we have no fear of anything, much less what others might think or say in reaction to our words. We are not part of the Sheep Brigade who goes along because we feel if we stray from the group attitude we have to worry about a negative reaction. It's just so much easier to go along. Conscious people don't usually make waves. We seek to try to keep our life flowing in a seamless fashion. We also don't go along just to go along. There has to be a valid reason for us to speak or act. We might not always conform but if we don't it's for a sound reason. When I say conform I don't mean you mindlessly follow the crowd. I just mean you try to accommodate others' wishes as much as possible. So, in both speech and actions be sure to be clear regarding your intentions. That's just old fashioned, plain and simple honesty.

If you've ever watched "Seinfeld," the character Kramer is an example of stream of consciousness speaking. It's part of his character. Whatever is thought is verbalized no matter how inane or inappropriate. He doesn't even take people's feelings into account when he opens his mouth. It's funny on the show but in real life it's not. The Bible, in Proverb 29:11 speaks to just that point: "A fool uttereth all his mind." Conscious people are the antithesis of the fool. Don't take that to mean you shouldn't talk. But, think first, talk second. It's like a carpenter who wants to do the job right: he always measures twice and cuts once. Think twice before speaking once, or as Epictetus put it two thousand years ago in his *Discourses*: "First learn the meaning of what you say, and then speak." Just as with anything else in our lives, if you want to be the very best you can be, it's always quality over quantity. It's obvious this way of thinking goes back to ancient times, so given it's history, and the fact that it actually works, it does have validity. When words are measured, speech also becomes more lucid. You will notice the quality of your self-expression will improve. You'll have a tendency to get to the point in a more timely manner and even your vocabulary will change for the better. That's due to the fact that you'll spend a lot more time thinking than saying. Your ideas will naturally have more time to formulate.

Some people will almost always tell you what they think you want to hear, not what they really think. They do that for a number of possible reasons. One reason being that they're insecure and want to be liked. They feel if they have the same opinions as you, you'll like them better. Human nature being what it is, many times that's true.

Another reason is that they're trying to pull the wool over

your eyes. How many times have we seen a politician or nominee for a high-ranking government position have a sudden and miraculous transformation? The positions they espouse while sitting in front of a Senate committee are diametrically opposed to the positions they've espoused their whole lives. For them it's a convenience that helps them get the job they court. Whether they follow up and take the new positions seriously is a matter of debate. If they don't, then they've been dishonest and aren't worthy of the position they sought.

The most familiar "agreeable talkers" to most of us are some salespeople, who, in order to make the sale, will tell you how marvelous you look I whatever you're trying on, no matter how bad it really looks. Or, the used car salesman, who'll omit certain things in his sales pitch. For instance, they might "forget" to inform you about an accident the car you're looking at was involved in.

I used to pride myself on my ability to always get the last word in. That was especially true in confrontational situations. You know how after an argument you always think "I should have said this or that," or "Oh, I wish I had thought of that ten minutes ago"? And you reproach yourself because you didn't think of the right zinger when you had the chance. "If I could only re-do it," so the thinking goes, I could have gotten that so-and-so really good. For some reason I always managed to say what I wanted to exactly when I wanted to. I was incredibly good at shooting people down. Especially those I thought deserving of it and who I thought needed a lesson. I never thought "what if" because I said it all in the heat of the argument. I developed the knack over the years and I was especially adroit at withering sarcasm. Thinking back on it I realize that was a really dumb thing to have pride in. I was so expert at the useless art of sarcasm when I should have been directing my energies to something that was actually worthwhile. And, although the people I zinged the hardest were the kind you'd love to see get it, especially the arrogant and snobbish, my favorite targets, that really wasn't my place.

Sometimes I almost felt I was performing some kind of community service. It was as if I were a Highway Patrolman pulling over a dangerous driver on the freeway. I was more than willing to provide that service. I'd do it for myself and for others if I thought they were being bullied and needed a little help. To be honest I sometimes enjoyed it immensely, especially if I thought I was helping the underdog. I don't do that anymore. Because I enjoyed doing it so much it was quite a challenge for me to give it up. But being conscious I know now that whatever someone's attitude, I don't need to humiliate them to feel good about myself, or put them down for sport. As my ego shrank I understood the need to be non-confrontational and more relaxed in my thinking. If someone wants to act the fool or walk around feeling superior, I don't really care anymore. My only job is to make sure I'm the best person possible and all other things are secondary. I now feel I can be of more help to people this way because now my words have more meaning and aren't spoken in anger, thus getting my point across more clearly without making enemies. But, still, on occasion, the urge strikes.

Especially in certain situations. For instance, I could never understand the truly snooty attitude of sales clerks in exclusive shops. It's as if they thought they actually designed and manufactured the items, instead of just selling them. Unless you look like you have money, good luck trying to be waited on. I think it's their condescending attitude more than anything that gets people's goat. I don't look like I have two nickels to rub together, so I'm used to it. I don't take it personally, no matter what the intent, and neither should you, if it happens to you. I'm probably the only customer of Nordstrom, whose reputation was made on good customer service, that's been ignored even if I needed help. I never get upset about it, but just move on to another store whose salesclerks make a point of helping me and who obviously appreciate my business. There's absolutely no resentment on my part if I get ignored. I accept it and it doesn't matter.

I always disliked Sears, not only because they got caught ripping off consumers in their auto repair shops, but because of the way my father was treated there just before he passed away. There's a store close to where I live but, until recently, I've avoided it. But, on one occasion, they had something I needed and no one else had it. I went there with no expectations but was pleasantly surprised to find the salespeople were actually friendly and helpful. When I had a problem with a piece of electronic gear I'd bought there, the sales-clerks made it as easy as possible for me to get it exchanged. There were no hassles and they actually upgraded the piece of equipment without charging me more. They are the first place I shop now. I'll only go somewhere else if they don't have what I need. Their per-ception of me was that I was a customer who had as much value as the next guy, and because of the good treatment my perception of Sears changed for the better.

Now when I come across someone whose nose seems to be stuck in the "up" position, instead of trying to put them in their place I pretty much ignore them. I've come to realize that they're playing a part, like an actor in a play. For some reason they perceive them-selves as the lead and the rest of us are no more than extras. And, it seems that the less stature they actually have, the more prominent the role they project. It gives them a feeling of self worth to boost them-selves up and put others down. It's hard to get angry at someone who's so delusional.

Speaking of delusional, when I worked in L.A., many of our clients were very famous people. With only a few exceptions, and these are people everyone's quite familiar with, they were very gra-cious and most seemed like very nice people. They were mostly TV, stage, and movie actors, actresses, singers, directors, studio execu-tives, and just about anyone connected with the entertainment indus-try. They liked coming to us because we treated them like regular people. Having hundreds of celebrity clients we weren't at all star struck, and they didn't ask for anything special and we never offered it. The only concession we made was, since they usually had some-one else handle their money, we would bill them, instead of having them pay on the spot. My philosophy has always been to treat every-one the same. I never take into account their stature in society or wealth or lack thereof. That's even if they were big spenders. As a matter of fact this week I had a celebrity come in to my shop to buy some expensive sunglasses for his staff. He had to pay full price just like everyone else. We make it a practice not to discriminate in any way because I would expect the same treatment myself if I shopped somewhere else.

But there are always exceptions to any rule. There are a couple of those celebrities, and one in particular, who literally feel that the world revolves around them. They're reminiscent of the old time Hollywood, where outrageous behavior was the norm even more than today. It's a surreal experience dealing with someone like that, if you've never done it. I remember getting a call from a client who happens to be a famous fashion designer. He droned on and on detailing to death a perceived slight by another optician. The poor optician had made one minor mistake that had been quickly rectified, but that wasn't nearly enough to mollify this particular gentleman. He took the innocent mistake as a personal affront. At first I thought something terrible had happened. But, when he finally got to the point around twenty minutes into his monologue, I was flabbergasted to find out the cause of all this melodrama. I've never in my life heard a person complain so much about so little. He went on and on about a fashion show he was now going to have to cancel and how much money he would lose because of it. He also tried to enlist me into an effort to have the optician put out of business. And all this was after he'd already gotten his glasses corrected, which took all of one day. He even went into great detail about how he felt he could no longer write a weekly newspaper column and how that would be such a great loss for the city. I told you it was surreal. What one thing had to do with another is way beyond me. He had no idea what he sounded like, but I have a feeling if he realized how very small he came off, he'd have been mortified. (Then again, knowing him, maybe not.) I've thought about that conversation from time to time and often wondered how he would have dealt with a real problem. He affected an aire of royalty. I'm surprised he didn't want to have the poor optician's head chopped off.

He was so pompous that the slightest thing caused him an incredible amount of angst. He had built up in his mind a small, easily corrected mistake and made it into Armageddon. What he perceived to be a personal attack on him was in reality nothing of the kind. He was about as far away from the conscious ideal as one could imagine, and he easily could have been the poster child for how not to be.

Nobody is perfect. We all need some minor adjustments from time to time especially to be more objective and not let our biases cloud our views. But, the egomanic designer was the most deluded individual I've ever met. With all his wealth and fame he's still as miserable and petty a person as there is. I would rather die poor in the gutter and have lived a relatively happy life than to have his fame, money, and miserable outlook on life. Aesop could have been speaking of this man when he wrote in "The Gnat and the Bull": "The smaller the mind the greater the conceit."

CHAPTER TEN
LISTENING

At least as important as the concept of good speech is good listening. Many of us have the habit of interrupting others when they're speaking. That's not only rude but annoying. I'm sure you've been involved in a conversation where you can tell the other person isn't listening. They're just waiting for a slight pause so they can jump in and have their say. Unfortunately, that's an all too common trait. You could be trying to make a valid point but you might as well have been whistling Dixie for all they hear. They're thinking of one thing only, and that's what they're going to say next. If the conversation doesn't revolve around them they lose interest and at the first opportunity steer the conversation back in their direction.

"I" is the most frequently used word in the English language for a reason. (Notice how many times I use the word "I" in this book.) If "I" were removed from the language many people would be left with nothing to say, which might not be a bad thing. Conscious people do a lot more listening than speaking and allow whoever's speaking the floor. I can usually tell if someone is trying to do the right thing and allow other people their time without interrupting. For the most part, you can tell when they're very consciously trying to do just that. I always attempt to figure out if someone mentioned the fact that they had a habit of interrupting people or if they figured it out for themselves, and are trying hard to correct it. Either way I think it's admirable that they're making a conscious effort to improve.

It's important to people that they be heard out. We're more willing to listen if given the opportunity to finish our thoughts. It's very frustrating when either you can't get a word in edgewise or if you do, to be talking to yourself. My best friend's name is Mike and we've known each other for forty-seven years. Mike has a habit of talking more than most and he sometimes trails off at the end of a sentence so it's hard to hear the tail end of what he's saying. I developed the habit of tuning people out a long time ago if they were either speaking too long or what I thought they had to say was extremely boring. Mike definitely likes to talk. But, years ago I caught myself tuning him out. Now, what kind of friend would I have been to someone as close as Mike, if I didn't even listen to what he had to say? So, I made it a point to listen when he was speaking and if I did catch myself drifting, I brought myself right back. I figure that's the least I owe him considering I was the best man at his wedding and we've been good friends since first grade.

Mike's an interesting man. He and his wife adopted two Russian children and are in the process of adopting a third, one with multiple handicaps. Mike's extremely religious and is a very active member of the Roman Catholic Church that he attends every week. He even goes on yearly retreats to a monastery. He stays home to raise the kids while his wife works. Mike considers me a heathen because I don't attend church anymore. He also feels that because of that, I'm going to hell. I'm just hoping he's wrong, but you never know. Mike takes the time to write me long letters imploring me to actively believe in Jesus Christ, Our Lord and Savior, as he's wont to say in the letters. I appreciate the fact he takes the time to try to "save" me. But, I don't think I get more than twenty words in during one of our conversations. And now, I've trained myself to show him the courtesy of listening to his every word. So I feel a little better about myself because I corrected a deficiency in my character that he never realized I had. Until now.

As William Hazlitt wrote in *On the Conversation of Authors*: "The art of conversation is the art of hearing as well as being heard." As I've said I was as guilty as the next guy and the habit got to be pretty ingrained. It's actually not that hard to change because in every conversation you have the opportunity to consciously keep your mouth shut and wait until the other person has finished their thought. Once a person starts talking, you need to monitor yourself to take care to listen to what they have to say, and wait your turn. If you find what they say boring or irrelevant, that's no excuse for being rude and interrupting them. How bad can it be?

Speaking of people not listening, my former business partner and I would work three and a half days each, or did until he left the business. The schedule was set and didn't vary. Every day I worked I'd receive a call from one of my partner's friends. This woman was a very nice person so I didn't mind. The weird part is that over the course of two years I literally gave her our schedule at least fifty times.

For some reason that didn't seem to register with her, and even if I gave her the schedule on Tuesday I'd get a call Wednesday looking for him. She didn't listen. She sounded like she was but she wasn't. Don't do that. If someone is speaking, listen. It's only courtesy. This woman invariably called when I was busy and if she did this with someone else I don't know if that person would be as patient.

As with anything else there are exceptions. On Main Street in Santa Monica where my shop is located, there is a window washer who has an opinion on everything. He's a Berkeley graduate who will harangue you with his point of view on everything under the sun. We were still reliving the O.J. Simpson trial on a daily basis for years after it. He's the only white guy I ever met that thought O.J. was innocent. It's very amusing when he walks down the street because all the merchants run inside so as not to get lectured on whatever the topic du jour is. Once he gets hold of you the monologue starts, and doesn't end till you can find a way to escape. He's the exception around here.

With everyone else you can always change the subject, but only after giving them their say. I don't know how many times I've had someone tell me the same story. I might have heard the same tale literally half a dozen times. I don't interrupt the speaker to tell them I've heard it before because I realize that person enjoys relating the particular tale or they wouldn't be telling it so often. And the topic is usually themselves. I think it's something we all do to a certain extent. I'd much rather listen again than cut them short by telling them I've heard it before. We've all heard it before. It's not a big deal. It costs me nothing and makes them happy. The reason we have two ears but only one mouth is obvious. You should listen at least twice as much as you talk. Since people love to talk about themselves so much, why not let them? In *Idees et Sensations*, De Goncourt wrote: "Never speak of yourself to others; make them talk about themselves instead. Everyone knows it and everyone forgets it."

I don't speak loudly at all. Much of that has to do with all the congestion caused by my allergies, so I just can't get the volume. I can't count the times I started to speak before someone will say "What?" I might not get three words out and already they're "whatting" me. "Pardon me" instead is a lot less harsh to the ears. I've found that if I don't repeat myself they actually understood me in the first place but were too lazy to really listen. It's much easier for them to interrupt me than to listen to me. If people have the perception of you as a good listener they'll be more likely to want to include you in their conversations. Always try to remember that and when you want to be heard, they'll be a much more willing audience.

CHAPTER ELEVEN
BABY STEPS

I know this might sound a bit silly but if the stresses of everyday life get to be too much, and even if they don't, do a little something for yourself—smile! I'm serious. I make it a point to put a smile on my face for no apparent reason dozens of times a day, usually when I'm alone. In the beginning I had to keep reminding myself to do it, but now it's an ingrained part of my every day. It absolutely can lift your spirits and change your attitude. It certainly does mine. I'm not sure why, but I was never a big smiler although until I got ill, I enjoyed life. But, it was and still is always hard for people to tell if I'm having a good time or not. I remember when I was a cub scout, each member of the pack got to play engineer on a real locomotive. I can distinctly recall my den mother asking me if I was enjoying myself. She couldn't tell by looking at me. I was having the time of my life, what eight year old wouldn't if given the same opportunity? But I never cracked a smile once. When it comes to smiling you don't have to be stressed to do it or to have an impact on your feelings of well-being. On the contrary, I suggest you start with maybe twenty "for no good reason" smiles every day. No one has to see you do it if you get embarrassed for looking like you're having a good time when no one can figure out why. I urge you starting today to make it an everyday habit—and I'm positive if you go about it with the right attitude you'll see results.

The same goes for singing to yourself. It doesn't matter if your voice is as terrible as mine, you aren't doing it to entertain others. I sing to myself all the time. Sometimes I find myself singing a tune I don't even like, which goes to show how much control we have over our thoughts. It's definitely a spirit lifter or a spirit enhancer when you're already feeling good. Things like these are the little niceties you can use to enhance the overall quality of a happy life. Every small thing you do is a benefit to your well-being. And believe me, they do add up. There are lots of small things that you can do for yourself or for others that will improve the quality of your life. Don't think it has to be anything dramatic or any kind of regimented thing, but every time you make your life or another's just a little more pleasant, you're getting closer to your goal of an all-around happy life.

Another little thing you can do to improve your overall well-being is to take your time while eating. Again, I know it might sound simplistic and maybe even a waste of time but it's not. If you sit down to a well-prepared meal, consciously take the time to enjoy it. Experience the flavors, the subtleties of taste and smell, and appreciate all the effort it took to prepare it. We have a tendency to eat and run. Many of us think of eating as utilitarian, and sometimes a nuisance that takes time out of our busy day. Grab a quick burger at McDonald's and off you go. Experiencing good food is one of life's great pleasures. We've been given taste buds for a reason so we should take advantage and enjoy using them. It now takes me twice as long to eat dinner than it used to. I chew slower and eat smaller bitefuls. Originally I started doing that because of the Irritable Bowel Syndrome but I found it increased my enjoyment of food so much I stuck with it. If you're fortunate enough to be with family or friends or if you're eating alone it doesn't matter. What matters is that you allow yourself the time to fully appreciate the meal. I've been enjoying food so much more since I slowed myself down and concentrated on tasting the food rather than just consuming it.

One of the reasons I enjoy spending time with my brother Joe is that he's such a good cook. He could walk into any four star restaurant and start cooking and there would be no drop off in quality of the food prepared. He's a much better cook than I am, even though I cooked in my own restaurant. I was cooking twenty years before it became such a cool thing. I can still cook a bit but for some reason food always seems to taste better when someone else cooks it.

Since life is made up of moments, we can make each one special. No matter how small or seemingly insignificant, our actions add to the richness and fullness of it. Each small act has a profound influence on the overall. La Rochefoucauld in *Maxims* said it perfectly: "The tranquility or agitation of our temper does not depend so much on the big things which happen to us in life, as on the pleasant or unpleasant arrangements of the little things which happen daily." Take care to make the small things special and the bigger matters will, to a certain degree, take care of themselves.

Everyone has something simple they enjoy more than most. In my case it's reading books and the daily newspaper. I've always felt reading the newspaper to be one of life's great pleasures, and one of the world's greatest bargains. Where else could fifty cents take you around the world on a daily basis? When I have time I'll read two, sometimes three. My day would seem incomplete without that pleasure, although I don't always get a chance to do it. I'm sure there's one thing or maybe a number of small things you consider pleasurable.

Since pleasant little things add so much to the whole picture, whatever your favorites are, you need to try to take the time out of your busy day to treat yourself. You might even need to think awhile to remember some. Maybe it's something that's gotten pushed aside because of time constraints. Make a point to make the time. But, don't stress about it if you can't find the time as much as you'd like. You're doing this to reduce stress, not add more. At least make the effort, and if you can find the time you'll feel the difference.

It's important to take baby steps to avoid slipping into the negative, too. Sometimes our perception of what is right or wrong gets a little lax. We would never go into a store and shoplift, because the thought would be out of the question for most of us. But, if we take a "to go" order from a fast food place, we might bring enough napkins, forks, spoons, and condiments home to start our own restaurant. When I owned the restaurant in Northern California, my partner and I were invited to one of our customer's houses for dinner. The first thing we noticed on their dining room table was a milk pitcher they had obviously taken from our restaurant, without our permission. Restaurant supplies are very expensive because they're built to last. To me that is as bad as shoplifting from a department store. We didn't bring it up at the time but from then on our perception of that couple was clouded by their dishonesty. Is it really worth taking a chance like that for such a little gain? Not in my mind, under any circumstances is that the right thing to do.

You always need to remember, no matter the intent the result is the same. For instance, if you take a shopping cart home from the grocery store and do it for your convenience, whether you intend to keep it or not, the result is the same. The grocery is out one shopping cart that costs them over $100. Even if you leave it at the curb you are still responsible for their loss.

In fast food places the plasticware and condiments are left out for our convenience but that certainly doesn't mean they expect us to stock up. Though, I don't consider this at all the same as, for instance, going to a six-dollar all-you-can-eat buffet and bringing a shopping bag. I don't know anyone who would do such a thing because that would be abusing the intent. If you went through anyone's kitchen, you'd find enough little packets of ketchup, mustard, salt, and pepper, honey, and wet naps to cover a family barbecue. I don't think it's a big deal by any means, but I do think it's an interesting phenomenon. Also, it can be used as a practice situation if you're trying to live more consciously. For you to take only what you actually need for what you've bought, is a conscious thing. Instead of just grabbing a handful of everything, decide what you need and only take that much. People usually don't really take too much with any malicious intention. I just think for the most part, it's just easier to grab a handful off the counter stand and get out. Besides, now you don't have to buy napkins for the next few weeks. It's not condoned by management but I'm sure we're paying for those "freebies" in higher prices. So, as I've said, I don't think it's a major deal, I do think, when we do it, we let our morality slip a little. And, that's something you never want to be playing fast and loose with because it's the foundation for everything we do in our lives. But, in this case, as I said, I think it's an excellent practice tool. Instead of mindlessly, or maybe not so mindlessly grabbing, you take the time to stop and think first. Because being conscious entails thinking before acting, anytime you do, you make it that much easier to do with something important the next time. I always found if I practiced on unimportant matters, and this qualifies as one of them, it definitely helped when I really needed to consciously slow down in stressful situations. It just reinforces the habit of thinking first.

The following scenarios are included as practice for more important matters: As far as acceptance goes, sometimes it takes a lot of self control to keep from getting frustrated while waiting in line to order at fast-food restaurants. The only fast food I eat is El Pollo Loco chicken, but I used to frequent others. What I noticed is when some people finally get their turn after waiting in line, no matter how long they had to wait, they're not prepared to order. It's as if the menu wasn't in huge letters staring them in the face. Everything is listed with prices above the register and many times there are pictures for those who aren't sure what a chicken leg or burger looks like. And, it's almost always the same dumb questions. I used to think that if I heard someone ask what the side dishes were, the ones right in front of them, one more time, I'd have to kill someone. These people remind me of those who, after waiting in a long line at the bank, ask the teller for a deposit ticket and stand at the teller's window writing up their deposit, and then ask for the balances of all their accounts; as everyone waits and fumes. I find things like that rude and very inconsiderate.

In fast food places they either ask obvious questions because they didn't bother to take the twelve seconds to read the menu as they were supposed to do (that's why it's posted), or they're so busy being goofy with their friends in line they have no clue what's even on the menu. That's always fun when the order taker tries to take their orders. These are usually the same people who invite their friends to join them in the front of the line, without a thought to all the other people who've been patiently (or impatiently) waiting their turn. It makes you wonder how these people grew up and if they were taught any manners or consideration for others.

The situations I've described are commonplace and we've all experienced them. There was a study done recently where people were timed in parking lots on how long it took them to pull out of a space once they reached their car. What the study found was the person would actually take considerably longer when they knew another car was waiting for their spot. It belongs to them now and when they're good and ready, and not a second sooner, they'll give it up. It's just childish and shows a total lack of consideration for others. It's a possession thing. Maybe for one of the few times in their lives these people were in control of a situation, and they're going to milk it. On all these occasions, once you start living life consciously, you'll be very glad you did.

Instead of getting impatient or starting to resent people, use the techniques I've previously described. Take a few deep breaths and consciously relax. Right away realize that no matter how upset you get, you're not going to speed the situation up. Accept what's going on for what it really is, just a minor inconvenience, and no more. You're not going to change the way people act so you're just going to have to learn to accept it and adapt to it. When these things happen, consciously direct your attention to something else. Imagining your favorite spot with all its vivid colors is a very pleasant way to go about it. Plan tonight's dinner, or you could people-watch or concentrate on completely letting go and starting from your head down, relax each group of muscles in your body, or anything you can think of to pass the time without resorting to resentment. Resentment can easily build a head of steam if allowed to. Since the situation is out of your control, that's unless you want to make a scene or get into an argument, it's best to keep yourself on an even keel. No matter low long it feels, these things usually last no more than a few minutes, although that time perception thing comes into play, and if you don't make it a point to relax, the time will seem much longer than it really is.

There could be many small things in our lives that, if changed just a little, would make life a bit more pleasant. For instance, if you're at all like me, you like to come home to a neat and clean house. I don't like clutter, so I always make it a point not to leave dishes in the sink or newspapers lying around. Before I leave for work every morning, I straighten up. When I get to my front door before leaving I give the place one last scan to make sure when I come home that night I'll be greeted with the place looking just as I want it to. If I come home to a sloppy place, although it's not a huge deal, it's just not as inviting. I didn't always do that. One day I decided to make a list of all the little things that were in my control to make each day a little more pleasant for me. The list encompassed large things and small, but what they all had in common was the fact they would all, to a certain degree, make my life happier. What I'm doing now is working on cleaning up my language. I feel I can be a better person if I watch what I say and how I say it. Growing up, my friends and I all got into the bad habit of peppering our speech with curse words. I no longer want to do that, so I've made it a conscious self-improvement task not to curse at all any more.

It's funny how many men, at least the men I've known, speak differently when they're together and there are no women around. You wouldn't realize it was the same person. Every once in a while, you slip, although you'd think it would happen a lot more since it is such a conscious thing and takes some effort not to. When my brother Joe was out for a visit we went to dinner with my sister Nikki. As he was speaking he slipped and let a curse word fly, which seemed very odd, and he apologized immediately, although my sister didn't care. Five minutes before she arrived he and I were talking, the way guys do, and every few words things were said that we'd be mortified about if my sister heard us say them. Five minutes later we sounded like a couple of priests. We were the same guys, but our language changed so dramatically that we could have fooled everyone.

I blame my brother for being a bad influence on me. It's all his doing that I let a few fly without realizing it. If he weren't here,

I wouldn't have done it, so obviously it's all his fault. See, I know how to lay blame on others and not take responsibility for my actions.

A lot of guys slip into that mode of speech because it's just the way they've spoken since they were kids. If that's something that you've noticed about yourself, it's a great practice tool for conscious living by trying to learn to control what you say, and to keep it clean. I've been pretty successful at it and only occasionally let one fly when I'm a bit tired and not on my guard as much as usual.

We all act differently around different people. We don't treat any two people exactly the same. If you have contact with a dozen people in a day, you most likely will tailor your approach to each one a little differently. It's almost as if we're human chameleons, in our ability to act differently depending on who we're with. We talk differently, act how we feel is appropriate for that person, and talk about different things, or the same things, but from a different angle. Our approach is modified, usually without us realizing it, for the situation we're in at the moment. I don't think it's in any way dishonest, but more of a situation where we show respect to different people by acting and talking in a different manner depending on who's around us at the time. But, if you're trying to live a conscious life, it's always good practice to try to keep things the same, on a high level when approaching others. If you wouldn't want someone else to hear particular words spoken with them in the room, it's best not to talk that way at all. If you do that, you'll find there's never a reason to have to modify your speech or actions so you won't offend someone.

Again, it's an easy thing to do, because we always think before speaking or acting, so there's always enough time to get our act together in all circumstances. Instead of tailoring your approach, always keep it on the same level no matter who you're with or when you're with them. I've gotten to the point of being a bit uncomfortable when I'm around guys who speak of women more from an anatomical aspect than from a human aspect. If women heard how some men speak about them, they'd be quite upset, and rightfully so.

They're spoken of not as individuals, but as body parts. For example, it's not at all uncommon when some men see a woman with a nice figure to say something like: "Get a load of the rack on that one." She's not a human being anymore, but a set of breasts, at least as far as the speaker is concerned. Remarks like that are not only unfair, but downright insulting to the women in question. Many guys have been doing that since they reached puberty, and it's as natural as getting out of bed in the morning. But, that's very changeable with just a little effort, and if you find yourself in that position, it's best to get away from people who talk that way, and to make sure you're never guilty of participating in that kind of speech yourself. It just shows respect to others to treat them as an individual, rather than just a body or a pretty face.

Getting back to keeping a home where you can be most comfortable, I especially make it a point to straighten up if I'm going on vacation or on a long weekend. In those cases I'd usually prefer to still be where I was, doing whatever I was doing, so I don't want the double whammy of coming home to a mess. It might seem to be an insignificant little thing, but, again, it adds to the overall quality of life. If you like to come home to a neat place but run out of time in the morning, get up ten minutes earlier, it won't kill you, and when you get home that first night, you'll be glad that you did. You'd be surprised how much you can accomplish in a short time when properly motivated. In my case, it takes no more time than ten or fifteen minutes. Consciously make it a point to take the time to do small things that you'd consider worth the few minutes it takes to do them.

That's especially if you've never taken the time before. It could be anything—and might just involve changing the time you do something. If, for example, you don't like crowds when shopping, it's best to always make a point to shop when the stores are emptiest. Do that even if you have to change your schedule around to accommodate it. If you like to hike but find the popular trails too crowded for your taste when you can make the time to use them, get a book on local hiking trails and start hiking less popular ones. If you can juggle your schedule a bit, you'll find that the things that brought on dread before, and that could be almost anything, are now not nearly as distasteful. You're not going to make your life perfect, but you can make each situation you encounter as pleasant as possible. And, that's the way of conscious living.

Always strive to make the best out of any situation you're in, willingly or not. Because that's what's happening at the time, and you're pretty much stuck with it until you move on. And, it's important to continually remind yourself that this is indeed your life at this very moment, and that being the case, it's your responsibility to yourself to enjoy it as much as possible. Consciously tell yourself, when you can start to feel yourself slipping a little in the attitude department, "I'm going to enjoy this as much as I can," and keep reminding yourself until you can feel yourself coming around. This is just a conscious way to remind yourself that this is what you need to try to do. Your ultimate goal is reached through practice.

I have a friend whose golf game is affected when the courses are full and we either have to wait at each hole to tee off or there are a couple of foursomes waiting behind us. It makes him very nervous when there's an audience and it negatively affects his game. He allows the fact that others are watching to affect him and many times he allows it to speed up his swing. If he approached golf consciously, none of that would matter. Instead of fearing looking foolish in the eyes of strangers, by say, "worm-burning" a drive, their presence would be no more than part of the scenery, and their comments about his game wouldn't be a source of concern. Most guys waiting don't give a crap about how well you shoot. All they care about is you teeing off and getting the hell out of there so they can go. And, besides, we'll probably never see these people again, so why care what they think?

My friend and I played together for years, and to accommodate his comfort level, we chose courses and times where there were usually fewer crowds. I personally couldn't care less if I had the course to myself or had a thousand people watching. My brother and I have the same theory on golf: "If you practice it becomes work." So my game reflects that and I score in the mid-nineties usually. I

might not play very well, but I have a great time. And, I keep reminding myself that I'm doing this for the pure pleasure of doing it,
so, number one, I don't take it too seriously like a lot of golfers, and,
number two, I'm determined to have a good time. I might remind
myself of that fact as much as ten times in one game.

    In the beginning of conscious living it's extremely important
to remind yourself that no matter what you're doing, you intend to
get the most out of it and enjoy it as much as you can. The longer
you live consciously, the less you need to remind yourself what you
true goals really are. Don't ever forget that the ultimate goal is a
serene, stress-free, happy life, and if you need to remind yourself
fifty times a day initially, then that's what you should do.

    As a friend, I want my golf buddy to be as comfortable as
possible so he can enjoy the game. Trying to accommodate others
who are close to us is just a little part of friendship. It's not a big deal
to me when we play, anyway. Besides, if you're flexible, you get to
experience more in life.

    Everyday frustrations that plague us all. Taken alone they're
not that big of a deal, and can be easily handled. When there is a
little frustration here a little frustration there, we get the feeling we're
being nickeled and dimed to death. It's a cumulative thing and by
the end of some days all we want to do is go home and forget the
outside world exists. By the fifth little nit-pick of the day we can get
the feeling that may of the things we'd like to do aren't worth the
hassle. It can be anything from circling a parking lot for half an hour
trying to find a parking space to having someone driving half the
speed limit in front of you when you're late for an appointment, to
waiting for the cable guy to show up when you've taken the afternoon off work and he never shows.

    Frustration can take the most enjoyable, and under normal
conditions, the most straightforward thing and make it a nightmare.
The following is the final example of an everyday situation and how
best to cope with it. It's something we've all experienced. I included
this because the example cited encompasses four tenets of conscious
living: *staying in the moment, keeping expectations reasonable,*

accepting what is out of our control, and doing what is in your power
to make the result what you'd prefer it to be.

Nowadays, if you need to call your bank to straighten out a discrepancy or almost any company to inquire about any thing you get the distinct feeling nobody there really wants to talk to you. Every thing is automated and once in the system you start to feel like a rat in a maze. Make one false move and you're back to where you started. That's especially true with banks. Much of the time trying to find their phone number is a process in itself and you're guaranteed to either get the wrong branch office or no answer at all. Once you think you're on the right track that doesn't necessarily mean you are going to get a human being to help. When you finally do get through to a real person, it's almost never one who can actually help you. They'll give you the phone number of the place you're really supposed to call which doesn't necessarily mean anything or get you any closer to where you want to be.

The feeling grows that no one on the other end wants to take responsibility for anything and if there is any chance to pass you off to someone else, they'll do it. If you do finally locate the right person after you've spoken to every computer-generated voice they have, you have a better than even chance to get the person's voicemail with the message: "I'm away from my desk right now." (Doesn't anyone stay at their desks anymore?) By now, a routine matter that should have taken five minutes to resolve is going on it's second hour and at that point you're willing to speak to the janitor if just so you can hear a human voice and not another damn machine. Besides, he'd be as much help as you've gotten so far. If you do get a voice mail and leave your number and an explanation of the problem, good luck in getting a call back. You've got a fifty-fifty shot at that. That usually entails a few more phone calls. We get to the point where we start to resent these people for wasting our time and making an ordinary transaction so difficult. It seems like nothing is straightforward anymore and we feel like circus animals who are required to jump through hoops to get our reward. Then to add insult to injury a voice comes on apologizing for the delay and telling us how important our call is to them. If we're so important to them why are we talking to another machine, and if we're so important why don't they have enough staff so we don't have to spend so much time on hold every time we call? Instead of having a hold button, they should label it for what it really is. A more appropriate term would be the "ignore button," as in, "I'll be with you in a minute as soon as I get off ignore." No matter how many times you hear that apology you get the distinct feeling the people answering the phone wish you'd never called. When you're pushed a little too far and have lost all patience with then, that little voice comes back on telling you how much they "appreciate your patience". How do they know you're patient? By this time, patience is just a memory. Just to annoy you a little further the latest twist is to try to steer you to their web site so they can guarantee no human contact at all, and this way any hope of a resolution can now truly be considered a pipe dream. If these people really believed in customer service you wouldn't only be getting lip service, but even that, from a real human being would be an improvement. That's a perfect example of saying one thing and doing another. You're so important that they put you through all this nonsense.

Since all of that is part of our lives in the technology era we're now stuck with it, we have to learn how to handle it, or go crazy in the process. We have to deal with these people even if they don't seem to want to deal with us, and even if they do everything in their power to avoid us. No matter how often you wonder "if anyone at all is doing their job?", you still must need them or you wouldn't be calling and putting up with all this nonsense.

Since frustrations have a tendency to build to resentment this is one of the situations where consciously living only in the present moment really comes into play. As a conscious person we need to make it a point to realize that each incident is separate and unique. One frustration has nothing to do with the next so you don't want to carry over the negative feelings to your next encounter. Once one frustration is finally resolved it's to be forgotten so it won't add fodder to the next one when it comes along. Wipe the slate clean. Then consciously relax. You need to always remember you're not being singled out and this is the way they treat everyone, so don't personalize it. Accept it only for what it is, an inconvenience and usually no more. It's important for your peace of mind that when you place the call go in with the realistic expectation that it could take a lot longer and be more difficult then you'd prefer. If it gets too bad just hang up and try again later. While you're waiting to speak to someone, do other things to occupy your mind. Do something constructive so it won't feel like you're wasting time. Don't keep track of how long the wait is or how many calls you had to make to accomplish what you wanted in the first place. That just adds to you frustration and doesn't' help the matter because they don't really care or want to hear it.

Don't blame or get angry at the person who finally speaks to you because for the most part they're just part of a system over which they have no control and it will make it more difficult to get what you want. Getting angry will only take you out of a flowing state. If you're truly disgusted speak to a manager or write a letter to the head of the company. Their name is usually a matter of public record. I've done that a number of times with excellent results. I remember one time I was having trouble with my phone at home. I called Pacific Bell and was given a time when a technician would come out. I took the morning off and waited for him and was surprised when he actually showed up on time. As we all know, after dealing with cable companies, that's not a realistic expectation anymore. Even if the cable company is not involved, they leave such a bad after taste that you have trouble believing anyone. But, I was pleasantly surprised and he "fixed" the problem. Unfortunately, the fix didn't work. I called the phone company again and explained what had just happened. The operator gave me another appointment and again I took half a day off from work to try to get the problem resolved. But, the same thing happened. I again called and was given another appointment. Each time the appointment was made for about a week from when I placed the call. I thought that was wrong because I'd already had their repairman out twice. The lady I spoke to said there wasn't anything she could do about it, No matter how many times the problem was supposedly fixed, when I called I was again put at the bottom of the list. That was their system and that was that. I went along with it and the third time was no charm. Same scenario, same results. By this time my phone was out for three weeks and I figured if I tried the same thing again, I'd get the same results. So, I decided to go to the top and wrote a letter to the president of Pacific Bell up in San Francisco. I explained exactly what happened with no invective or whining. Three days later I received a letter back from him apologizing and guaranteeing an immediate fix. That same day I also received a phone call (at my office) from Pac Bell's Southern California manager, explaining that the problem wasn't with my phone, but was in the underground wires leading up to my house. He had it checked out before calling me. He gave me his private number and said if I had another problem I was to call him directly so he could handle it. When I drove home that afternoon there was a crew from Pac Bell at the bottom of the hill from where I lived. They had the street dug up and we're at that very moment, fixing the problem. That night my phone was working. The reason I finally got the prompt service was that I was very businesslike in my approach with the letter. I didn't threaten or even complain. I just stated the facts as they occurred and left it at that.

People do appreciate that type of approach. What others don't appreciate is people whining instead of explaining. I didn't allow myself to get upset even once and made it a point to flow with the situation and accept the results. If the matter was important (priorities) to me I would have written the letter sooner but I'm not a phone person and if I didn't need one, I wouldn't have one.

Recently, I had a young lady come into my shop to look for new glasses. I showed her a number of things I thought would work and when she left after picking out two, she said she needed a few minutes to walk and think about it and she'd be right back. Ten minutes later I got a call from her optometrist's office asking if I had the frames in stock the young woman had chosen. She had absolutely no intention of buying them from me, but basically just lied about the fact that she was thinking of purchasing them. What she did was surreptitiously jot down what she thought were the frame name and color off the frame temples. Unfortunately for her she wrote down the wrong information. That's a pretty common practice in my business. Since we carry nicer frames than most optometrists, people come in to browse with no intention of buying. They just want to see what's available so they can order them from their doctor. It used to bother me that these people would think nothing of taking up to an hour of my time when they knew what I didn't. Fifteen minutes passed and in she walked, this time looking a little sheepish.

Now, most of us don't like being lied to or used in that way. If she had been honest up front she wouldn't have come in with her tail between her legs like she did. She still wanted to know the name of the frames but was afraid to ask this time because she'd just gotten "caught." I could tell she was trying to figure a way to finding out. I could see the wheels turning. I made life easier for her and wrote the names and colors of both frames on my business card and handed it to her. Most people would have called her on her sneaky approach but I saw no point. I didn't say a word except I hoped she enjoyed her new glasses. I sold the frames to her optometrist at my cost as a favor to them, although I'd never done business with them before. It was just professional courtesy. As the young lady left she turned around and said, "I appreciate you being so nice, most people wouldn't have been in the same situation." I thought nothing of it. That's what conscious living is all about.

When I first started living consciously, the afore mentioned would have been a big deal and I would have been proud for acting as I did, and rightfully so. Now, that type of reaction on my part is just second nature. That's the way I've trained myself to think, so I expected myself to do what I did and it was no biggie. It was a surprise to her, not me. The lesson is to be up front, be honest, say what you mean and mean what you say, and your life will flow that much smoother. Again, this is not at situational thing or only when it's convenient. It's a way of life that you should follow no matter what the circumstance.

All of this is especially true when things aren't going your way or you're feeling down. At that time you need to talk to yourself and to remind yourself that you're taking things one at a time and you're just living in the very moment you are in, and that it is your responsibility to yourself to accept whatever is going on if you can't change it, and to make the absolute most of it. When you're feeling depressed a very good way to go about rectifying the situation is to try to discover exactly what is causing you to feel that way, and usually you'll come to realize it's not anything earthshaking or even very critical. Remind yourself that now you are taking everything that comes along in a conscious and measured fashion. If you can figure out what's causing the negative feelings in you, you can much more easily and thoughtfully realize that's it's nothing that can't be handled. Your job is to get yourself feeling good about yourself before going on with your day. Take your time, remember that you're naturally not going to feel on top of the world every minute of every day. Even conscious people have bad days. What sets us apart is that we make the effort to get on top of the situation immediately, because we don't want to waste any of our precious time out of a flowing state. Besides, who wants to feel deflated any longer than necessary?

Recently my brother Joe came out for a visit. I met him at the airport and his flight was supposed to arrive at 11:00 p.m. but didn't show till almost 1:00 a.m. Both my niece and nephew offered to pick him up because they knew that going out so late would be a major strain on me, but I wanted to do it. I try to do as much as I can while I'm still able. It turned out to be very difficult for me and the next day I was not feeling well at all. On top of the fatigue my allergies were acting up very severely, and I actually started to feel a little down mentally. That's something that hadn't happened in a long time, probably eight months or so, so I recognized immediately the negative feelings that were starting to develop. I also knew I had to consciously get on top of the situation before it could develop any further. So, I made a point to just stop whatever I was doing, and tried to sort out why I was beginning to feel that way.

I knew I couldn't allow it to go on one second more than necessary and I had to develop a plan to get myself righted. I soon came to understand the problem was mostly physical, I was just feeling lousy and in reality had been for the best part of a month, and it was starting to get to me. Now that I knew what the root cause of my negativity, I could go about fixing it. So, I had a little talk with myself. I reminded myself that this is the reality of the situation and I'm not going to feel good a lot of the time. That's just a fact of my life. I reminded myself that the way I felt was nothing unusual, I've been feeling that way for years, and if I let myself get down mentally it would only make matters that much worse. I also soon came to the realization that I was doing the exact thing that I've repeatedly cautioned you about. I was projecting into the future and starting to worry about my health. I always know that the stage I'm now in is temporary, and my health will start to deteriorate again, which I can feel happening now, and that remission I'm enjoying will not last. I also found myself projecting into the future about the business. My partner is leaving the business in a little over a month, which means from now on I'm the only one that's going to be there. I'll be working seven days a week and I became concerned if my health would allow me to handle it. Since I can already feel the deterioration happening to me, I began worrying about how I would be able to maintain my business as a viable entity. All those thoughts were coming to me at the same time, and I could feel myself starting to get overwhelmed a little.

So, again, I stepped back to give myself a chance to reassure myself that if I took care to consciously slow myself down and to think clearly about the situation I could get a grip on it. I very consciously told myself that I would handle both the business and my health problems when the time came, and thinking and stewing about it now was only causing me problems in my present life. I reminded myself that whatever or however the situations would develop, I've always found ways of constructively dealing with them in the past and there is no reason to think this time would be any different. I didn't allow myself to proceed any further without resolving my negative feelings that were starting to build, and affect me in a negative fashion. I determined that very minute I would get a handle on my feelings and not go a minute more until I got a good start. I'm the exact same person I was yesterday, and the only difference was my attitude. I still was living where I wanted to and had family and friends that I've always had, so nothing of substance had changed except how I looked at it. Since that was the one thing in my power to control, that's what I concentrated on. It took me a good part of a day to accomplish that, but when I woke up the next morning I started working on my attitude from the second I got up until I could feel myself starting to come around. This time it was a little more difficult than usual because I know what to expect when I get sicker and the memory of how very bad I had been feeling physically was still fresh in my mind from my last episode.

But I convinced myself that the terrible physical problems were indeed a thing of the past and what will happen the future is just conjecture at this point, and I got myself to where I could forget them again. Through all that conscious effort my mood made a sharp U-turn and I found myself on track again and able to enjoy my brother's visit, without a hint of negativity. The reason I was able to get the situation under control is because I never gave it a chance to develop. As Barney Fife was fond of saying, I "nipped it in the bud," and so should you at the first sign of trouble. The less it is given a chance to develop the easier it is to get a handle on. Don't be leisurely about it, take care of it at the beginning and you'll get to a point where you can develop your own techniques to cope, as long as you consciously accept your feelings for exactly what they are and try to understand what's causing them.

PART VI

CONCLUSION

I think now would be a good time for one final review of the cornerstones of conscious living to make sure everything is clear in your mind. Concentrate on the areas we are reviewing and refer to them often until they become second nature:

- **Control**
- **Living In The Moment**
- **Expectations**
- **Acceptance**
- **Eliminating All Fear**

<u>Control:</u> The glass is always half full, never half empty. Your attitude about things determines the level of happiness you'll achieve, especially with those things out of your control. There is nothing more important. As you know, no matter what the situation you're confronted with you have a myriad of choices as to how you'll respond and that all starts with how you choose to view whatever is transpiring. Never forget—that is your choice. Keeping a good attitude when dealing with those things in your control is easy, anyone can do that. The trick comes when things don't go as planned, due to forces outside your control. That's why you take each situation as it comes, and make it a point not to assign things more importance than they deserve. Unless it is a life and death situation you should never put undue pressure on yourself. We all would like everything to work out as planned, and we have a responsibility to ourselves to do everything in our power to make it so, but even then, we lose as many as we win. Frustration takes hold because we just don't have control over most things that occur in our lives. When you get to the point of still feeling good about yourself and what you've accomplished even in a losing cause, then your attitude about whatever transpires is positive and correct. The end result is no longer the only goal, now of equal importance is keeping it in perspective, and that encompasses the whole process from beginning to end. If your attitude about something puts undue pressure on yourself by making things all win or all lose propositions, then you are putting urgency where none should

be. You're losing control of the situation when you needn't. Attitude is perspective. Your reality is how you view things and not only the things themselves. The more realistic yours is the less chance of overreaction. And, overreaction to a situation or words of another is all too common, and causes us to complicate matters when they're really not complicated at all. It also causes us to read into things what's not there, and imagine things that only exist in our minds.

Since you are a hundred percent responsible how you view things, outside pressures should no longer come into play, once you've progressed that far. No matter who tries to sway you for or against something ultimately you get to decide how you will feel about it. That's totally in your control. And, since now, instead of just using a willy-nilly approach to things, you get to consciously determine the best way to view them. Always do that with an eye toward keeping your life flowing seamlessly. *If viewing something one way takes you out of a flowing state of mind then it's in your power to change that attitude until it fits the concept of living consciously.* Your attitude determines if something you do, whether it's in your control or not, is easy or hard. It's all in the way you look at it. If your attitude regarding something is that it is a problem, a problem it will become for you. When you dedicate yourself to conscious living there will no longer be any occasions of you having a "bad attitude" because you now know that you don't have to allow that.

Every morning when I walk into my store the first thing I say to myself is how lucky I am to have such a beautiful place to come to. I say it and I mean it. If I'm to run a small business successfully I must be very committed and always have a positive attitude about it. That is the one area I have control over. If I allowed it to start to become a chore, then my commitment will lessen because of that. My attitude about what I do and how I treat people needs to be positive in order for me to enjoy my work, maximize the store's potential and treat all our clients the way I would like to be treated. If I went in with a negative frame of mind none of that would be possible. This is my profession that I chose seventeen years ago but it took me that long to come to really appreciate it, and now I have gotten into the habit of remembering that each day. I do that now because my attitude had a tendency to wax and wane with the ups and downs of the day-to-day operations.

That's a big part of the reason I consciously make it a point to keep my attitude ahead of the problems encountered daily, and don't let those problems affect it anymore. This is another example, if this strikes a personal chord and you're doing something you enjoy but allow petty annoyances we all deal with daily get to you, make it a point to be thankful that you too are a fortunate person for having such a good job to go to. Take control of the situation. And do it on a daily basis. If your attitude allows you to appreciate the big things such as your job or good friends then there's no reason it shouldn't allow you the pleasure of appreciating the small things. Things that we've always taken for granted. Things such as a beautiful day, a good book, no traffic, a delicious meal, an enjoyable movie, a kind gesture or any number of a hundred things good that happen to us every week. If you can keep a "gee-whiz" attitude about things you'll enjoy them even more and appreciate them, maybe for the first time in a long time.

Although I do very much now enjoy what I'm doing, I know because of my health situation, in the near future I won't be able to do it anymore. That is out of my control. I've accepted that as part of my life, and I know the day is coming much sooner rather than later. But, as long as I accept it and don't try to fight the inevitability of the reality, the transition will be much smoother. It would be much more difficult to accept the fact that I now have severe limits in what I can do and can't do. But, that's fine, and now, at least I realize when I leave my business I have an opportunity to do other things with my life that the business kept me from doing.

Living In The Moment: This is how you lead each moment of your life. It's in reality not each moment but each second. A lot can happen in one minute so that's actually too large of an increment for our purposes. The only reality in our lives is the very second we are living-at the present time. While you are reading this, this is your life. A minute from now the phone could ring with someone giving you pleasant or unpleasant news, but you are not living even one minute in the future so as far as you're concerned that moment doesn't exist. Something can't exist that hasn't been. So, why worry about it? Even if you know that something you really don't want to happen, will in the near future, that in no way should affect how you feel in this minute. If you do, that's worry. Worry comes from what Ken Keyes, in *The Handbook to Higher Consciousness* calls, "futuring." Projecting your thought into the future is very harmful when you're trying to make the most of what you're doing in this very second. You can't concentrate on two things at once, and when you project thoughts into the future, that has a tendency to dominate your thinking, and that in turn causes worry, it also causes impatience and frustration.

That also means that whatever is happening now can't be fully enjoyed. For example, right now my leukemia is in remission. Unfortunately for me there isn't a cure for my type at the present moment. Each time I go to my oncologist my blood counts inch up a bit. To be considered in the normal range, my white blood cell count should be between four thousand and eleven thousand. Four months ago mine was at six thousand, after having received treatment. At my last visit it was over thirty-five thousand. When I go back to my doctor, which I'll be doing this week, it will probably be even worse. So, obviously, I'm going in the wrong direction. When it gets to a certain point I can really start to feel it, and it makes even minor chores very difficult. Every day becomes more of a struggle just to make it through. It's quite unpleasant. I still have to show up for work just as everyone else. When I do reach the point where I no longer can function I know I'll have to undergo chemotherapy again. I also know the treatment will last anywhere up to a year. When that time comes, since I've already experienced it I know what to expect. Hopefully you'll never have to go through it, but I wouldn't wish it on my worst enemy, which, to my knowledge, I don't have. The treatment is necessary but while I'm undergoing it, I feel even worse than if I wasn't. If I want to live, I absolutely have no choice in the matter. So, I'll do it. But, what I won't do is spend even a second of

my present life worrying about it. That future event, which is draw-
ing closer by the day, in no way concerns me now. What good would
that do? How would that benefit me in any way? Even if I were to
start treatment tomorrow, I would not allow it to affect my day today.
One of the reasons I'm writing this book at this time is because I
have a window of opportunity in which to do it, before I won't be
able to concentrate due to the fuzzy thinking caused by the medication and the exhaustion they cause. I also know that there will be a
lot of ancillary problems caused by the chemo. But, that's just a fact
of my life, and I feel fortunate that there is a form of treatment that
keeps it at bay for a while. If, for some reason, it doesn't work the
next time, I'll cross that bridge when I come to it, but not a second
before. I have great faith in my doctor so I know I'm in very compe-
tent hands. If there was anything I could do to keep myself from
having to go through it again, I would in a second. Since there's not,
there's not. I can't wishful think it away so I don't even try. It took
a lot of conscious effort to get to this point, but having developed this
attitude, I can fully enjoy whatever I'm involved in as much as my
illnesses will allow.

   **Every moment that you worry about what might happen
is a moment of lost happiness.** If we had a hundred lives it wouldn't
matter that much, but we don't. As I've said, we have only one shot
at this, so why waste precious time worrying about the future? As
I've mentioned, the vast majority of things that worry us either don't
take place or aren't as bad as we've built them up to be by harping on
them. If they do occur, and are as bad as our imaginations built them
up to be, what good did worrying about them do? All the worrying
did was to make the situation worse and ruined your peace of mind
leading up to it. Thomas Jefferson once wrote to a friend: "How
much pain have cost us the evils which never happened?" It's a very
simple concept but it makes a whole lot of sense.

   That doesn't mean you live your life blundering from one
moment to the next without any foresight or a plan of action. What it
means is you don't spend any more time than necessary out of the
present, where your life is being lived. As Albert Camus wrote in

Beyond Nihilism: "Real generosity towards the future lies in giving all to the present."

The same rule of thumb applies to spending an inordinate amount of time with your thoughts in the past. That's already history and although it's not harmful as worrying about the future, it too takes you out of the reality of now. That's the reason many of us do it. I don't think there's anything wrong with recalling fond memories, doing that can make us feel better. Half of the fun of say, going on vacation is the memories we bring back with us to enjoy, again and again. If you had a particularly happy childhood as I did, I never would want to forget it. But, it's also true that most of us have memories of things that transpired in our past that even the thought of can make us cringe. Thinking of those things can dredge up old feeling that have nothing to do with the life we are now leading. We can't relive them to correct them, so why bother going over them in our minds years after the fact. Why cause ourselves pain all over again?

George Washington once said that if he were to reflect on his past it might reduce him to tears. He'd rather live in the present and let history judge his life. Washington was a wise man who, even with all the baggage of an eighteenth century gentleman, knew what was important and what wasn't. If you do find yourself spending a lot of time reminiscing about past events then there's a good chance that you need to address some problems in your present that are causing you to not want to spend your time here. If you find yourself spending much of your time in the past, at least try to take lessons from it so in the future you won't make some of the same mistakes.

Over the centuries much has been written about the subject of focusing on what needs to be done in the here and now, and not reliving what's already transpired. You can't change it and since much of it is painful for many of us, it is your obligation to yourself to move on with your life, and not keep replaying it. Whereas, you can return to the place of your youth, you can't go back to your youth. If you think of your life as a book, you've already written what's already transpired, so now it's time to start writing some new chapters. Or, as Charles Edward Wilson wrote over forty years ago regarding the uselessness of past thinking, "It's futile to talk too much about the past—something like trying to make birth control retroactive." It's just a waste of time.

If you can't get over the past you won't have an easy time of it in the present or future. That's because living your life in the past is a way of denying the present, and that's no way of going about life if you wish to make the most of it and to enjoy it as much as possible. Most of us don't spend an inordinate amount of time there, and in reality spend much less reliving the past as we do worrying about the future. But, for some, as billionaire inventor Warren Buffet said: "The rearview mirror is clearer than the windshield." And, that can be a problem. If you're into the past, read a book or watch a documentary, but leave your thinking in the present.

When you're getting ready for work in the morning and you're applying make-up or shaving, are you thinking about everything you have to do during the day? If you're lying in bed at night are you replaying the events of the day? If you're at home watching television or reading, do you find it hard to concentrate due to the fact that your mind keeps returning to a conversation you had in the afternoon? *There always seems to be a running commentary going on in our minds that has nothing at all to do with what we're trying to do at the moment. We spend more time being distracted than not. As you know that's not the best way to go about things. No matter where your mind drifts off to, and no matter how often, keep bringing it back to the matter you're attending to in the present moment.* Your day will happen when it happens, the day you lived and kept reliving is no longer, and whatever you said during the day is now old news. When your mind drifts, bring it back, when it wanders, rein it in. It's as if you're trying to herd cattle. Every time you think you've gotten a good hold on them, some slip away and you constantly have to bring them back. It never ends. It's difficult to keep up, so keep at it.

Expectations: When you expect too much from anything you'll easily be disappointed; when you expect too little, you might be shortchanging yourself. It's a fine line.

If I hire someone it's with the expectation that they'll do a good job. I also have the realistic expectation that since they don't have a personal stake in the business, they won't be nearly as committed as me. But, I have every right to expect, regardless if they have a stake in the business or not, that they'll do a good job. The person I hire expects certain things from me and rightly so. But, until that person actually starts working, I never really know if they'll live up to my expectations. There are certain minimums but really no maximums when it comes to such things.

Recently, in Kentucky, there was an instance of where even the minimum expectations of an employee were way too much. It happened at Dairy Queen. A customer paid for his two-dollar order with a two hundred dollar bill, and got a hundred and ninety-eight dollars in change. Now, that would usually raise some red flags, for a number of reasons. Least of which is the fact that a two hundred dollar bill doesn't exist. Even if the clerk was unsophisticated enough not to know that, the fact that the bill had George Bush featured on it, with the slogan "We like broccoli" emblazoned across it should have been a clue. I mention this as an extreme example of why you should never expect others to act the way you do, as you would like them to, or even in a logical way. You can't control how others' act so you should always go in to any situation with low or no expectations of others until their actions dictate what you can expect from them in the future.

One thing. Our expectations of others should never be anywhere near what we expect from ourselves, in any circumstances. We have no control over anyone but ourselves, in any circumstance. We have no control over others' motives, motivations, attitudes, skill level, desire, determination, or anything else that goes into how a person will perform any given task. As with anything out of our control, in most situations, we should go in with no expectation at all, or very minimal ones. Before we can expect certain results, we need to see how the person or product actually performs.

That goes for everything you undertake. Keep your expectations reasonable, and there'll be much less chance that the situation will cause frustration. Realistic expectations keep you in control of whatever you're experiencing, and allow you to reach you goals without wanting more. You'll also find that the cause of much of your impatience is also eliminated.

As I've said, expectations, in order to have any meaning, have to be realistic. Much of that has to do with experience. Through experience we come to realize that most things take longer than anticipated, are usually more difficult to accomplish, and if there is money involved, cost more than originally thought. For instance, have you ever heard of a government contract that didn't come in over budget and late? Sometimes that has to do with the specifications changing, but it's more than likely that the original expectation were totally unrealistic. Did you ever know of a person who did a major renovation on their house who didn't go through hell with the contractor for the entire length of the project? It just doesn't happen and to think you'd be the one person spared from that is just not a realistic expectation. When going into anything new the only thing you can realistically expect is to be confronted with the unexpected.

If you go in realizing that, whatever you're involved in will go much smoother, because you'll be expecting the unexpected. There will be fewer unpleasant surprises lurking around every corner. Since your perception of things is basically your reality, the more honest yours in the greater change to keep your life flowing in a straight line and the easier it will be to handle the "surprises" when they pop up.

Acceptance: As we know, there is much in our lives we need to accept even though we'd prefer not to have to. But, we learn to accept the reality of certain things and come to realize they are out of our control–so acceptance is the only way to realistically deal with them. If these things were in our power to change–we would. As you become conscious through practice, that becomes easier and easier to do. As you now know, it's extremely important that we never equate acceptance with quitting or caving in. It's very simple: if something is in your power that you feel needs changing, do it. If, on the other hand, it is out of your power, you are left with no other alternative but to accept it, no matter how galling it might have previously seemed. Falling short here could lead to a life filled with frustration, non-fulfillment, and longing for things there is no chance in your ever attaining. As I've said, accepting the previously unacceptable is a hard pill to swallow until you get the hang of it.

Another type of acceptance we've touched on is the acceptance of the consequences of our actions. Many don't spend the small amount of time it would take to think things through before jumping in. Then, when the results don't come out as hoped, people have trouble accepting that it did indeed come out wrong, and they alone are responsible.

That's just another case of living life hoping for things to turn out well instead of being prepared and making sure they do. People who do that live life with the "Even a blind pig finds an acorn every once in a while" attitude. That is, blindly going through life in the hope that things will turn out the way you'd like them to with out planning or foresight.

An extreme example of not thinking things through, is this wave of school shootings that seems to be sweeping the country. I'm sure in many of these cases the shooter doesn't even fully understand why they did what they did and they certainly didn't think through the consequences of their actions. If they had, there would be a good chance the shootings would be much less frequent. Although, it certainly wouldn't be expected to stop them (some of these kids are trying to commit suicide). If the student sat down and analyzed the ramifications of their actions, for example, never having the basic freedoms to sleep in their own bed again, enjoy a movie with friends and not cellmates, walk on the beach, enjoy a cream soda, go to restaurant for dinner, enjoy the company of their family, bask in the sun of a beautiful dawn, or any of a million things, we all take for granted, that might give some of them pause, and change their minds, or at least make them think twice. These kids are obviously under a lot of mental pressure and are not thinking straight. They're going on emotions and in many cases are seeking revenge.

We, on the other hand, aren't under the same pressures. One reason for that is, we learn how to deal with them before they reach a critical point, so there is absolutely no reason for us to rush into things without thorough examination first. We need to make sure we fully understand any consequences of our actions, and are willing to accept those consequences if necessary. If we do feel pressured to act before we should, then it's usually ourselves applying the pressure, and we'll just have to accept the results if we decide to go ahead prematurely. Remember, you put more pressure on yourself than all outside forces combined and if you're finally tired enough of having to accept less than hoped for results, it's in your power to change, and slow down and think so you'll have to do a lot less accepting things you' rather not, and a lot more enjoying the positive results you'd rather have.

A very good way to keep the pressure off yourself and make the task of acceptance a whole lot easier and less frequent, is not to impose arbitrary rules on yourself. We're taught at home and in school as children how to conduct ourselves to be a functioning member of society. You already know how to behave so as not to embarrass yourself or family, before you're let out on your own. We all know our basic Emily Post types. So, we know just about all we need to to get around pretty comfortably. We might not know where the fish knife goes in a formal place setting, or even what it looks like, but almost no one really cares about that.

Many times rules that govern the conduct of our lives are created by others for us. An example of that is all the laws on the books that govern our society and many times are passed in response to new societal problems.

Making arbitrary rules that are, in reality, artificial, is as bad as setting arbitrary and artificial deadlines for yourself. That is just putting undue pressure on yourself and is something that can easily be avoided, unlike many outside pressures that we have to accept.

Eliminating All Fear: As you're well aware, fear is one thing that keeps you from reaching your potential. Once you've learned to eliminate fear or reduce it to a more manageable level, all sorts of possibilities open up that can substantially improve the quality of your life. When you've conquered your fears by facing them, you'll find you'll be more willing to experience new things that you might have previously been reluctant to try for fear of failing at them.

If you can think of fear as the schoolyard bully, once you've had enough of being intimidated and frightened, you'll finally stand up for yourself. When you do that, there's a good chance the bully will back down. If he doesn't, and you put up a fight, he'll more than likely leave you alone in the future because you'll now present more of a challenge than he's willing to deal with, and he'll move on to others. So even if you lose the initial battle, you still win the fight. You might get your nose bloodied, but your spirit will be stronger for having the courage to stand up to your tormentor.

That's what facing fear will do. You may not be able to conquer all your fears completely, but you have to stand up for yourself and at least make an honest effort to overcome them. If you do make a concerted effort, you will definitely see the results, and you'll no longer have to look over your shoulder when you venture out.

Plus, when you're no longer shackled by the fear of rejection, that might embolden you to try for a more challenging job, or ask someone out to whom you've always been attracted. When rejection *does* occur, as it sometimes will, you can now view it in context and realize it's not the end of the world.

Eliminating or minimizing fear as much as possible is one of the most important things in taking the stress out of your life. As long as you assess things on a completely realistic basis and no longer magnify their threat to you, living a more open and fulfilled life becomes an attainable goal.

If you can view new challenges, things you might have previously feared, with the mindset of "what's the worst thing that can happen?" you'll quickly realize that the worst thing that can happen in most cases is really nothing that is detrimental to you, at least not in the long term.

You'll never know if you're good at something or enjoy participating in it if you're afraid to try. Once you develop the confidence to attempt new things, that will significantly increase your confidence level when it comes to all other matters. It has everything to do with realistically assessing situations, accepting those situations and the results of your efforts, and moving on after you've done everything in your power to get the desired results.

One very important note: Some of us may start to feel a little guilty when we begin the task of conscious self-improvement. We might feel that trying to lead a happy life is a bit selfish. What about all the people who go to bed hungry at night, are homeless, or fear for their lives on a daily basis? We know that they don't enjoy the same opportunities that we do for leading a happy life—and it's just not fair.

Well, it isn't. Due to circumstances beyond our control, we happened to be born in a place and time that affords us that opportunity. Feel very fortunate and remember to appreciate that fact every day.

I would hope that if you're in a position to help those less fortunate than yourself, you do. Being a happy person will help you accomplish that because, as you know, when you're in a good frame of mind, you're more willing and able to be generous and giving. When you're in a poor frame of mind, all your energies are directed toward coping with that. So, trying to achieve and maintain a happy and tranquil frame of mind is not at all selfish—just the opposite. Remember that.

Sometimes I take my own advice a little bit too much to heart. I'll get to that soon. As I've mentioned, Kauai is my favorite place in the world. I just came back from spending eleven heavenly days there. I'll tell you how I made a conscious effort to maximize the enjoyment of my trip. If you decide to try what I did and make your next vacation a more conscious one, you'll see that you'll wring so much enjoyment out of even minor things, you don't need to concern yourself with doing "everything." This might give you some ideas for your next vacation as to how to get the most from it without having to run around and cram in as much as possible, for the fear of missing something.

First off, I allowed myself to get excited leading up to the trip and I found myself singing "Going to Kauai" to the tune of Smokey Robinson's "Going to a Go-Go." I allowed myself the time out of the present to fully enjoy the anticipation of my upcoming trip, and made it a point not to even think about the travel part.

In Kauai every morning I woke up and immediately went out on the lanai to look at the beautiful scenery and to thank God for making the trip possible, and the day beautiful. By 8:30 a.m. after a few cups of coffee, shave and shower, and before walking to the café for breakfast, I'd stop at a secluded spot on the beach (which are everywhere on the island) and just enjoyed the breeze, the water, and on a couple of occasions was lucky enough to see whales out in the distance. I just happened to be there at the time of year whales come to the area. I made it a point to focus on all the vibrant colors of the ocean and the wisp of clouds in the bluest sky and the lush vegetation. I again gave thanks for the trip, especially after all I've been through, and made a point just to stand there and quietly just drink it all in. It was a form of meditation that I found very relaxing to start every day. As you see I'm consciously making it a point of each moment of my trip to remember where I am and how much I'm enjoying it, and especially to be thankful for the opportunity to be there. As you'll experience when you do it, that attitude adds a lot to the enjoyment of everything you do. Remember, conscious living isn't only something you do to get you through the rough patches, it's the way you lead your life at all times. It makes the good times even better. Once you've reached a certain point, conscious living becomes like happiness: it follows you wherever you go. Most people leave much of their happiness wherever they vacationed, and are sad to see it end for two reasons: They miss the carefree atmosphere a vacation allows them to have, and they now have to return to their humdrum daily existence and the reality of that. Vacations allow us to live in a fantasy world for a short time that's free of job pressures, bills, sitting in traffic, cleaning the house, and just everything that makes up our humdrum life fifty weeks of the year.

If you can lead your life consciously, you'll get to the point where you actually can even enjoy the flight home, believe it or not. I know I did. When I alluded to the fact that sometimes I take my own advice too much to heart, this is one occasion of that. On the way home I was having such a wonderful time in Honolulu Airport checking out all the shops and people watching, I almost missed my flight back to L.A. That is the complete opposite of all my other vacations, pre-conscious living, where I dreaded coming home and the flight back. I had a two-hour stopover there and lost track of time (I never wear a watch). I barely made it to the gate, even though I was within a hundred yards of it for most of those two hours.

Remember when I alluded to the fact that a conscious person is so relaxed and basically easy going, thus making others more comfortable in their presence. I noticed a major improvement in how I was treated by all I came in contact with compared to any previous vacations in Hawaii. For instance, one morning I headed out to do some kayaking and, as is the usual case with me, I couldn't find the river (I found it the next day). On the trip I was very happy to find that if I took everything very slowly, I could do more than I expected. For example, when I snorkeled I used to spend an hour at a time under water. On this vacation I spent no more than 10-15 minutes at a time. I didn't find the river but I did find a golf course, even I couldn't miss that. I hadn't played in a number of years because of my health, so I figured I'd just hit a few. As the course was right along the ocean I decided I'd just enjoy the scenery and see if I could get my swing back. I live by the ocean in California, but the water off Kauai is just the most beautiful aqua color that it's like seeing the ocean for the first time. My swing was about as bad as I thought I would be after a two-year layoff. Normally, since I was hitting so poorly, I would never attempt to play a full 18-hole course. Other golfers have a very low tolerance level for people who are so bad that it slows their game down. But, the course was pretty empty which really surprised me. I found that I was much more willing to do things on my own that previously I wouldn't have without a partner. I had no fear of looking foolish at all. So, I decided to play. I rented clubs, bought some balls and tees, and went to the starter's window. On most golf courses there are the regular rates and after a certain time, twilight rates, which are usually much lower. I was there an hour before the twilight rates took effect so I expected to pay full price. I also needed a cart because there's no way I can physically walk a course. The starter and I hit it off right off the bat and he gave me the twilight rate and cart at half price. I didn't ask for that but, as I've said, conscious people, because we tend to make others comfortable in our presence, are just naturally liked, even by strangers.

I played the course, terribly, and had the time of my life. I don't know how many times I stopped and made it a point to be thankful for where I was and what I was doing. I wanted to absorb the entire atmosphere. It wasn't just a game of golf, it was a wonderful afternoon. When I brought the clubs back, I also gave back the balls (I'd lost two) and the tees I didn't use because I didn't need them. The club pro actually gave me a refund on all of that. I asked him if that was what he usually did and he said "no," but he enjoyed our time together so much, he decided to do it. As I've said, that kind of treatment from others, you'll find, is a side benefit of leading your life in a conscious, relaxed an open fashion. It's almost as if you develop an aura about you that people find quite pleasing. You're relaxed and at peace, which automatically translates to those around you.

Getting back to the trip. Each morning after my meditation at the beach, I picked up a local paper and headed off to breakfast. I walked just about everywhere so I could enjoy the little things. I determine that in order to get the full enjoyment from my vacation I'd eat only fresh, healthy food. I usually eat well anyway. I'd have breakfast at the same café every morning because I like the relaxed environment. Each morning I'd order the fresh fruit plate, which was huge, and a stack of pancakes. On vacation I usually only eat twice a day so I packed it in. When I got back to my condo I'd rest for a while before deciding what I would do for the day. Since I'm limited as to what I can do, I chose just one activity.

One day I'd hike, another I'd bike, a third I'd snorkel, then kayak, then golf, and so on. I didn't just do those things as I always had, but I consciously stopped to "smell the roses" and made a point to be thankful for and take my time over each thing I did.

The thing you need to consciously steer clear of is spending even one moment out of the present thinking about having to go home. The last day of your trip should be approached as if it were the first day. You're not on the plane heading home so why even think about it? I didn't leave the resort until 6:00 p.m. (I had a 7:20 flight) and not once during that day did I concern myself with anything but wringing as much enjoyment as I could from the day with no thought at all of leaving. When the time comes to go home, go home, but don't anticipate. Make it a point to anticipate your trip but not to anticipate the return flight. This way you'll guarantee yourself the maximum possible enjoyment and at the same time keep yourself from stressing about the vacation being over. Do that and you'll be able to enjoy the best vacation of your life till the very end. I guarantee it!

It was the first vacation where I consciously approached every little thing. It was incredible. I thought that vacationing alone, something I'd never done, wouldn't be as much fun as sharing. But, when done consciously, i.e., thoughtfully and appreciatively, I found there is no limit to the enjoyment I could have. I approached it as I approach everything in my life now and because of that, my vacation was as "perfect" as it could possibly have been. First change I get I'm back there.

There was only one aspect of my trip that was less than perfect, and it taught me a lesson that I'll take on my next vacation. From now on I'll only book reservations at a place where I'll have no upstairs neighbors. I've found that vacations resorts aren't built to the standards of regular housing. To give you some idea, if the people upstairs turned the water on in their kitchen I couldn't even hear my TV. For the first half of my stay I had a family with two small kids (or was it 50?) staying in the condo above me. To say that their discipline was lax would be overly generous. I could literally hear every word they were screaming, and when the kids played tag, I thought the ceiling was going to cave in, and they never stopped. And, of course, we'd have the hourly crying game. They were replaced in the second half of my stay by a family with only one child. I thought I caught a break when the first family left, but I was soon jolted back to reality. This was one of those cases where I learned a lot more about these people than I ever wanted to. Basically, anything I learned about them was more than I wanted to. The woman in this family was a screamer, with a capital S. And, she was relentless. I don't know what that poor kid did, but it couldn't have been less than murder the way she was carrying on. I must have missed that part, but she went after him with a vengeance and just wouldn't stop. She was literally screaming at the top of her lungs and it would last for maybe an hour at a time. Throughout each episode the kid was bawling his head off. This woman was literally out of control.

Living a conscious life certainly came in handy staying under these people. I was in no way going to allow these out of control and extremely inconsiderate people to ruin even one minute of my stay. The first thing that entered my mind, after my homicidal thoughts were discarded, was "How must these people behave when they're not on vacation?" If this is their idea of a good time, I couldn't even imagine what they would do in real life. My second thought was "Thank God they're not my real neighbors." And my third thought was that since I was stuck with them, I'd have to do my level best to ignore them (there were no other rooms available—I know because that's the first thing I checked). So, that's what I decided to do and when it got too bad, I'd sit out on the lanai for some peace and quiet. But, I made it a point not to let it bother me.

I handled these people just like I knew I would. When you lead a conscious life you develop a very strong confidence that whatever the situation, once your brain computes what's going on, you'll do whatever it takes to stay in a peaceful, flowing state, and not allow circumstances to drag you down. I did and it didn't.

All of this has a lot to do with priorities. If you determine that, no matter what chaos is going on around you, your top priority is to keep a level head, that's where your attention will naturally be drawn. That might not be a priority for others or it might not even be on their list, but as conscious people we realize that many other beneficial things just naturally flow from that concept, and it makes everything else so much easier to deal with. You develop the confidence to know that the actions or words of others can't rattle you or take you away from your core beliefs or your flowing state.

Priorities are a strange thing. What might be completely unimportant to some might mean everything to another. Since I meet so many different people, this is something I've noticed over the years in my work. Some people's priorities seem completely out of order. There was one client who came in for years who really stood out because his priorities were so weird. He never had any money because he was always out of work, so his brother would pay for his glasses, which I thought was rather nice. He wasn't only chronically unemployed, but was at least eighty pounds overweight, short, and bald. I'm not picking on him, I just want you to visualize him. He always dressed in ratty looking clothes when he really didn't have to. His family had quite a bit of money and they watched out for him. So, I'd have this shabby looking, short, fat, bald guy coming in all the time. Why? Because if his glasses were one half of one tenth of a millimeter askew he noticed it and couldn't stand how they looked on him. Never mind the fact that everything else in his life was all over the place, his glasses had to be just so. Everyone else in the office would run to the back room and hide when he approached. I soon found out that that's due to the fact his average adjustment could easily take an hour. Sometimes he'd even bring a friend specifically to help him make sure that the glasses were absolutely perfect on his face before he left. He stared in the mirrors so much I'm surprised he didn't get eyestrain. The first time he came in for an adjustment I thought he was kidding. I couldn't see anything wrong, but after a half hour, I realized why everyone else in the office magically vanished when he showed up. And, the worst part is, if he liked the way you adjusted his glasses, he'd only want you to do it from then on. I literally must have spent fifty hours over the years adjusting his glasses when most of the time I couldn't see anything wrong in the first place. To me, this man's priorities were completely topsy-turvy, and he put emphasis on the "wrong things."

The best thing about priorities is that we get to set our own. Everyone's priorities are personal, different, and ever changing. What might have meant everything to you three years ago might not even make the list today. As we mature our priorities of what we feel important also mature. When you're a teen the greatest priority was to fit in with the crowd, to feel you're part of something. When we enter the working world many people's priorities shift to finding the best job they can and raising a family. In the 60s the top priority for many students was social change and equality. Now it's more ego-centric and the priority of most students, as I read recently, is to make a lot of money.

To a conscious person the top priority is to lead a peaceful and flowing life. We come to realize that money, fame, or any other things many hold people dear mean absolutely nothing if we're not happy. We learn that everything else flows directly from that, and without happiness, everything else is totally meaningless.

You could be with your favorite people, on the most beautiful day of the year, participating in your most pleasurable activity, on the first day of a long vacation, after having just won the lottery. But if you've never learned how to sustain happiness if it comes and goes with the whims of the ever-changing world around you, even with all that you'll find maintaining a happy and secure state of mind will be impossible. And that's a far cry from being selfish, and ego-driven, which when you look closely and get past the rhetoric, is actually the priority for many. You could have the greatest job in the world, with a seven-figure salary, a house overlooking the ocean, and anything you heart desires or money can buy, and still be unhappy.

As we know, there is only minimal relation between external success and happiness. Prioritizing helps us realize that. How we set our priorities determines how we live our lives and pretty much what makes us do the things we do. But, it's not something we give much conscious thought to—and that's where many of us are short-changing ourselves. It's like anything else, if we put thought and time into deciding what we should hold dear, and what is expendable and really not that important, we'll find we make better choices that will benefit us in the long run.

For instance, if the most important thing to you is conscious self improvement, and you make it a point to make your life's work doing just that, you'll find greater satisfaction than if your priority is, say, taking home a huge paycheck. Money comes and goes, happiness, with a strong foundation, doesn't. Anybody who has even minor skills can make money, maybe not as much at they want, but money nonetheless. But, in actuality, the vast majority of people will never consciously improve their lives. That's for a number of simple reasons. They don't even realize there's a better way. They don't know how to go about it. They don't consider it important. It takes constant hard work which most people aren't willing to put in, there is no instant gratification because it's a process that takes time, they're afraid of the reaction of others (many think conscious improvement is selfish and a waste of time), they don't want to break from the crowd (the hard mentality), or a dozen more reasons. Each one of those reasons is valid to those who use them.

You can't make someone want to become a better person if they don't want to, no matter how beneficial you feel it would be for them. If it's not a priority of theirs, then there's really no use in trying to steer them to a better way. That's their choice. But, as you're well aware, with your attitudes you do have subtle effects on others. That's one reason consciously setting priorities is so important if we want to reach our goals of leading a life free of stress and worry and take others we love along for the ride. We do realize there certainly is a better way and with reaching that as our top priority, we have a very great chance of realizing it. When we do achieve that goal, we elevate all those who come into contact with us, especially friends and family, and through our examples, set the tone for them to become better (happier) human beings. That's even if they don't realize it at the time, and even if it's not on their list of priorities. So, the bottom line is, if you want to be more successful at the art of conscious living or just life in general, you have to decide what you consider important and what you consider not so important. You can't be expected to do "everything," or give everything the same emphasis. Since life is ever-evolving, it's in your best interests that you keep on top of the situation and are willing to reevaluate your priorities from time to time, to make sure you get the most out of the life you have.

Since others' priorities won't be the same as yours, you shouldn't allow others to influence you when it comes to what you consider important. That's as long as you develop faith in yourself to make the right choices. That also goes for the way we think. Many people have no opinion or even like and dislikes until they get a cue from another. A good example of that is some of the rabid followers of Rush Limbaugh. If they didn't turn on the radio and find out what Rush thinks about a certain subject, they'd be lost, and not know what or even how to think. Once they get their cue from him, that becomes their opinion.

I know people who are type-A personalities and are continually on the move. Every second they are driven by the need to be doing something or else they feel they're wasting time. On the other hand, I have a good friend Miki who, if she calls me on a Sunday will almost apologetically tell me she's been lazy and hasn't accomplished anything all day. She usually just relaxes or takes her dogs for long walks or rides her horse on her day off. For some reason she feels guilty about it. I tell her the same thing all the time: "That's what days off are for!" You don't always have to be "accomplishing" something or filling every minute of every day with some activity. That in no way means you're lazy. If you can be satisfied sitting in the shade of a tree reading a book or just relaxing watching the world go by, there's absolutely nothing wrong with that. If everyone else is running around cramming all they can into a day, that's fine for them, more power to them. If you can be just as satisfied relaxing and enjoying a quiet day in the park or even at home, then you're a fortunate person. Always remember-your happiness does not depend on how much you do, it depends on how much you appreciate and enjoy the things that you do.

If it's a priority to kick back and recharge your batteries for the upcoming week's work (even during the week), then that's what you should do. As long as you're comfortable with it, there's nothing wrong with it. It reminds me of when I was in school. If I finished well before the other students I would feel very uneasy because I thought that there must be something wrong, something I must have missed. It couldn't have been that easy. That's how many of us feel when everyone but us seems to be busy and always seem on the go. The more you have internally, the less you need externally. You might get the feeling that somehow you're missing out. If I didn't have to work another day in my life, I'd be quite happy about that. Am I lazy? Not in the least. I don't derive my happiness or feel my self-worth has anything to do with the amount of hours I put in. To me, they're mutually exclusive things.

Many people's priorities change only when something calamitous happens in their lives. For some it takes a major life-changing event that opens their eyes and makes them reassess what they view as important. We've all heard people who, having come close to death, say how they now realize what they never before did. Their life's focus could have been their work, or any number of things, but when they come so close to losing everything, realize for maybe the first time what it really means to live their life to get the most out of it. Often the people who've gone through such catastrophic events say they can see what they couldn't before. They now realize the importance of things that before held little importance for them, and appreciate things they've always taken for granted. From now on they're going to lead their lives differently and "stop and smell the roses." Maybe they will and maybe they won't. After the initial shock of the event that caused them to re-evaluate their lives becomes more of a memory they might easily go back to their former lifestyle. If they're not living life consciously, i.e., thoughtfully making it a point to do what they just said they would, all the time, they might easily drift back to their old ways. If they do realize the emphasis of their former lives needed reevaluation, that means when they finally did look at their priorities, they found them to be askew. If the life-changing event happens later in life, that tells them they were emphasizing what they now consider to be the "wrong" things.

We don't all have to wait for some calamitous event to see what others, who never realized that it's the little things that make life pleasurable, discovered. Most of us are fortunate enough not to experience an earth shaking event such as a near death experience, but we can see clearly nevertheless. It's analogous to us witnessing a bad car accident, or it's aftermath while we're driving. Immediately, our driving improves. We become more cautious, maybe drive a little slower, and might even go so far as to actually use our turn signals, make safer lane changes, etc. That's obviously because we see right before us the consequences of an action and realize it can happen to us. You could go to twelve hours of traffic school but that won't have near the same impact on us as seeing firsthand a mangled car or body draped with a sheet lying in the road. But, that more attentive driving usually lasts only a short while, and soon, we're back to our old ways.

I suggest that it is in your best interest to lead a conscious life so there'll never be a need for some catastrophe to make you change what you're doing or how you're going about it. There should be no need for a B.C. (before catastrophe) and an A.C. (after catastrophe) because if you're leading life as you should, they're one and the same.

Well, that's it. I hope you have the tools you need to begin living life in a conscious fashion. To get the most out of your life and everything that goes into it takes constant and thoughtful effort. Good things happen for a reason. People who are successful at the art of living have usually worked very hard. Now you know that you too are capable of reaching that plateau. The dedication you are willing to devote to the task of consciously working towards sustainable happiness will result in achieving the desired result.

Take your time, be patient with yourself and your progress, and as you've discovered, you will discover that the secret to a happy life is not really a mystery at all.

I would suggest that once you've read this book and started living consciously, you re-read it and mark the passages most relevant to your life. You might want to keep it with you wherever you go. Refer to it often until everything in it becomes second nature.

To order additional copies of
OUTWARD ANXIETY - INNER CALM
please complete the following.

$19.95 EACH
(plus $3.95 shipping & handling for first book,
add $2.00 for each additional book ordered.

Shipping and Handling costs for larger quantites
available upon request.

Please send me _____ additional books at $19.95 + shipping & handling

Bill my: ❏ VISA ❏ MasterCard   Expires _____

Card # _____

Signature _____

Daytime Phone Number _____

For credit card orders call 1-888-568-6329
TO ORDER ON-LINE VISIT: www.jmcompanies.com
OR SEND THIS ORDER FORM TO:
McCleery & Sons Publishing
PO Box 248
Gwinner, ND 58040-0248

I am enclosing $_____   ❏ Check   ❏ Money Order
Payable in US funds. No cash accepted.

SHIP TO:

Name_____

Mailing Address _____

City _____

State/Zip _____

Orders by check allow longer delivery time.
Money order and credit card orders will be shipped within 48 hours.
This offer is subject to change without notice.

Home In One Piece
While working alone on his parent's farm one January morning in 1992, eighteen year old John Thompson became entangled in a piece of machinery. Both arms were ripped from his body and he was knocked unconscious. He was awakened by his dog, got off the ground, and staggered to the house. John opened a door with his mouth and grasped a pen in his teeth to call for help on the phone. A truthful journey with themes of survival, recovery and enduring hope.
By John Thompson as told to Paula Crain Grosinger, RN.
(162 pgs.)
$16.95 each in a 6 x 9 paperback.

Blessed Are The Peacemakers
A rousing tale that traces the heroic Rit Gatlin from his enlistment in the Confederate Army in Little Rock to his tragic loss of leg in a Kentucky battle, to his return in the Ozarks. He becomes engaged in guerilla warfare with raiders who follow no flag but their own. Rit finds himself involved with a Cherokee warrior, slaves and romance in a land ravaged by war.
By Joe W. Smith (444 pgs.)
$19.95 each in a 6 x 9 paperback

Pycnogenol®
Pycnogenol® for Superior Health presents exciting new evidence about nature's most powerful antioxidant. Pycnogenol® improves your total health, reduces risk of many diseases, safeguards your arteries, veins and entire circulation system. It protects your skin - giving it a healthier, smoother younger glow. Pycnogenol® also boosts your immune system. Read about it's many other beneficial effects.
Written by Richard A. Passwater, Ph.D. (122 pgs.)
$5.95 each in a 4-1/8 x 6-7/8" paperback.

Remembering Louis L'Amour
Reese Hawkins was a close friend of Louis L'Amour, one of the fastest selling writers of all time. Now Hawkins shares this friendship with L'Amour's legion of fans. Sit with Reese in L'Amour's study where characters were born and stories came to life. Travel with Louis and Reese in the 16 photo pages in this memoir. Learn about L'Amour's lifelong quest for knowledge and his philosophy of life.
Written by Reese Hawkins and his daughter Meredith Hawkins Wallin. (178 pgs.)
$16.95 each in a 5-1/2x8" paperback.

Whispers in the Darkness
In this fast paced, well thought out mystery with a twist of romance, Betty Pearson comes to a slow paced, small town. Little did she know she was following a missing link - what the dilapidated former Beardsley Manor she was drawn to, held for her. With twists and turns, the Manor's secrets are unraveled.
Written by Shirlee Taylor. (88 pgs.)
$14.95 each in a 6x9" paperback.

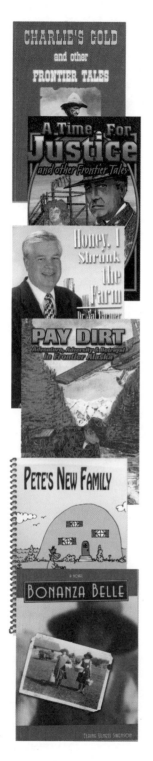

Charlie's Gold and Other Frontier Tales
Kamron's first collection of short stories gives you adventure tales about men and women of the west, made up of cowboys, Indians, and settlers.
Written by Kent Kamron. (174 pgs.)
$15.95 each in a 6x9" paperback.

A Time For Justice
This second collection of Kamron's short stories takes off where the first volume left off, satisfying the reader's hunger for more tales of the wide prairie.
Written by Kent Kamron. (182 pgs.)
$16.95 each in a 6x9" paperback.

Dr. Val Farmer's
Honey, I Shrunk The Farm
The first volume in a three part series of Rural Stress Survival Guides discusses the following in seven chapters: Farm Economics; Understanding The Farm Crisis; How To Cope With Hard Times; Families Going Through It Together; Dealing With Debt; Going For Help, Helping Others and Transitions Out of Farming.
Written by Val Farmer. (208 pgs.)
$16.95 each in a 6x9" paperback.

Pay Dirt
An absorbing story reveals how a man with the courage to follow his dream found both gold and unexpected adventure and adversity in Interior Alaska, while learning that human nature can be the most unpredictable of all.
Written by Otis Hahn & Alice Vollmar. (168 pgs.)
$15.95 each in a 6x9" paperback.

Pete's New Family
Pete's New Family is a tale for children (ages 4-8) lovingly written to help youngsters understand events of divorce that they are powerless to change.
Written by Brenda Jacobson.
$9.95 each in a 5-1/2x8-1/2" spiral bound book.

Bonanza Belle
In 1908, Carrie Amundson left her home to become employed on a bonanza farm. One tragedy after the other befell her and altered her life considerably and she found herself back on the farm.
Written by Elaine Ulness Swenson. (344 pgs.)
$15.95 each in a 6x8-1/4" paperback.

First The Dream
This story spans ninety years of Anna's life. She finds love, loses it, and finds in once again. A secret that Anna has kept is fully revealed at the end of her life.
Written by Elaine Ulness Swenson. (326 pgs.)
$15.95 each in a 6x8-1/4" paperback

Country-fied
Stories with a sense of humor and love for country and small town people who, like the author, grew up country-fied . . . Country-fied people grow up with a unique aware-ness of their dependence on the land. They live their lives with dignity, hard work, determination and the ability to laugh at themselves.
Written by Elaine Babcock. (184 pgs.)
$14.95 each in a 6x9" paperback.

It Really Happened Here!
Relive the days of farm-to-farm salesmen and hucksters, of ghost ships and locust plagues when you read Ethelyn Pearson's collection of strange but true tales. It captures the spirit of our ancestors in short, easy to read, colorful accounts that will have you yearning for more.
Written by Ethelyn Pearson. (168 pgs.)
$24.95 each in an 8-1/2x11" paperback.

The Long, Blonde Pigtails with Big Red Bows
Teaching Children Not to Talk to Strangers
The story of three little mice who learn a heart-breaking lesson from a casual encounter with a "stranger" in their neighborhood. This is an integral message that appears throughout the book, to teach and protect our children.Written by Mary Magill. Illustrated by Barbara Scheibling. (24 pgs.)
$14.95 each in a 8-1/2x8-1/2" paperback.

(Add $3.95 shipping & handling for first book, add $2.00 for each additional book ordered.)

Prayers For Parker Cookbook
Parker Sebens is a 3 year old boy from Milnor, ND, who lost both of his arms in a tragic farm accident on September 18, 2000. He has undergone many surgeries to reattach his arms, but because his arms were damaged so extensively and the infection so fierce, they were unable to save his hands. Parker will face many more surgeries in his future, plus be fitted for protheses.

This 112 pg. cookbook is a project of the Country Friends Home-makers Club from Parker's community. All profits from the sale of this book will go to the Parker Sebens' Benefit Fund, a fund set up to help with medical-related expenses due to Parker's accident. $8.00 ea. in a 5-1/4"x8-1'4" spiral bound book.